The *Cross and Crown Series of Spirituality* is proud to present to the public an original work by an American Dominican, Father Paul Hinnebusch. This book fills a need in the spiritual reading of American Catholics, first, because it is written by an American for Americans, and secondly, because it treats of the mystery of Christ in the spiritual life, not as a goal of the spiritual life, but as the way to the Trinity.

With the ever-growing emphasis on a Christocentric spirituality, expressed especially in the liturgical participation and in the sacramental life of the Church, it may understandably happen that a number of Christians will think of Christ as the totality of the spiritual life and the unique goal of this life. Yet Christ himself said of himself that he is the way and that his entire mission was to fulfill the will of the Father. Moreover, he promised explicitly that he was also preparing the way for the Trinity, who would take up their abode in the souls of the just.

As in the beatific vision in glory, so also in the full flowering of grace and charity on earth, the Trinity is the focal point of Christian spirituality. It is therefore of the greatest importance that as the individual Christian approaches Christ through the liturgy and the sacraments and as he strives to transform himself into Christ through the practice of the virtues and a life of prayer, he should also realize that all this should be done with a view to the Trinity. Whether it be a question of the loftiest mystical experience on earth or the eternal enjoyment of the beatific vision in glory, the perfection of the Christian life is to be found in the knowledge and love of the Father, Son and Holy Spirit.

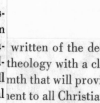

written of the deep-
theology with a clar-
mth that will provide
ent to all Christians.
doctrinal, and that
also eminently prac-
easily led from theo-
application in prac-

'HOR

O.P., is a native of
After receiving his
h School in Colum-
e College at Provi-
tered the Dominican
n to the priesthood,
most exclusively in
us Catholic colleges.
is chaplain at the
minican Sisters of
osaryville, Poncha-
ationally know as a
rticles on religious
lity. He has written
numerous articles for *Cross and Crown, Review for Religious* and *Sponsa Regis.*

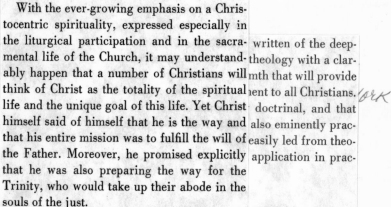

Like the Word

Cross and Crown Series of Spirituality

LITERARY EDITOR

Reverend Jordan Aumann, O.P., S.T.D.

NUMBER 29

Paul Hinnebusch, O.P.

LIKE THE WORD

TO THE TRINITY
THROUGH CHRIST

B. Herder Book Co.

ST. LOUIS AND LONDON

IMPRIMI POTEST
Gilbert J. Graham, O.P.
Provincial

NIHIL OBSTAT
J. S. Considine, O.P.
Censor Deputatus

IMPRIMATUR
Most Rev. Cletus F. O'Donnell, J.C.D.
Vicar General, Archdiocese of Chicago
September 29, 1964

© 1965 by B. Herder Book Co.
314 North Jefferson, St. Louis, Missouri 63103
London: 2/3 Doughty Mews, W.C. 1
Library of Congress Catalog Card Number: 65–17849
Manufactured in the United States of America
Designed by Klaus Gemming

Contents

PART ONE

To the Trinity in the Word

CHAPTER I

LIKE THE WORD

For just as from the heavens
    the rain and snow come down
And do not return there
    till they have watered the earth,
    making it fertile and fruitful,
Giving seed to him who sows
    and bread to him who eats,
So shall my word be
    that goes forth from my mouth;
It shall not return to me void,
    but shall do my will,
    achieving the end for which I sent it.[1]

"SO SHALL MY WORD BE. It shall not return to me void." In this magnificent passage from the Book of Isaias the Lord God is speaking of his prophetic word in which he has just foretold the return of his people from the Babylonian exile. What has been spoken shall certainly be, for when God speaks, what he says is infallibly accomplished.

God had once said: "Let there be light," and there was light. Likewise, whenever he speaks through his prophets, the prophetic word is always fulfilled. The very word seems to contain within it the divine power to accomplish what is spoken: "My word . . . that goes forth from my mouth . . . shall not return to me void, but shall do my will, achieving the end for which I sent it."

This sentence bursts into the brilliance of a wonderful new meaning when the Word, who is God, is made flesh, and

[1] Isaias 55:10–11.

3

dwells among men. The Word, Son of God, is sent into the world on a mission, and returns to the Father who sent him, but not empty-handed. He does the Father's will; he accomplishes the work he has been given to do.

At the very instant he comes into the world, he says: "Behold, I come to do thy will, O God." [2] As a boy of twelve, he says to his mystified parents: "Did you not know that I must be about my Father's business?" [3] At Jacob's well, he says to his disciples: "My food is to do the will of him who sent me, to accomplish his work." [4] The night before he dies, he says: "Father, I am coming to thee. I have accomplished the work thou hast given me to do." [5]

The Father's work, accomplished by the Word, is the salvation of men, the "gathering into one the children of God who were scattered abroad." [6] The Word brings back to God the human race which had departed from the divine presence by the sin of Adam. As he enters the crowning stage of his mission on earth, the Word, speaking to his disciples of his imminent return to the Father who sent him, says: "I go to prepare a place for you. And if I go and prepare a place for you, I am coming again, and I will take you to myself, that where I am, there you also may be." [7] And where is the Word? He is with God!

This promise of Jesus to take us where he is, is perfectly fulfilled, of course, only when man attains the beatific vision. However, because of the mission accomplished by the Word, even now in this life man can be, like the Word, with God. The Word has not returned to the Father fruitless. In the course of this book, we shall endeavor to show how man lives with God by living the interior life of prayer. Christianity is life with the Holy Trinity.

[2] Hebrews 10:7. [3] Luke 2:49. [4] John 4:34. [5] John 17:13, 4.
[6] John 11:52. [7] John 14:3.

But Christ alone is the way to this life. Only in him does man return to God; only in him does man live with God. There is no other way. "I am the way, and the truth, and the life. No one comes to the Father but through me." [8]

And how is he the way? How does the Word bring us to the Father? *By* his grace and truth, and *in* his grace and truth. "The Word was made flesh, and dwelt among us . . . full of grace and of truth . . . and of his fullness we have all received." [9]

Though the work accomplished by the Word is the Father's own work, the work is carried out in our individual souls only when we join in this work, becoming co-workers of Christ in our own sanctification. When the Jews asked Jesus: "What are we to do in order that we may perform the works of God?" in answer Jesus said to them: "This is the work of God, that you believe in him whom he has sent." [10]

In other words, God's work of salvation can be accomplished in man only if by faith man gives himself over to him whom God has sent—to Jesus Christ, the Word of God. Just as the word of God spoken in times past by the prophets carried in it a kind of divine power to accomplish God's work, so Christ the Word is himself the power of God. "We preach . . . Christ, the power of God and the wisdom of God." [11] When by faith man gives himself to Christ the Word, the divine power of the Word sanctifies him, bringing him to God, restoring him to divine sonship. "To as many as received him, he gave the power of becoming sons of God, to those who believe in his name." [12]

Man's sharing in this power of the Word is sanctifying grace. But man returns to God with the Word, not only in his grace, but also in his truth; that is, not only in the power of

[8] John 14:7.   [9] John 1:14, 16.   [10] John 6:28–29.
[11] I Corinthians 1:24.   [12] John 1:12.

the Word, but also in the likeness of the Word. It is only in the likeness of the Word that we can return to God.

The likeness of the Word's return to the Father is impressed upon us first of all by the baptismal character. The character is the likeness in us of Christ's priesthood and sacrifice by which he goes to the Father. Again and again, at the Last Supper, Jesus spoke of his sacrifice on the cross as his going to the Father. No one goes to God except through this sacrifice of Christ, and with him, and in him. The baptismal character in the soul is the re-orientation, the re-direction, of fallen man to God, by the power of Christ's priesthood and sacrifice. Original sin had disorientated man from God, giving man's nature an evil bent, away from God. Adam's disobedience had impressed itself like a brand on the whole of human nature, turning the whole of mankind away from God. Human nature's powers, disordered among themselves, were left by Adam with a bent toward created goods in opposition to God.

Original sin, then, is the mark of Adam's disobedience impressed upon human nature; the character of baptism is the impress of Christ's obedience, re-directing man back to God.

The disorder of original sin, in the very essence of man's soul, tends to express itself in man's personal sinful actions. So too, the character of Christ, the impress of his obedience upon the soul, has to express itself in a man's personal actions. The character of baptism is not static, not lifeless; it is a dynamic, living power, a sharing in Christ's priestly power, orientating the powers of the soul to God, so that by the actions of these powers man can return to God in the grace and truth of Christ's sacrifice. Thus, the character of Christ, imprinted upon the soul itself, expresses itself in human actions in the likeness of Christ's own actions, actions which indeed are Christ's own action; i.e., Christ acting in and through man's action. Only by acting thus in the likeness of the Word of God does man go to the Father. "We may know that we are in him by the following test: He who says he abides in him ought to conduct himself just as he conducted himself." [13]

Man's action in the likeness of the action of the Word of God is "the work of God" accomplished in us by the Son of God sent to us for this very purpose. The Christian has "put on the Lord Jesus Christ." [14] He declares in all truth with St. Paul: "It is no longer I that live, but Christ lives in me. And the life that I now live in the flesh, I live in the faith of the Son of God, who loved me and gave himself up for me." [15] Our likeness to the Word of God, in which alone we can return to God, is therefore no mere exterior conformity to his virtues; it is Christ living interiorly in us by his grace, living all his virtues in our actions, taking us to the Father.

We can go back to God, then, only in the likeness of the Word of God, only in the likeness of his obedience, which obliterates in us the likeness of Adam's disobedience. The obedience of Christ is first rooted in us by the baptismal character, but it develops and grows and bears fruit in us only by our actions in the likeness of his virtues, as we, too, do "the work of God" and are "about the Father's business," doing his will.

This is the "work of God" which we must accomplish by our labors with Christ, and which he must accomplish in us. It is the work enjoined upon us by Christ when he said: "Labor not for the food that perishes, but for that which endures unto life everlasting," and when he said, a few

---

[13] I John 2:5 (Spencer).   [14] Romans 13:14.   [15] Galatians 2:20.

moments later: "This is the work of God, that you believe in him whom he has sent." [16]

The food that endures unto life everlasting is the bread of life; it is Christ himself, the Word of God. For "not by bread alone does man live, but by every word that comes forth from the mouth of the Lord." [17] Christ is the living Word of God. The bread of life is God's truth in Christ, which man must contemplate for the satisfaction of his hungry soul. "I am the bread of life. He who comes to me shall not hunger, and he who believes in me shall never thirst." [18]

The contemplation of God in his Word, in the beatific vision by the light of glory, is the final goal and happiness of man. But when man is still on the way to this goal, the same Word of God who will be the goal is also the way.

In the Scriptures, the word of God expresses to us the will of God, which is also our bread of life. Christ himself found his nourishment in the will of God: "My food is to do the will of him who sent me, to accomplish his work." [19]

Thus we can distinguish several senses in which we must labor for the food that endures unto life everlasting. The food which alone satisfies man's hungry soul is the contemplation of God. This is to be our food even in this life, but we can enjoy this contemplation only if we labor for it in the sweat of our brow. For the worst part of the curse put upon Adam when it was said to him: "In the sweat of your brow you shall eat bread," [20] is the difficulty which our fallen nature finds in nourishing itself on this heavenly food in the practice of prayer. The impression of Adam's disobedience, left on our whole being by original sin, expressing itself in the disorder of concupiscence within a man and in the disorder of his relationships with his fellow men, takes away

---

[16] John 6:29.   [17] Deuteronomy 8:3.   [18] John 7:35.
[19] John 4:34.   [20] Genesis 3:19.

the calm and peace so necessary for the contemplation of divine things. The true curse of the effects of original sin is the difficulty man experiences in contemplating God, his true bread of life. The curse takes its fatal effect when man, in spiritual sloth, abandons the effort required for prayer, gives up the labor for this divine food of the soul.

If man would feed his hungry soul by the contemplation of divine things, he must labor for this contemplation by striving to conquer the disorder within and without, by obedience to the will of God, sincerely sought and eagerly carried out at every moment of his life. He must labor to perfect in himself the likeness of the Word's obedience to the Father. By the work of obedience, man gradually brings his whole being and his whole life into the orderly harmony of perfect subjection to God, so that his every action is directed to God, so that in every action he goes in love to the God from whom he came.

Therefore, in the opening sentence of his rule, St. Benedict appeals for obedience to the rule and to the superior, so that, as he says, "by the labor of obedience you may return to him from whom you had departed by the sloth of disobedience." The whole goal of St. Benedict's rule and of every religious rule is to order the lives of the religious in such a way that they may live in the contemplation of God. Obedience to the order prescribed by the rule brings order into man's whole life and being, so that the obstacles to the contemplation of God are at a minimum, and in peace and calm of soul, man is open to the inspiration of the Holy Spirit.

In addition to the general labor of always doing God's will, there is the specific labor of the continuing effort to be recollected in the presence of God, the labor of fighting persistently the distractions that proceed from the disorder of our fallen nature and the fallen society in which we live.

"Do not labor for the food that perishes, but for that which endures unto life everlasting, which the Son of Man will give you." [21] Contemplation, the bread of life, is the gift of the Son of Man. We must labor to prepare ourselves for the gift. By the labor of obedience to God's will, we open ourselves for Christ's gift of the Holy Spirit, who by his inspirations brings us to the contemplation of God even in this life. "To him who overcomes, I will give the hidden manna!" [22]

Such is the theme of this volume. We shall endeavor to show how the interior Christian life is an interior likeness to the eternal Word of God in his life with the Father, in the unity of the Holy Spirit. But the essential predisposition to this interior life of contemplation is obedience to the will of God by a moral life which conforms with the obedience of the Word made flesh. We shall treat of many details of this predisposition and of other aids to life in the divine presence.

Only in the likeness of Christ's obedience does one return to the Father, to dwell forever in that presence from which we had been cast out by sin. We, too, were sent forth by the creative word of God, which brought us out of nothingness so that we might come to him. But because we went astray, the Word came forth in person to bring us back. In him alone do we return to God.

> So shall my Word be
>   that goes forth from my mouth,
> It shall not return to me void
>   but shall do my will,
>   achieving the end for which I sent it.

[21] John 6:27.   [22] Apocalypse 2:17.

CHAPTER II

LIFE IN THE TRINITY

THE GRACE OF ADOPTION as sons of God forms us in the likeness of the Word, of whom it is written: "The Word was with God." The grace of adoption makes it possible for us to be with God, ever living in the divine presence by continual recollection. It is said that St. Dominic spoke "only with God or of God." When he spoke with God, he was like the Word: with God. When he spoke of God, he was like the Word-made-flesh: speaking to men.

In this and in the next chapter we shall show how the grace of baptism, adopting us as divine sons, makes it possible for us to be like the Word: with God. The poet Dante, recalling the marriage of St. Francis with Lady Poverty, tells how Faith was the bride of St. Dominic, whom he took to himself in holy baptism:

> At the sacred font were perfected
> The espousals pledged between faith and him.[1]

St. Dominic was ever faithful to this spouse. The eternal Father pointed out to St. Catherine of Siena, when she saw Dominic, like the Lord, coming forth from the bosom of the Father, that one reason why Dominic is so like the Lord is the fact that he always preserved the grace of baptism by obedience to the divine will, like the obedience of Christ himself. He was indeed a true son of the Father.[2]

Moreover, it was at Dominic's baptism that the strange light, represented in art as an eight-pointed star, was seen for

---

[1] *Paradiso*, Canto XII, 61.

[2] Raymond of Capua, *The Life of St. Catherine of Siena*, tr. by George Lamb (New York: P. J. Kenedy, 1960), p. 184.

11

the first time upon his brow, for it was then that the eternal Word, the light of the world, was begotten in the soul of Dominic by the eternal Father.

It is upon the brow that every Christian traces the sign of the cross in perpetual commemoration of his own baptism. Let us examine the wonders of our adoption as sons of God, beginning with a consideration of the sign of the cross as a profession of faith in the things accomplished in us in baptism.

Some of the most profitable aids to sanctity are also the most simple, so simple that they are the first things we teach to little children, and through their use, even children can become saints. One such valuable aid to sanctity is the sign of the cross.

The sign of the cross sums up the whole Christian way of life; it is indeed a complete rule of Christian perfection, for it expresses the indispensable essentials of Christianity in a brief phrase. It tells us that Christianity consists in living the life of the Holy Trinity, by dying to self on the cross of Christ.

The sign of the cross is a reminder of what took place in our baptism. Baptism was a death to sin through the power of the cross of Christ, and a resurrection to the divine life of grace, which is a participation in the very life of the Holy Trinity. Water was poured three times over our head, each time in the form of a cross, while the name of the Holy Trinity was invoked upon us: "I baptize thee in the name of the Father, and of the Son, and of the Holy Spirit." In that instant, the Holy Spirit, by entering our souls in person, consecrated us temples of the living God and sanctified us by his personal presence.

But the three divine Persons are inseparable, living in one another, living one and the same life together. By sending their Holy Spirit of love into our souls, the Father and the Son entered into us with him and made us their dwelling-place, their heaven. By sending his Spirit into us, the eternal Father begot us in the likeness of his Son, so that, like Christ himself, spontaneously we go to the Father in an embrace of love, crying in the Spirit, "Abba, Father!"

Baptism also bestowed upon us the grace of vigorous, living faith, which gives us the power to live the life of the Trinity ever more fully. It is true that faith is presupposed to baptism—"He who believes and is baptized shall be saved" —but the sacramental grace of baptism does something to that faith. It turns it from a mere acceptance of revealed truths, a mere assent to their veracity, into a living power for living those truths. It is only a beginning when we say: "I believe in three divine Persons in one divine nature, Father, Son and Holy Spirit." But living faith, a faith that is lived, actually carries us into the inner life of the Holy Trinity, so that we live their life with them.

We should not be content merely to remain in the state of grace, in a static condition, as it were; rather, by vigorous, active faith and charity, we must enter ever more deeply into the life of the eternal Three. It was for this reason that the truth of the Trinity was revealed to us. God did not reveal this staggering mystery merely to confuse us and humiliate us by its brilliance. He made known the mystery of the Three-in-One out of infinite love so that, in infinite love, he could communicate the Trinity's own life to us, so that we could enter into the Trinity and live in intimate relationships of knowledge and love with Father, Son and Holy Spirit, and thus share their infinite bliss.

St. John the Evangelist tells us all these things magnificently. "No one has at any time seen God," he says. "The only-begotten Son, who is in the bosom of the Father, he has revealed him." [3] No one has seen God; that is, it was impossible for any creature to have even the slightest suspicion that a Trinity of divine Persons existed. Only the Word of God himself, eternally living in the bosom of the Father, could reveal that truth. Our Lord said it thus to Nicodemus: "No one has ascended into heaven except him who has descended from heaven: the Son of Man who is in heaven." [4]

And how has the Son revealed these things, and why has he done so? Again, St. John gives the answers. Referring to Christ as "the Life," "the Word of life," "the eternal Life," John writes: "The Life was made known, and we have seen and now testify and announce to you, the Life eternal which was with the Father, and has appeared to us." [5] This is how the Trinity was revealed to men: the Word of life, who was with the Father, was made flesh and dwelt among us, and we saw his glory, the glory of the Only-begotten of the Father.

But why did the Life eternal appear among us, why did he reveal the Trinity? John answers: "In order that our fellowship may be with the Father and with his Son Jesus Christ . . . that you may rejoice, and our joy may be full." [6]

Fellowship, companionship, intimate friendship with the three divine Persons—that is the fruit of living faith. For St. John and St. Paul, faith is not merely the acceptance of a cold formula of truth; for them, living faith is a total surrender of self to Christ, so that he may form in us this life of the triune God. We see, then, that Christianity is not merely a list of articles to believe and a set of commandments to observe. It is not just a complex of multiple activities; nor is it primarily a system of morality. First of all, and essentially, Christianity is a new manner of exist-

[3] John 1:18.   [4] John 3:13.   [5] I John 1f.   [6] I John 1:14.

ence, a divine state of being. What counts above all else in a Christian is what he is, rather than what he does. And this is what he is: an adopted son of God, living the life of the Holy Trinity; and this life is love—charity. "God is love, and he who abides in love abides in God, and God in him." [7] Christianity is fellowship with God, an intimate relationship of life and knowledge and love with the divine Three.

Christian morality, truly a divine way of living, is the consequence of the life of the Trinity within us, the consequence of our divine mode of living. For example, St. Paul uses only one all-sufficing argument to convince us that we should be chaste: "Do you not know that your members are the temple of the Holy Spirit who is in you, whom you have from God, and that you are not your own?" [8] Notice how he says, "You *have* the Holy Spirit," you possess him.

St. John tells us the same thing about the Father and the Son; he writes: "He who confesses the Son *has* the Father also." [9] Christianity, therefore, is the possession of Father, Son and Holy Spirit, not only in the next life, but right here and now; it is living the life of the Trinity even here on earth. "Our life is hidden with Christ in God." [10] "Our citizenship is in heaven." [11]

Jesus told us all about this at the Last Supper. He pointed out that we would know Father, Son and Holy Spirit as intimate friends, so that we will be able to speak familiarly to them, either to each one of them in turn, or to all of them together. And we would so know the Three, precisely because they would be living in us:

> I will ask the Father, and he will give you
> another Advocate to dwell with you forever,
> the Spirit of truth, whom the world cannot

[7] I John 4:16.   [8] I Corinthians 6:18.   [9] I John 2:23.
[10] Colossians 3:3.   [11] Philippians 3:20.

receive, because it neither sees him nor
knows him. But you shall know him, because
he will dwell with you, and be in you.[12]

"He who loves me will be loved by my Father, and I will love him, and will manifest myself to him." But how will this manifestation take place? "If anyone love . . . my Father will love him, and we will come to him, and make our abode with him.[13]

St. John explains how this divine indwelling is brought to its perfection: "No one has ever seen God. If we love one another, God abides in us, and his love is perfected in us." [14] In other words, "God is love, and he who abides in love, abides in God and God in him." [15]

If these things are true, if the Holy Trinity truly does so dwell in us as in his temple, then we can draw only one conclusion, the one expressed so succinctly by St. Teresa of Avila: "Remember how important it is for you to have understood this truth: that the Lord is *within* us, and that we should be *there with him*." [16] Sister Elizabeth of the Trinity says the same thing: "The Blessed Trinity is our dwelling place, our home, our Father's house, which we should never, never leave!" [17]

And why should our souls be in the Trinity as our dwelling? So that the three divine Persons may sanctify us. Their presence in us is the formal cause of sanctity. Sanctifying grace, which alone makes us holy, is so called because it gives us the sanctifying presence of the Trinity. The swiftest way to great sanctity is recollection, living an

---

[12] John 14:16f.   [13] John 14:21, 24.   [14] I John 4:12.   [15] *Ibid.*, 16.

[16] St. Teresa of Avila, *The Way of Perfection*, Chap. XXVIII.

[17] M. M. Philipon, O. P., *Spiritual Doctrine of Sister Elizabeth of the Trinity* (Westminster: Newman, 1955), p. 192.

interior life in the presence of the divine Persons who dwell
in us.

The spiritual life consists less in multiplying personal
efforts than in letting oneself be possessed by God. It is not
primarily what we do that sanctifies us; it is not a multitude
of activities which makes us holy; rather, the all-holy One
sanctifies us when we put ourselves in his sanctifying
presence, opening ourselves to his light and his love. For this
reason, by making the sign of the cross at the beginning of
every activity, we remind ourselves that we are temples of
the Trinity, who are in us only to sanctify us, and our work is
holy only if they work in us.

It should be our aim to be as conscious as possible of this
sanctifying presence within us, so that the Trinity will work
in us. All we have to do is to remove the obstacles to their
sanctifying presence; and this we do by mortification. The
cross which we trace upon ourselves in the name of the
Trinity reminds us to die to self all day long, so that we can
live to God. "Consider yourself as dead to sin, but alive to
God in Christ Jesus." [18] We must silence our senses and all
our desires so that nothing can interfere with the interior
working of our three divine Guests.

The Eternal Father speaks his Word—his Son—in our
souls; we cannot hear him unless we are in peace and silence; we must learn to listen to him. Our Blessed Lord com-
plained of those who do not listen when the Father speaks
his Word to them. He says: "No one can come to me unless
the Father who sent me draw him. . . . It is written in the
prophets: 'And they shall all be taught of God.' Everyone
who has listened to the Father, and has learned, comes to
me." [19]

[18] Romans 6:11.   [19] John 6:45.

When the Father has spoken his Word in us, and we have listened, love flames forth in us, that divine love which is the special work of the Holy Spirit within our souls.

This silent listening to God, this docility to the divine Teacher, is all-important. "They all shall be taught of God." How sad is the mistake of those souls who, when they pray, do all the talking, multiplying vocal prayers endlessly, staying on the surface, never truly entering into their souls to listen to the Father. Prayer is a conversation—not man's chattering monologue.

Let us, then, go straight to the source of sanctity, the God who is in our hearts. With Elizabeth of the Trinity, let us cry out to the divine Three:

> O my God, Trinity whom I adore!
> Help me to become utterly forgetful of self,
>   that I may bury myself in Thee. . . .
>
> Give peace to my soul; make it thy heaven,
>   thy cherished dwelling place, thy home of rest.
> Let me never leave thee there alone,
>   but keep me there all absorbed in thee,
> In living faith adoring thee,
>   and wholly yielded up to thy creative action! [20]

Let me bask in the sanctifying power of thy love, thy love which longs to communicate to me the fullness of thy life. Father, speak in me thy Word, who spirates in me thy love!

[20] Philipon, M. M. *The Spiritual Doctrine of Sister Elizabeth of the Trinity* (Westminster, Md.: Newman, 1955), pp. 53–54.

CHAPTER III

THE MYSTERY OF CHRIST
WITHIN US

OUR ADOPTION as sons of God is not a mere resemblance or copy of the eternal Son of God, but we are like him because he himself lives in us. His own life in us makes us like him. Nor is it a likeness only of his divinity, but also of his humanity, which makes us adopted sons of God. For it is not merely the eternal Word, but this Word made flesh who lives his life in us: *Christ* lives in us, and we in him.[1]

We cannot be sons of God except in Christ. Note how many times St. Paul (for example, in the first fourteen verses of the epistle to the Ephesians) insists that it is only "in him"—in Christ—that we have divine sonship, "for the praise of his glorious grace with which he has made us gracious *in the well-beloved*." [2] It is only when Christ lives in us and we in him that we have divine sonship; it is only in and through Christ's humanity that God forms in us the likeness of his divinity.

It is unfortunate that we do not meditate more on this "mystery that Christ is in you." [3] We speak often of the other mysteries—the Holy Trinity, the Incarnation, the Holy Eucharist, and so forth—but this mystery that Christ is in us and we in him [4] is the completion and fullness of the mysteries of the Incarnation, the Redemption and the Holy Eucharist. We, the members of the Mystical Body, are the completion of Christ; his work of redemption is meaningless

[1] John 15:4; Galatians 2:20. [2] Ephesians 1:6. [3] Colossians 1:28.
[4] John 15:4.

19

without us. The mystery of Christ in us is, therefore, of tremendous importance in our spiritual life.

Like the mystery of the Trinity, this mystery is something which infinitely surpasses human understanding. It can be known only in the light of faith and, as it were, in a dark manner. And yet it is so vital to spiritual progress that it deserves continual meditation. Under the influence of the gift of understanding we must endeavor to penetrate it ever more deeply.

When St. Paul says that Christ is in us, he means the man who is God: Jesus, son of Mary. It is indeed a great mystery how this man can live in other men. The divine life of sanctifying grace is Jesus Christ living in us in some mysterious way. At the Last Supper, Jesus said: "I will not leave you orphans; I will come to you. Yet a little while and the world no longer sees me. But you see me, for I live and you shall live. In that day, you will know that I am in my Father and you in me, and I in you." [5]

And a little later that same night, Jesus commanded us to live this mystery when he said: "Abide in me and I in you." [6] In other words, there must be a mutual indwelling; he lives in us so that we can live in him. We and he must achieve a kind of identity of life; we must live one life together. Jesus prayed for this at the Last Supper, asking the Father to admit us into that unity of life which he himself enjoys with the Father and the Holy Spirit: "As thou, Father, in me, and I in thee, that they also may be one in us. . . . I in them and thou in me, that they may be perfected in unity." [7] In these words Jesus is telling us that, just as three divine Persons live one divine life in common, so we are to live one life in common with Christ; the life we live in Christ is a sharing in the very life of the Holy Trinity. We can enter into the divine

[5] John 14:18–20. [6] John 15:4. [7] John 17:21, 23.

life of the Trinity only by entering into Christ, by living in him; he alone is "the way, the truth and the life. No one comes to the Father but by me." [8]

It is this mutual indwelling of Christ and the soul to which St. Paul refers in his famous words: "It is now no longer I that live, but Christ lives in me." [9]

We in Christ

But how can we be in Christ and he in us? "This is a great mystery." We are in Christ not as water is in a jug, nor as a man is in a house. This is not a matter of material dimensions; this abiding in Christ is something out of this world; it is a totally new manner of existence, a supernatural mode of being. This existing in Christ is a new world of things, "a new creation," says St. Paul.[10] "If then any man is in Christ, he is a new creature." [11]

This new world of grace is beyond our understanding, so we cannot think of it in terms of ordinary, natural existence. We are in Christ and he is in us in a mystical way. When we are in the state of grace, we have a mystical union with Jesus. We are not speaking now of that mystical union which is the highest perfection of the Christian life, but of a mystical union possessed by all who are in the state of grace. According to the dictionary, the word "mystical" refers to something which is not apparent to the senses, nor within the grasp of the intellect; it is something greater than the things of this creation; it is entirely supernatural, beyond our natural powers of comprehension. But that does not mean that a mystical thing is not real; in fact, it is more real than anything we can know with our natural powers; it is a

[8] John 14:7.   [9] Galatians 2:20.   [10] Galatians 6:15.
[11] II Corinthians 5:17.

greater reality, so great that we cannot fully grasp it in this life.

This presence of Christ in us and we in him is something very real indeed. Christ is the head of his Mystical Body and is immediately present to all his members in that mysterious mystical way. The whole Christ, both his divinity and his humanity, is continually acting in each living member of his Mystical Body. The sacred humanity of Jesus Christ, into which we are incorporated as members, is the sole source of divine life in each one of us, his members. As Jesus said, "Without me, you can do nothing."

In the present order of things, all supernatural life derives from Christ; we can live it only in him; it is impossible to live it except in him. Jesus makes this point by using the metaphor of the vine: "I am the true vine . . . abide in me, and I in you. As the branch cannot bear fruit of itself unless it remain on the vine, so neither can you unless you abide in me. I am the vine, you are the branches. He who abides in me, and I in him, he bears much fruit; for without me you can do nothing." [12]

A vine and its branches are one living thing. The vine does not live without its branches, nor the branches without the vine. Vine and branches are one complete entity, one living substance. So it is with us and Christ. We have but one supernatural existence together. Christ is the vine; he is the whole vine, including its branches. We are the branches, only because we are in him, living the divine life in him. We have been incorporated into him so that he can live his life in us and we can live in him. As the vine gives its life to the branches and lives its life in the branches, so he gives us his divine life and lives it in us. We can live the divine life of grace only because Jesus Christ is immediately present to us

[12] John 15:4–5.

in that mystical way, continually causing his divine life in us. The redemptive, sanctifying power of Christ is always present, sustaining our supernatural life of grace.

A person lives the divine life of grace only because the Holy Spirit is actually dwelling in his soul. But, says St. Thomas Aquinas, "Christ works through the Holy Spirit. 'If anyone does not have the Spirit of Christ, he does not belong to Christ's (Rom. 8:9). Therefore, whatever is done by the Holy Spirit is also done by Christ." [13]

Christ in Us

Pope Pius XII, in his encyclical on the Mystical Body, echoes the words of Aquinas, saying: "Christ is in us through his Spirit whom he gives to us and through whom he acts in us in such a way that all divine activity of the Holy Spirit within our souls must also be attributed to Christ." [14] The Holy Spirit comes to no one unless Christ Jesus sends him. "For if I do not go," Jesus said at the Last Supper, "the Advocate will not come to you; but if I go, I will send him to you." [15]

St. John the Evangelist, who heard these words of Jesus and recorded them for us, understood from them that Jesus, by going to the Father through his obedient death, merited the right to send us the Holy Spirit. The same God-Man who died on the cross and is now glorified at the right hand of the Father, has the exclusive right to bestow the Holy Spirit upon redeemed mankind. This was the explanation given by St. John in recording the words of Jesus about

[13] *Commentary on Ephesians 2:18.*
[14] *Mystici Corporis* (N. C. W. C. edition), p. 76; AAS, XXXV (1943), p. 230.
[15] John 16:7.

rivers of living water. Jesus had said: "He who believes in me, from within him shall flow rivers of living water," and John commented on this: "He said this of the Spirit whom they who believed in him were to receive; for the Spirit had not yet been given, seeing that Jesus had not yet been glorified." [16]

Since it is only the glorified Jesus—the man who is God—who sends us the Holy Spirit from the Father, the Pope is right in saying that Christ is in us through his Spirit, whom he gives to us, and through whom he acts in us, in such a way that all divine activity of the Holy Spirit within our souls must also be attributed to Christ.

Since we have access to the Father only through Christ, who sends us the Holy Spirit, our whole spiritual life must be centered upon Christ, who said: "No one comes to the Father but through me." [17] We should, therefore, strive to be aware of the presence of Christ in us. He is not far from us, not hard to find, not hard to contact, but he is immediately within us, closer to us than we are to ourselves, maintaining us in the divine life.

In fact, we may say that, in the order of grace, Christ is everywhere. Just as in the natural order God is everywhere, in all creatures, maintaining them in existence by his creative power, so, too, the God-Man, Christ Jesus, is everywhere in the "new creation"—the Mystical Body—by his redemptive power, maintaining each member in the divine life. It is in his humanity, says St. Augustine, that the Son of God is the true vine. Therefore, in his humanity, we must abide, as branches of the vine, if we wish to live the divine life. Just as "all things (in the original creation) were made through him," the Word, [18] so through the Word-made-flesh, Christ Jesus, all things are restored and pre-

[16] John 7:38.   [17] John 14:7.   [18] John 1:3.

served in the supernatural life. Nothing happens in the "new creation" except by the actual working of Christ its head, working in it by his Holy Spirit; for all grace since the Fall is the grace of Christ, merited by him, and—since his glorious resurrection—caused in souls only through the instrumentality of his glorified humanity.

Consciousness of Christ's Presence

Christ, therefore, truly is in us by the grace he is producing in us, as truly as God is in all things by causing their existence. But Christ's presence in us causes divine life, while the universal presence of God in all creatures causes only natural being in them. The more conscious we are of this presence of Christ in us, the more perfectly we will live the supernatural life.

Since Christ lives in us, it is incumbent upon us to cultivate the habit of repeatedly surrendering to his divine influence. Again and again, we must offer our whole being to him, saying with St. Augustine: "O sweet Jesus, live thou in me!" Let my life be yours, Lord, let my work, my prayers, my sufferings be yours. Lord, all these things really belong to you; you have a right to them, for my whole being bears your mark. The baptismal character marks me out as belonging exclusively to you; I am not my own but yours. You have bought me at a great price; use my life as your instrument for glorifying the Father.

Although the Redeemer has absolute rights over each of us because he has purchased us by his blood, so that we have no right to live except in him and for him, he does not force his divine life upon us; he does not live in our actions against our will. It is very important, then, that we repeatedly express to him our willingness that he take over our life completely; we should fervently ask him, invite him again and again, to begin and complete all our actions, so that we will never act independently of him. To give confidence in asking that our life be completely merged into his, let us remind him that he has a right that we live exclusively in him, he has a right to act even in our slightest action. So, Lord, take what is yours; live in me. Do not permit me to rob you of what belongs to you.

When we say our Office, or any of our prayers, let us tell him: "Lord, pray in me. Lord, let us pray together as one, you and I. This is not just my prayer, but yours. The Father will not accept it unless you present it with me."

When we suffer, let us offer no word of complaint, but let us say: "These pains are yours, Jesus. This headache belongs to you just as much as my prayers and my apostolate do. Let me not rob you of it by my complaints and my unwillingness to endure it for you. Suffer in me; fill up in me what is wanting to your sufferings on the cross, for the benefit of your body, the Church."

Or, when things go wrong, when efforts seem to be wasted, let us remember that Christ does nothing in vain; if we let him work in us in all our undertakings, if we begin each work by asking him to live in all our actions, then nothing we do will be in vain, no matter how fruitless it may seem to us. So, in all our frustrations, let us try to see the hand of Christ. "Lord, my life is yours; you know what you are doing with me; do with me what you will."

Finally this awareness of Christ within us is the perfection of devotion to the Holy Eucharist. For Christ is present in the tabernacle of the altar only for the sake of being tabernacled in our souls. When Christ comes to us in Holy Communion, he comes intending to remain permanently. He does not leave us when the sacramental species has dissolved, but after Holy Communion our mystical union with him is stronger and closer than it was before. But we lose many of the greater benefits of this union if we never think of it, if we are unmindful of the mystery that Christ is in us. In Holy Communion, the whole Christ comes to us— body, blood, soul and divinity. And our lasting mystical union with him is also a union with the whole Christ; every part of Christ—his body, blood, soul and divinity—works in us for our sanctification. This is because the whole Christ, the living Christ at the right hand of the Father, is the instrument used by God in forming the divine life in us.

Since the ascension, God's action in souls is always theandric; that is, the divinity of Christ works in souls only through his humanity. It is only when we are united to Christ the head, only when we abide in his humanity as branches in a vine, that we have supernatural life. That head, that true vine, is the God-Man, with body, blood and soul, as well as divinity; through his humanity, he gives us divine life.

Therefore, not only after Holy Communion, but any time of the day, we may say with great profit that wonderful prayer to Christ within us: "Soul of Christ, sanctify me; Body of Christ, save me; Blood of Christ, inebriate me." For the whole Christ is mystically present to us and the purpose of each Holy Communion is to tighten the bonds of our mystical union with him. Any time of the day we can be in communion with him, imbibing the benefits of his presence, thus reaping to the full the graces of Holy Communion.

In this way, we will guarantee that his prayer to the Father at the Last Supper will be answered in our case: "As thou Father in me, and I in thee, that they may be one with us . . . I in them and thou in me, that they may be perfected in unity." [19]

[19] John 17:21, 23.

PART TWO

Like the Word, in the
Interior Life

CHAPTER IV

CHRIST, THE PRIMORDIAL SACRAMENT

THE SACRED HUMANITY of Christ is an instrument; it is like a signet ring used by almighty God to impress upon us the likeness of his divine Son. Or rather, not just his humanity, but his whole being as God-Man impresses its likeness upon us, so that the adopted children of God are in the likeness both of Christ's divinity and of his humanity. Even our lowliest human actions should resemble the human actions of this Man who is God, for Christ must live in everything we do.

These truths about divine adoption are illustrated for us in St. Catherine's vision of St. Dominic in the likeness of Christ. The eternal Father, after pointing out to Catherine six points of resemblance of Dominic to Christ, summarized by saying; "In all his actions, he was like my natural Son in some way." Then he added a seventh point of similarity: "Even his body bore a great resemblance to the body of my most sacred, only-begotten Son," [1] as if to emphasize the perfection of the life of Christ in Dominic.

"We also," says St. Paul, "eagerly await a Savior, our Lord Jesus Christ, who will refashion the body of our lowliness, conforming it to the body of his glory by exerting the power by which he is able also to subject all things to himself." [2] This power of Christ is already at work in us,

---

[1] Raymond of Capua, *Life of St. Catherine of Siena*, p. 185.
[2] Philippians 3:20.

forming first our souls, then all our human actions, and eventually even our bodies, in the likeness of Christ.

Christ our Lord is a living sacrament; he himself is an efficacious sign of what his power and grace will produce in us. The seven sacraments instituted by Christ are efficacious signs, signs which contain his own divine power to accomplish what they signify. The sign itself tells us what effect it is producing in our souls. But Christ himself is the primordial sacrament; the seven sacraments are only so many extensions or continuations of Christ, which make him and his sanctifying power present to us. The sacraments can sanctify only because Christ is working through them; they are his instruments. The sanctity which Jesus gave to human life by living it, he communicates to us in the sacraments.

But he himself is the great sacrament because he himself is an efficacious sign; that is, he is the model, the exemplar of what his sanctifying power produces in us. Everything he was, everything he did, everything he is now, signifies to us what he does for us by the divine power which is in him. This power, producing the life of grace in us, refashions us in Christ's own likeness. The mysteries of our Lord's life, which he accomplished in the past when he was on earth, remain present to us by the divine power which is in them. All the actions of Christ's life have this divine power to reproduce in us what they signify.

This fact is indicated for us by St. Paul when he says, for example: "Christ was delivered up for our sins, and rose again for our justification." [3] His death is the cause of our death to sin, his resurrection is the cause of our resurrection to the life of grace. "If we have become united with him in the likeness of his death, then we shall also be in that of his resurrection." [4] Though the apostle mentions explicitly only

[3] Romans 4:25.   [4] Romans 6:4.

two mysteries, the Church, guided by the Holy Spirit, teaches that Christ's grace reproduces in us all the mysteries of Christ's life.

For this reason, in the course of the liturgical year, in celebrating the greatest of the seven sacraments, the Mass, Holy Mother Church dramatizes for us in turn, in the propers of the Mass, all the mysteries of our Lord's life, so that by the power of his grace, given to us through the Mass and Holy Communion, Christ may reproduce in our souls the particular mystery of his life which the Church is reliving at that particular liturgical season. And in the collects, secret prayers and postcommunions, the Church prays for the effects of grace in our souls which correspond to that mystery.

In this way, the celebration of a mystery in the sacred liturgy is a sacrament which produces in us what it signifies. For example, at the Christmas season, the mystery of Christ's infancy, working in our souls through the Mass and Holy Communion and our meditation on that mystery, strengthens in us the virtues of Christ's infancy and hidden life.

In Advent we celebrate the mystery of the preparation for Christ's coming. Cooperating with the special grace of this mystery, brought to us in the Masses of this season, we meditate on our helplessness without Christ, and the grace of the season forms in our souls the burning desire of the patriarchs and prophets for the Savior, so that our souls are more perfectly prepared to receive the fullness of the life of Christ.

Or, in that same season, we meditate on Christ's conception in the womb of Mary by the overshadowing of the Holy Spirit, realizing that we, too, have been conceived as children of God by that same Holy Spirit in baptism, which is the womb of Mother Church. Or rather, it is Christ who has been conceived and formed in us; we are children of God because he lives in us. In Advent we are in the womb of Mother Church, being nourished by her doctrine and her sacraments as we await our birth into the eternal life of heaven. We eagerly look forward to our full birth in heaven, just as Mary in expectancy breathlessly awaited the birth of her divine son. Or we ask Mary to form us in the womb of her love, in the likeness of Christ.

In Christmastide, by the grace of the season, we continue to meditate on our adoption in Christ as children of God, and the grace of adoption grows in us, forming us more perfectly in the likeness of Christ. For the Son of God became Son of Man so that men could become sons of God. In the Christmas season we strive for the poverty and humility of Christ's hidden life at Bethlehem and Nazareth and we re-live his obedience to his parents, who took the place of God, just as our superiors do.

And thus, by the time Lent comes, we are strong enough —for we have grown with Christ "in wisdom and age and grace" [5]—to receive the great grace of the Lenten season to re-live Christ's passion and death with him by our Lenten penances. In this season the mystery of Christ's passion produces in us a death to self and to sin. If we are thus united to Christ in the likeness of his death, we shall have the grace of overflowing joy and deep hope brought to us by the mystery of Christ's resurrection. The grace of this mystery also causes in us a resurrection to a more vigorous super-natural life than we have ever lived before, because Christ's resurrection signifies and causes "that we should have life, and have it more abundantly." [6]

And thus the liturgy, which primarily and essentially is the celebration of the Sacrifice of the Eucharist, produces in

[5] Luke 2:52.   [6] John 10:10.

us the likeness of the eternal Word of God, that Word who in the beginning was with God, that Word who was made flesh and dwelt among us.

It forms in us the likeness of the Incarnate Word, fashioning in us the virtues of Christ's sacred humanity—the obedience and humility of his hidden life, the self-denial and patient suffering of his Passion—but it forms in us also the likeness of Christ's divinity—the likeness of the Word with God. In fact, the likeness to the virtues of his humanity flows from our interior likeness to his divinity.

For the Word-made-flesh is a sacrament, a living sign. Everything that the Word of God did in his human nature signifies to us, manifests to us, what he does eternally in his divine nature. And since Christ is a sacramental sign with power to accomplish in us what he signifies, he reproduces in our souls the very things that occur eternally in the Trinity; he forms the very life of the Trinity in our souls.

The mysteries of Christ, then, the things the divine Word did as Man, reflect the things he does eternally as God, and they contain divine power to reproduce these things in us. In the following chapter we shall illustrate this point, showing how the grace of the mystery of the Incarnation reproduces in our souls Christ's eternal birth of the Father as the Word of God.

CHAPTER V

"ABBA, FATHER!"

JESUS CHRIST, the Son of God, the Son of Mary, has two birthdays, an eternal one and a temporal one. His first birthday is the eternal day in which he is begotten of the

Father, of which we sing in the psalms: "Thou art my Son, I this day have begotten thee"; "before the daystar, like the dew, I have begotten thee." [2] His second birthday was a day measured out in time by that daystar, the sun.

The Son of God was born into time so that we could be born into eternity. The Son of God was born of a woman so that we might be born of God. "When the fullness of time came, God sent his Son, born of a woman . . . that we might receive the adoption of sons. . . . . Because you are sons, God has sent his Son into your hearts, crying, "Abba, Father!" [3] Christmas, therefore, is really our birthday as well as Christ's. He was born on earth so that we could partake in his eternal birth. He entered into the womb of a woman so that we could enter into his eternal generation by his Father.

That is, when we live the divine life of grace to which we were born in baptism, we share in the very life of God; God lives his life in us. His divine life consists in eternally giving his divine nature to his Son, the second Person of the Blessed Trinity, and in these two Persons, Father and Son, eternally giving the divine nature to the Holy Spirit. When we are born of God, by grace, the Father gives us a sharing in that same divine nature which he eternally gives to the Son and the Holy Spirit, and thus indeed we begin to live eternal life, God's own eternal life. For by grace, says St. Peter, "you are made partakers of the divine nature." [4]

The great Dominican mystic, Tauler, says these things in this way: "God is present most intimately in this depth of the soul, and there he continuously engenders his Word; for wherever the Father is, it is necessary that he generate. He also engenders us that we may be his sons through the grace

---

[1] Psalm 2:7.   [2] Psalm 109:3 (Confraternity Edition).
[3] Galatians 4:4–6.   [4] II Peter 1:4.

of adoption." [5] In other words, when God dwells in our soul, even in our soul the Father is eternally giving birth to his divine Son, the Word. He is present in our soul precisely so that he can give us a sharing in that divine sonship of the Word; the Father in our soul begets us in the likeness of his divine Son. Thus we are "conformed to the image of his Son, so that he may be firstborn among many brethren." [6] Therefore, of us, too, the Father can say, "This is my beloved son in whom I am well pleased." [7]

Because we share in the sonship of Jesus, it follows that we share in his eternal birth of the Father. That is why we can say that the Son of God had a birthday in time, like us, so that we could share his eternal birthday with him. He entered into time so that we could enter into that eternal day, when the Father begets us, with Christ, in the image of his Son.

We receive divine life from the Father, and that is why we call him "Abba, Father"; [8] but we do not have this divine life in the same way that the Son and the Holy Spirit have it. They have identically the same nature as the Father, and they have the divine nature in its infinite fullness. But we are children of God by adoption, and so we are not God, but nevertheless are true children of God, sharing in God's life. In the eighty-first psalm, God addresses us, saying: "You are gods and all of you the sons of the Most High." St. Augustine comments on this: "If we have been made sons of God, we have been made gods." [9] If baptism is a real rebirth in God, it means that there is a real communication of God's life to us, a real communication of nature between the Father and his adopted sons.

Augustine continues: "God calls men gods because they

---

[5] *Institutions*, 34.   [6] Romans 8:29.   [7] Matthew 3:17.
[8] Galatians 4:6.   [9] St. Augustine, *In Psalmis*, 49, no. 2.

are deified by his grace and not because they are born of his substance." [10] Eadmer, a disciple of St. Anselm, says: "God makes other gods, but in such fashion that he alone is the God who deifies and we are the gods who are deified." [11] No wonder that John the Evangelist exclaims: "Behold what manner of love the Father has bestowed upon us, that we should be called children of God; and such we are." [12]

As a proof that all these things are so, "God has sent the Spirit of his Son into our hearts, crying, 'Abba, Father!' " [13] The Holy Spirit cannot lie; he is the "Spirit of truth." [14] He tells the truth when he "testifies to our spirit that we are sons of God. But if we are sons, we are heirs also: heirs indeed of God, and joint heirs with Christ." [15]

"This gift by which God calls man his son and man calls God his Father exceeds all other gifts," says St. Leo the Great.[16] For it is the gift of himself, a sharing of his very own life. "Every good gift and every perfect gift is from above, coming down from the Father of lights. . . . Of his own will, he has begotten us by the word of truth." [17]

There is a vast difference between the adoption of a son by a man, and the adoption of a son by God. When a human being adopts a son, it is because he lacks something; he needs a son because he has none. But God has an eternal Son in whom he takes infinite delight, and therefore he does not need us as his children. We understand, then, what infinite love God is bestowing upon us when he spontaneousy begets us of his own free will, not because he has to, but simply because he loves us. And we upon whom he so lovingly

[10] *Ibid.*   [11] Eadmer, *Liber de similit.*, cap. 66.
[12] I John 3:1.   [13] Galatians 4:6.
[14] John 15:26.   [15] Romans 8:17.
[16] St. Leo the Great, *Sermo 4 de Nativitate.*
[17] James 1:17–18.

bestows this sonship were sinners, enemies of God, slaves of sin. He redeems us even as he begets us.

When a human being adopts a son, the adoption is a legal fiction; the process of adoption produces nothing new in the being of the adopted one. All the human adopter can give the adopted son is his name and his property. But when God adopts us as his children, he truly begets us, he truly does share his own life with us, he regenerates us in his eternal Son. When the heavenly Father adopts a soul as his child by grace, he forms that soul in the likeness of the eternal Word; we are "predestined to become conformed to the image of his Son." [18] However, we are not truly like the Son of God unless we are like him in his oneness with the Father, in the living love which is the Holy Spirit.

St. Thomas Aquinas explains our adoption as sons of God by grace as follows:

> The sonship of adoption is a certain likeness of natural sonship. Now the Son of God proceeds naturally from the Father as the intellectual Word, in oneness of nature with the Father. To this Word, therefore, something may be likened in three ways.
>
> First, on the part of the form but not on the part of its intelligibility. Thus, the form of a house already built is like the mental word of the builder in its specific form, but not in intelligibility, because the material form of a house is not intelligible, as it was in the mind of the builder. In this way, every creature is like the eternal Word, since it was made through the Word.
>
> Secondly, the creature is likened to the Word, not only as to its form, but also as to its intelligibility: thus the knowledge which is begotten in the disciple's mind is likened to the word in the mind of the master.

[18] Romans 8:29.

In this way the rational creature, even in its nature, is likened to the Word of God.

Thirdly, a creature is likened to the eternal Word as to the oneness of the Word with the Father, which is by reason of grace and charity: wherefore, our Lord prays: "That they may be one in us . . . as we also are one" (Jn. 17:21–22). And this likeness perfects the adoption, for to those who are thus like Him the eternal inheritance is due.

It is therefore clear that to be adopted belongs to the rational creature alone: not indeed to all, but only to those who have charity; which is "poured forth in our hearts by the Holy Spirit" (Rom. 5:5); for which reason the Holy Spirit is called "the Spirit of adoption of sons" (Rom. 8:15).[19]

Our adoption as sons of God, therefore, is perfect only in proportion to our likeness to the Word in his unity with the Father in the Holy Spirit of love, and this can only be by grace. We are sons of God only when God is speaking the Word in our souls, and simultaneously, Father and Word are spirating in us the Holy Spirit of love.

Therefore, our adoption as sons in the likeness of the eternal Word is attributed to the Holy Spirit. For just as the Word, eternally begotten of the Father, eternally goes to the Father in the embrace of love which is the Holy Spirit, so too, like the Word, the adopted son of God goes to the Father in love, in the Holy Spirit, crying, "Abba, Father!"

"Father!" is love's cry. This filial love for the Father is the sign of our divine sonship. It is the Holy Spirit's way of manifesting his presence in the soul. "You shall know him," said Jesus of the Holy Spirit, "because he shall dwell with you and be in you." [20] This knowledge that we have of

---

[19] *Summa Theologiae*, IIIa, q. 23, a. 3.   [20] John 14:17.

the indwelling Holy Spirit, says St. Thomas, is "quasi-experimental." [21] In the filial love he produces in us, we experience his presence. It is thus that he bears witness to our divine sonship: "The Spirit himself gives testimony to our spirit that we are sons of God." [22] Love's cry, "Father," springs from this conviction which he gives us.

All of this is the fulfillment in our souls of the mystery of Christ's nativity. St. Paul expresses the mystery in these parallel sentences: "God *sent* his Son, born of a woman . . . that we might receive the adoption of sons. God has *sent* the Spirit of his Son into our hearts, crying 'Abba, Father!' " [23]

"But if we are sons, we are heirs also. . . ." [24] The inheritance which God gives us is not some possession outside himself, not just the created riches he has made, but his very own life. He himself is our inheritance. We are "joint-heirs with Christ." [25] The inheritance of Christ, the thing he eternally receives from his Father, is the divine life. As joint-heirs with Christ, we receive this divine life with him from the Father. We, too, are begotten of the Father with him; we enter into that eternal birth of the Son and share in it.

We enter into Christ's eternal birth already in baptism, for then we are truly begotten by God: "Unless a man be born again of water and the Spirit, he cannot enter into the kingdom of God." [26] He who has been born of God already has eternal life—"He who believes in me has life everlasting" [27]—for grace is the seed of glory; the life of heaven is the full growth of the life of grace.

But our divine adoption and entrance into Christ's eternal

[21] *Commentary on the Sentences,* I, d. 14, q. 2. a. 2, ad 3.
[22] Romans 8:16.   [23] Galatians 4:4, 6.   [24] Romans 8:17.
[25] Romans 8:17.   [26] John 3:5.   [27] John 6:47.

birth is perfect and definitive only when we have entered into glory. Then, indeed, the Word of God has been perfectly begotten in our souls, for by the light of glory our souls are directly united to the divine essence; we see God face to face in his eternal Word and, like the Word, we are one with the Father in perfect love in the Holy Spirit.

This is the fullness of the inheritance which we will possess jointly with Christ: the fullness of the life of the Father. The divine life given to us in baptism was the pledge of the inheritance: "You were sealed in Christ with the Holy Spirit of promise, who is the pledge of our inheritance until its full possession is redeemed." [28]

The beginnings of divine life, given to us in baptism, must grow. If we are sons of God in the image of the Word, we must act accordingly. His life grows in us only with our cooperation, as we strive to conform ourselves more and more to his likeness, so that our divine sonship will become ever more perfect. In imitating Christ, lest we miss the whole point of the imitation, we must endeavor to imitate what is most basic in his life; namely, his relationship of Son to the eternal Father, his interior attitudes of soul toward the Father. This we shall discuss in the following chapter.

However, as we discuss other aspects of this filial relationship, we must never lose sight of the fact that this relationship is essentially love. Our adoption as sons makes us like the Word in his unity with the Father in the Holy Spirit of love.

[28] Ephesians 1:13–14.

CHAPTER VI

THROUGH CHRIST TO THE FATHER

THREE THINGS TAKE PLACE as the life of Christ grows in a Christian soul: incorporation into Christ, configuration to him and transformation in him. The life of Christ begins in us when we are incorporated into him in baptism. As this life grows in us, we are configured to him, we become more and more like him. When his life in us has reached its full perfection, we have been totally transformed into Christ, so that he lives in absolutely everything we do; he is in all our thoughts and actions; we do nothing independently of him. Then are the words of St. Paul fully verified of us: "It is now no longer I that live, but Christ lives in me." [1]

Christ in our soul has become the source of all our actions, so that he is indeed soul of our soul, life of our life. Just as the soul gives life to the human body and to every living part of it, so when we have been transformed into Christ, he gives divine life to our soul and to everything we do. Our whole being is transformed by the divine life of Christ which penetrates us through and through.

Incorporation, configuration and transformation are not three stages of the Christian life, which take place successively, but three aspects of one thing which is happening continuously in a soul that grows in grace. Configuration to Christ and transformation in him begin at the moment of incorporation into him. Configuration is a process which has its completion in total transformation. But our configuration progresses only because our incorporation into Christ becomes ever more intimate.

[1] Galatians 2:20.

To incorporate means to make one body with; baptism incorporates us into Christ—"we have been baptized *into* Christ"— [2] for it unites us to him in his Mystical Body, so that Christ our head can live his divine life in us. Just as a vine lives its life in and through its branches, so Jesus Christ lives his divine life in his human members, and we, his members, live the divine life in him. Only in him are we sons of God, sharing in God's own life.

The incorporation into Christ which takes place in baptism becomes ever stronger as we receive the other sacraments, especially the Holy Eucharist. Jesus said: "He who eats my flesh and drinks my blood abides in me and I in him." [3] In Holy Communion we become more intimately united to our head, more firmly attached to him, more deeply rooted in him. The bonds of union with Christ are faith and charity; as St. Paul puts it, you "have Christ dwelling through faith in your hearts," you "are rooted and grounded in love." [4] Holy Communion, more than anything else, strengthens our bonds of love, incorporates us more closely into Christ, deepens our roots in him so that we can bear more abundant fruit in him, so that nothing can uproot us from him.

But incorporation into Christ is for the sake of configuration and transformation in him. When Christ lives his life in us, he remakes us in his own likeness. God has predestined us, says St. Paul, "to become conformed to the image of his Son." [5] The grace which flows to us from Christ in his sacraments refashions us in his image. But this configuration to Christ takes place only with our cooperation. His grace in us bears fruit when we use it to imitate Christ, when we set our eyes on him, and do as he did. And

[2] Romans 6:3–4.   [3] John 6:52.
[4] Ephesians 3:17–18.   [5] Romans 8:29.

when, for love of him, we do what he did, he does it in us, he lives all his virtues in us. We must therefore work with Christ if we are to be configured to him. "Put on the Lord Jesus Christ," says St. Paul.[6]

However, configuration to Christ is something which must come from within. The imitation of Christ is not a mere aping of his exterior actions; it is acquiring his interior spirit. It must be an interior change, a change of soul, of will, of ways of thinking. If we learn to think as Christ thinks, to love what Christ loves, as a natural consequence our exterior actions will also become like his. Therefore, says St. Paul, "have this mind in you which was also in Christ Jesus."[7] And the Apostle goes on to describe our Lord's interior attitudes of soul, his humility and obedience, which were the expression of his filial love for his Father.

Our configuration to Christ is above all a configuration to his crucifixion; like St. Paul, we have to be able to say in truth: "With Christ I am nailed to the cross."[8] Configuration to Christ is impossible without mortification and sufferings; the cross is the only way which leads to complete transformation in him. "All we who have been baptized into Christ have been baptized into his death."[9] I have "become like to him in death," St. Paul continues, "in the hope that somehow I may attain to the resurrection from the dead."[10] "If we die with him, we shall also live with him."[11] Configuration is largely a dying with Christ, a being nailed to the cross; while transformation is living the life of the risen Christ.

But it is not just any kind of sufferings nor any kind of penances which configure us to Christ; it is only those which are endured with the interior spirit of Christ. Therefore, we

[6] Romans 13:14.   [7] Philippians 2:5.   [8] Galatians 2:20.
[9] Romans 6:3.   [10] Philippians 3:11.   [11] II Timothy 2:11.

must endeavor to imitate the mind of Christ, his interior attitude of soul toward his heavenly Father.

Transformation in Christ makes us perfect sons of God; God has destined us to be conformed to the image of his Son. In order that we have the mind of Christ, and thus become perfect sons of the Father, we must strive to imitate especially Christ's relationships to the Father, his attitudes toward him, his filial piety.

In reading the gospels, we should take care to note how Jesus is forever addressing his Father or speaking about him. His whole life and being are centered on the Father: from him he comes forth; to him he returns. We find him saying things like this: "Father, I give thee thanks that thou hast heard me"; [12] "I confess to thee, O Father, Lord of heaven and earth"; [13] "Father, I have glorified thee on earth"; [14] "Father, into thy hands I commend my spirit." [15] The attitudes expressed in these words, and many others like them, are to be imitated by all the children of God.

When St. Paul tells us to "have this mind in you which was also in Christ Jesus," he speaks chiefly of the humility and obedience of Jesus, his obedience unto death, even the death of the cross. But his humility and obedience flowed from his filial love for the heavenly Father. Jesus himself pointed this out at the Last Supper, when he said that he delivered himself up to his enemies so "that the world may know that I love the Father, and that I do as the Father has commanded me." [16]

But love for the Father produces unity of will with the Father; love makes two wills as one. The eagerness of Jesus to do the will of his Father is the keynote of his whole life; again and again he declares: "I have come down from

[12] John 11:41.   [13] Matthew 11:25.   [14] John 17:4.
[15] Luke 23:46.   [16] John 14:31.

heaven, not to do my own will, but the will of him who sent me . . . the Father." [17] "My food is to do the will of him who sent me, to accomplish his work." [18] Nor was Jesus content to declare this; he lived up to his declaration at the price of his death on the cross. In accepting the chalice of his sufferings, he did it with the greatest filial reverence for his Father. "My Father, if this cup cannot pass away unless I drink it, thy will be done." [19]

St. Paul points out that it was this filial reverence of Jesus for the Father which won our redemption. Speaking of the agony of Jesus in the Garden, the Apostle says: "For Jesus, in the days of his earthly life, with a loud cry and tears, offered up prayers and supplications to him who was able to save him from death, and was heard because of his reverent submission. And he, Son though he was, learned obedience from the things that he suffered; and when perfected, he became to all who obey him the cause of eternal salvation." [20]

The obedience of Jesus results from his reverence for his Father, and the reverence is the fruit of his filial love, the love of a Son for a Father. And this loving reverence produces the perfect humility of Jesus. Profound reverence for God as our Father is one of the best antidotes for pride. We must say "our Father" with childlike simplicity, for "unless you become as little children, you cannot enter the kingdom of heaven."

Our Lord's oneness of will with the Father is not merely a resignation to the Father's will, but a positive zeal for it, a burning desire to carry it out. And this eagerness to do the Father's will springs from a thirst for the Father's honor and glory. The apostles had noted how Jesus was eaten up with

[17] John 6:38–39. [18] John 4:34.
[19] Matthew 26:42. [20] Hebrews 5:7–9.

zeal for his "Father's house." [21] And on the first Palm
Sunday, as Jesus meditated on the Father's will that he die,
he was momentarily shaken at the thought, and said: "Now
is my soul troubled!" But then, thinking of his Father's
glory, he quickly recovered himself, and said: "Father,
glorify thy name!" [22] Again, at the Last Supper, he declares
why he has done the Father's will; it was in zeal for his
glory: "Father, I have glorified thee on earth, I have
accomplished the work that thou hast given me to do." [23]

Even the love of Jesus for souls flowed from his love for
his Father and his desire for the Father's glory. He told his
disciples to pray for the power to save souls so that the
Father may be glorified. "In this is my Father glorified, that
you may bring forth very much fruit." [24] And when Jesus
prayed, "Father, glorify thy Son that thy Son may glorify
thee," he was really asking that the glory of his own
resurrection would draw souls to him for the glory of the
Father.

Everything in the life of Jesus, therefore, is centered upon
his heavenly Father. He is always "about his Father's
business." [25] And his last act on the cross is an act of filial
surrender, of total abandonment of self to the Father:
"Father, into thy hands I commend my spirit." [26]

Such is the mind of Jesus which we must acquire in order
to be configured to him in his sufferings and death. Sufferings and death are inevitable in our life; it will be impossible
to escape them; they are the lot of every son and daughter of
Adam. But they will be of no profit unless they configure us
to Christ crucified. Our sufferings will not make us like
Christ crucified unless we accept them with the same spirit in
which he accepted his; that is, with filial love for the Father,

---

[21] John 2:17.   [22] John 12:27–28.   [23] John 17:4.
[24] John 15:18.   [25] Luke 2:49.   [26] Luke 23:46.

with reverent submission to the Father's will, with zeal for the Father's glory, with burning love for souls who will glorify the Father.

These sentiments can be produced in us only by Christ himself who lives in us. It is he who gives us his mind and his will; it is he within us who forms us in his own likeness and configures us to himself. Genuine Christ-likeness can come only from within, only to the extent that Christ is living his life in us, and we are living our life in him.

But we must work with him, imitating him, keeping our eyes upon him, to learn from him his relationships with his Father. When Moses gazed steadfastly upon God as he spoke with Him on Mount Sinai, his face became so bright with God's glory that the children of Israel could not bear to look at it, and he had to cover it with a veil. This veil on the face of Moses, says St. Paul, signified that Christ, the true glory of the Father, the full revelation of God, was still hidden under the figures and types of the Old Testament.[27] But now that the veil has been removed, continues the Apostle, all of us have the privilege of gazing directly upon "the glory of God shining on the face of Christ Jesus." [28] We see "his glory, glory of the Only-begotten of the Father, full of grace and truth." [29]

We must look at him, continually contemplating him, ever mindful of his presence with us. By thus gazing at Christ in our meditations and living in love the truth we have seen, we become like him, transformed into him. "We all, with faces unveiled, reflecting as in a mirror the glory of the Lord, are being transformed into his very image from glory to glory, as through the Spirit of the Lord." [30]

The light which so many noticed shining in the face of St.

---

[27] II Corinthians 3:7.   [28] II Corinthians 4:6.
[29] John 1:14.   [30] II Corinthians 3:18.

Dominic—was it there because he had gazed so steadfastly upon Christ in contemplation, that "the glory of God shining on the face of Christ Jesus" had transformed Dominic into the same likeness? In no other way but by contemplating Christ could Dominic have become so perfect an adopted son of the Father in the likeness of the eternal Word.

CHAPTER VII

WITH GOD, LIKE THE WORD

ST. PAUL SPEAKS OF CHRIST as "the image of the invisible God," who "in the fullness of time" was "made in the likeness of man." [1] Eternal image of the Father, incarnate in the likeness of men! Significant echo of the words of the Creator: "Let us make man to our image and likeness." [2]

This likeness of God, according to which mankind was originally patterned, was the Son of God himself, the Word of God, who is "the brightness of his glory and the image of his substance." [3]

But how was mankind made in the likeness of the eternal Word? What characteristics of the Word of God were found in the first man? It is written of the Word that "He was with God." [4] He lives eternally in the presence of the Father. The first man and his wife, until they sinned, were like the Word because they, too, lived in the presence of God. They were with God because they were in the state of grace, on terms of most intimate friendship with God, and conversed with him at will. These facts are taught in the Book of Genesis, under

[1] Colossians 1:15; Galatians 4:4; Philippians 2:7.   [2] Genesis 1:26.
[3] Hebrews 1:3.   [4] John 1:1.

the imagery of God walking in the garden with Adam and Eve in the cool of the evening. The man and his wife lived in God's own garden. Of course, it was by faith that they lived in God's presence, for they had not yet received the beatific vision.

But sin changed all of that. Man was driven from God's garden, driven from the divine presence. The likeness of the Word in them was destroyed. No longer were they with God; no longer were they like the Word, who is ever one with the Father in a bond of intimate love.

So that man could be restored to the likeness of the Word, the Word was made flesh, and by the grace of the redemption, once again we can be "conformed to the image of the Son." [5] To be "with God," to live in his presence and enjoy his friendship, is within the power of every soul in the state of grace. For the grace of adoption, given us in baptism, makes us beloved children of God, capable of living the intimate family life of the Trinity, at home with the Father, at ease in his presence.

Since the whole purpose of this grace is to make us "partakers of the divine nature," "so that our fellowship may be with the Father and with his Son, Jesus Christ," [6] it follows that as the life of grace in us more and more matures, we live more and more in the presence of God, we become more and more completely aware of his love for us, and we respond with an ever-increasing love of him. Knowledge devoid of love is not enough for living in the presence of God; fully living in his presence includes a tasting of his sweetness, a savoring of God that can come only from love. This savoring of God is the effect of the gift of wisdom, which works in close connection with charity.

All the powers of grace are directed toward this goal. God

[5] Romans 8:29.   [6] II Peter 1:4; I John 1:3.

enters the soul at baptism precisely so that his presence may be enjoyed. If grace does not lie idle in a soul, if the vital powers of grace are fully cultivated, then the soul will normally advance to a stage where it always lives in the divine presence.

These facts are evident from the words of St. Paul: "You are the temple of the living God, as God says, 'I will dwell and move among them, I will be their God and they shall be my people.' " [7] In explaining these words, St. Thomas says that it is in the saints that God dwells; that is to say, in souls in the state of grace. For in St. Paul's language, anyone sanctified by grace is called a saint.

"For although God is said to *be* in all things by his presence, power and essence, he is not said to *dwell* in all things, but only in the saints, by grace. The reason for this is that God is in all things by his action, inasmuch as he unites his power to them giving them existence and preserving them in it. But he is in the saints by the action of the saints themselves, by their action of knowing and loving God, by which action they are united to him and, in a certain manner, hold and contain him. For whoever loves and knows is said to have in himself that which he loves and knows." [8]

In other words, although God is in all things, upholding them by his power, he dwells in those whom he has adopted as his children by grace, for by grace they are able to be aware of his presence, which is impossible to the lower creatures. "Therefore, in a special way, God is in the rational creature which knows and loves him actually or habitually." [9] But it is possible for a soul to possess God by knowledge and love only because God is in the soul, producing in it the power of sanctifying grace.

[7] II Corinthians 6:16.   [8] *Commentary on II Corinthians*, 6:16.
[9] *Summa Theologiae*, Ia, q. 83, a. 3.

Since these things are so, St. Thomas makes a startling comment about the words of Jesus, "If anyone love me, he will keep my word, and my Father will love him, and we will come to him and make our abode with him." [10] St. Thomas says: "God is said to come to us not because he moves to us, but because we move to him." [11]

God is everywhere, preserving all things by his power, and he is in us also, preserving us in that same way. But that we can move to him by faith and love, and thereby be aware of his presence, he comes to us in a new way, in the sense that his all-present power produces in us a new effect, the supernatural effect of grace; "and through this effect of grace, he causes us to approach to him." [12]

Indeed, then, God's coming to us in the way described by Jesus—"we will come to him"—is really our going to him, for the effect of grace is to turn us to him in knowledge and love so that we are aware of his presence. Thus, he dwells in us as in his temple, where he is duly acknowledged and loved.

St. Augustine explains that God comes to us in three ways and in these same three ways we go to him. Each of his three ways of coming to us simultaneously causes our going to him. "First, he comes to us, filling us with his effects (of grace), and we go to him by (voluntarily) receiving the effects: 'Come to me, all you that yearn for me, and be filled with my fruits' (Sir. 24:18). Secondly, he comes to us by enlightening us, and we simultaneously go to him by considering (the truth with which he is enlightening us). 'Come ye to him and be enlightened' (Ps. 33:6). Thirdly, by helping us, and we go to him by obeying; because we cannot even obey unless helped by Christ: 'Come, let us go

[10] John 14:23.   [11] *Commentary on John*, 14:23.
[12] *Ibid.*

to the mountain of the Lord' " (Is. 2:3).[13] Notice that we go to God by considering his truth and obeying his commands, only because he is coming to us as we do these things, by giving us the grace to do them. "For it is God who of his good pleasure works in you both the will and the performance." [14]

Therefore, the dwelling of God in our souls by grace is really a case of love meeting love—our love meeting God's. "If anyone love me . . . my Father will love him, and we will come to him and make our abode with him." We possess him and enjoy his presence by our love which responds to his love. His love is efficacious; that is, it produces in us the power to love him. We can love him only because he is loving us, only because he is pouring out his love by his Spirit who has been given to us.

We have within ourselves what we love. "In that day," says Jesus, "you shall know that . . . you are in me and I in you." [15] That is, says St. Thomas, "by mutual love we are in one another." [16] "You are in me," that is, drawn by the grace of God, the gift of his love, you have come to me by knowledge and love, hearing my word and keeping it; accepting it in the enlightenment of faith, keeping it in love. And therefore, I am in you; for by this divine enlightenment, and by this love inspired by God, you possess and enjoy me.

Therefore, St. John writes in his epistles, "God is love, and he who abides in love abides in God, and God in him." [17] And all because God "has first loved us"—"not that we have loved God, but God has first loved us." [18] Or, as God expresses it through Jeremias the Prophet: "I have loved

---

[13] Quoted by St. Thomas, in *Commentary on John*, 14:23.
[14] Philippians 2:13.   [15] John 16:20.   [16] *Commentary on John*, 14:23.
[17] I John 4:16.   [18] I John 4:10.

thee with an everlasting love, and therefore have I drawn thee, taking pity on thee." [19] I have come to you in love, giving you the power to come to me in love. Whenever you turn to me in love, it is because I am turning to you in love.

So, although God is in the soul habitually as long as the soul is in the state of grace, the perfection of his presence in the soul consists in the soul's actually being aware of that presence, here and now, by active love and faith. It is up to the soul, then, to put its virtues of faith and charity into action; by acts of faith and charity, we actually contact God and enjoy his presence. It is within the power of the soul to do this, because by grace God is in the soul, giving it the power.

Living in God's presence by faith and love, therefore, is the maturity of our adoptive sonship of God. For by adoption as sons we are made like to the Son of God himself, whose likeness is formed in us by the Father. Every new grace of divine enlightenment is really a new likeness to the Son; or rather, a perfecting of his likeness in us, a deeper sharing in the Word who is eternal Light. Every new insight into divine things is a kind of new begetting of the Son in our souls by the Father, a new sending of the Son to us. All our supernatural knowledge of God is a sharing of God's own knowledge of himself, and he knows himself only in the Word, "the brightness of his glory and the image of his substance." [20] Each new divine enlightenment we receive is a more perfect living of the life of God who is Light.[21]

Just as each new enlightenment which we receive from God is a deeper sharing in the life of the Son who is Light, so each new increase in charity is a deeper sharing in the life of the Holy Spirit who is Love. The Father living in the

[19] Jeremias 31:3.   [20] Hebrew 1:3.   [21] I John 1:5.

depths of the soul begets the Word in it. But the soul, considering God's truth in this Word, breaks forth spontaneously in love of God in the Holy Spirit. This love of charity makes the soul one with the Father as the Son is one with him, and thus the likeness to the Son is perfected, the adoption as son is completed.

All of this is nothing more than the maturity of the grace of adoption given us in baptism, the fullness of the divine life of grace. It is a living of the life and light and love of the Trinity, a living in the presence of God. When we fully live this life of grace, like the Word we are "with God," one with him in the unity of the Holy Spirit, in fulfillment of Christ's prayer at the Last Supper: "That they may be one in us . . . even as we are one: I in them and thou in me, that they may be perfected in unity . . . that the love with which thou lovest me may be in them, and I in them." [22]

However, we must remember that no matter how perfect we become in this life, no matter how fully we live the life of grace, we are still living in the dark, as it were. On earth, the divine enlightenment given to us by the Word of God living in us is still only the enlightenment of faith, and by faith we always know things "in an obscure manner." [23] Hence, the marvelous realities we have been describing do not seem vivid to those who have not yet experienced them very deeply. If one's spiritual life is really healthy and fervent, these things are taking place in him, even though he may not always be very much aware of them. He lives these realities in the darkness of faith most of the time, and only now and then does he savor them. But as he makes more and more progress, he should more and more deeply experience the presence of God within him.

This is something to be greatly desired and prayed for:

[22] John 17:21–26.   [23] I Corinthians 13:12.

Come to me, that I may come to you. Live in me, that I may live in you. Father, form thy Son in me, that I may enjoy your presence by actual contemplation of you in the Word. Father and Son, enkindle the fervor of the Holy Spirit in me, that I may savor your presence in love. Holy Spirit of adoption, make me truly a child of God, that I may always be at home in the bosom of the Holy Trinity.

> We pray thee, O God, Three and One;
> Do thou so visit us, as we adore thee;
> Lead us by thy paths whither we take our way,
> To the light wherein thou dost dwell.[24]

[24] Matins Hymn, Feast of Corpus Christi.

CHAPTER VIII

FROM THE FATHER

WHEN MAN WAS FIRST MADE in the image and likeness of God, like the Word he was with God, living in the divine presence. Sin changed all this. Then the Word was made flesh and dwelt among us. Because the Word was with men, men could again, like the Word, be with God.

There is another way in which man must be conformed to the eternal Word, in order that his likeness to God be perfect. Speaking of himself, the Word-made-flesh has told us that all that he is and all that he does is from the Father, and that he never acts independently of the Father. "Amen, amen, I say to you, the Son can do nothing of himself, but only what he sees the Father doing. For whatever he does, this the Son also does in like manner."[1] And in his Last Supper prayer, he said: "Father, they have learned that

[1] John 5:19.

whatever thou hast given me is from thee. . . . They have known of a truth that I came forth from thee, and they have believed that thou didst send me." [2]

We see from these words that all that Christ is and has, not only in his humanity but even in his divinity, is from the Father. First, concerning his eternal divine life, Jesus says: "Father, they have known that I came forth from thee." That is, they have known that I am thy divine Son, eternally begotten by Thee. Within the divinity, the Son eternally proceeds from the Father. Eternally he is receiving all that he is from the Father. Eternally begotten of the Father, he is ever in the Father, living the one and the same life with him, but always receiving that life from the Father. And yet, he is equal to the Father; the Father does not exist prior to him; each always has the fullness of divinity.

Concerning his life in human nature, Jesus says: "Father, they have believed that thou didst send me." Everything Christ is and has and does as Man, is from the Father—his mission, his doctrine, his every action. "Father, they have learned that whatever thou hast given me is from thee, because the words that thou hast given me I have given to them." That is, they have received my words, Father, as thy very own; and such indeed they are, "for all things that are mine are thine, and thine are mine." [3] Whatever is thine is mine, for I have received it from thee.

Not only his words, but also all Christ's actions are from the Father. "The Son can do nothing of himself, but only what he sees the Father doing." "He who sent me is with me; he has not left me alone, because I do always the things that are pleasing to him." [4] "My sheep hear my voice . . . neither shall anyone snatch them out of my hand." And the reason for this is simply this, that "no one is able to snatch

[2] John 17:7–8. [3] John 17:10. [4] John 8:29.

anything out of the hand of my Father. I and the Father are one." [5]

We may say, then, that the Word, whether as God or as Man, receives all that he is from the Father, and does nothing independently of him. This is the likeness of the Word Incarnate which must be reproduced in us. If we are to be perfectly like the Word, we too must receive all from the Father and act only in him, so that we can say in perfect truth at the end of our lives, as did Christ at the end of his: "Whatever thou hast given me is from thee." I have done nothing independently of thee, nothing contrary to thee, Father, because thou hast given me thy life and hast lived it in me.

That this will be so, frequently we should recite the opening prayer of the Dominican Mass: "Precede our actions with thy inspiration, we pray thee, Lord, and follow them with thy assistance, that all that we do may begin always from thee, and through thee, being begun, may be finished. Through Christ our Lord. Amen."

But how is it possible that there be anything in us not from the Father, since "in him we live and move and have our being?" [6] It is impossible to exist or act unless God gives us being.

Sin is not from the Father, and sin occurs when man, with his free will, chooses to act contrary to the Father, attempting to be independent of him. Thus man repels from himself the likeness of the Word—who does nothing without the Father—and forms in himself the image and likeness of the proud and rebellious Satan. Jesus tells his enemies that their actions are from the devil, not from the heavenly Father. "If God were your Father," He said to them, "you would surely love me. For from God I came forth and have

[5] John 10:28.   [6] Acts 17:28.

come; for neither have I come of myself, but he sent me. . . . The father from whom you are is the devil, and the desires of your father it is your will to do." [7]

Through pride, we acquire the image of Satan—a rebellious, independent spirit, a tendency to go our own way, not God's. But the Word-made-flesh had no such spirit. "Behold, I come to do thy will, O God," [8] was the theme-song of his life.

There is another reason besides the instigation of the devil, and besides pride, to explain why everything in us is not from the Father. As a penalty of Adam's departure from the presence of God, all his children experience in themselves the rebellion of their lower nature. God mercifully allows this sting of concupiscence in man to humiliate his pride, in the hope that he will learn how helpless he is without God, so that perhaps he will return to him.

Because of his concupiscence, man's actions tend to begin not with God, but from below. They tend to begin in his lower nature, in the flesh, in the emotions, rather than in the soul, where God dwells. Man has a strong tendency to live only on the level of the senses and the emotions, rather than on the spiritual level, and if he gives in to this tendency, he becomes more and more like an animal, less and less like God. This is the penalty for withdrawing mind and heart from the presence of God. Unless man fights very strenuously to keep mind and heart on God, he will inevitably be drawn downward. Without a continual fight to remain in the divine presence, he will tend to live at best a very shallow natural life, concerned only with the world, or at worst, a degraded animal life, or even a diabolical one.

These downward tendencies are not from the Father in heaven; they do not bear the likeness of the Word, who is

[7] John 8:42f.   [8] Hebrews 10:7.

entirely from God. "God is no tempter to evil," says St. James. "Everyone is tempted by being drawn away and enticed by his own passion." [9] According to St. John: "All that is in the world is the lust of the flesh and the lust of the eyes and the pride of life, which are not from the Father, but from the world." [10]

How, then, can we ever hope to succeed in being perfectly like the Word, in whom everything is from the Father? Only by abiding in the Word-made-flesh, whose flesh is for our salvation. "Abide in me, and I in you. . . . For without me, you can do nothing." [11]

The Word is entirely from God not only in his divine life, but even his human flesh is totally from God. Although he was "born of a woman," [12] "the offspring of David according to the flesh," [13] son of Abraham, and son of Adam, the flesh that Christ received from Adam came from God, who made it from the dust of the earth and breathed into it a living soul. When St. Luke gives the list of Christ's ancestors, showing how he is son of David, son of Adam, he ends the list by saying that Adam "was son of God," [14] thus assuring us that even Christ's flesh was from God.

But our flesh too, like that of Christ, is from God, through Adam, with this difference: in us, it is a fallen, rebellious flesh. And there is another difference, which explains why Christ's flesh is not rebellious, but everything in it, its every movement, is from God. The flesh of Christ is from God because it was conceived in the womb of Mary by the working of the Holy Spirit. Therefore, even though it is truly of the stock of Adam, the flesh of Christ has nothing in it of fallen Adam, nothing of sin or sinful tendency. Only those conceived in the normal way of carnal relations have

---

[9] James 1:14.   [10] I John 2:16.   [11] John 15:4–5.
[12] Galatians 4:4.   [13] Romans 1:4.   [14] Luke 3:38.

rebellious flesh. (This is not to say that carnal relations are sinful, but that original sin and its effects are transmitted through carnal generation.)

But Christ was not so conceived. Since by the flesh of Christ our fallen flesh is to be restored, his flesh had to come anew from God, by a sort of new creation. Even though it was taken from the stock of Adam, and therefore was from God by way of Adam, Christ's flesh is from God in another way—it was directly conceived by the power of the Holy Spirit. When God formed the first man of the slime of the earth, he breathed into his face the breath of life and, says St. Paul, "the first man, Adam, became a living soul." [15] We note that in the Hebrew, the word for breath is the same as the word for spirit. At the creation of Christ, the New Adam, the Holy Spirit of God was, as it were, breathed again upon human flesh, in the womb of Mary, and the second Adam, says St. Paul, "became a life-giving spirit." [16] That is to say, the Holy Spirit was upon Christ so that he could give new life to all.

"If then any man is in Christ," says the Apostle, "he is a new creature: the former things have passed away: behold, they are made new. But all things are from God, who has reconciled us to himself through Christ." [17] Only "in Christ," only by our incorporation into his holy humanity, can all that is in us again be from God. No wonder that Christ declared so emphatically that he is totally from God: to show us how to aspire to the same, to teach us that only in him can we be so.

We are born again of God in baptism in the likeness of Christ, by that same Holy Spirit who formed his spotless flesh in the immaculate womb of Mary. And Christ was always led by that Holy Spirit. "Led by the Holy Spirit into

[15] I Corinthians 15:45.   [16] *Ibid.*   [17] II Corinthians 5:17f.

the desert," [18] he fasted, to show us that "if by the Spirit we put to death the deeds of the flesh," all our actions can again be from God. "For whoever are led by the Spirit of God, they are the sons of God." [19]

So that we will never act independently of the Father, Christ insists: "Abide in me. Without me, you can do nothing." [20] "He who eats my flesh"—that holy flesh formed by the Holy Spirit in the womb of Mary—"and drinks my blood, abides in me and I in him." [21] Abide in me by continual recollection, because sacramental Holy Communion is also for the sake of spiritual communion; that is, we receive the physical body of Christ in the Sacrament, so that by the grace received from contact with his humanity, we may live all day long in spiritual contact with his divinity by faith and love, continually walking in the divine presence in prayerful recollection. Such continual communion with God in recollection is not at all impossible, for the all-powerful Sacrament of the Eucharist makes it possible to those who work for it. Living in continual spiritual communion with God is the normal effect of fervent Holy Communion. [22]

Abide in me, then, through Holy Communion and continual spiritual communion, so that through me you may receive all things from my Father. "As the living Father has sent me and as I live because of the Father, so he who eats me, he also shall live because of me." [23] The Son eternally receives the fullness of divine life from the Father who begets him; when we abide in Christ, the Father begets that same divine life in us, forming in us the likeness of his eternal Word.

That is the goal of the Christian life: to receive all things

[18] Matthew 4:1.   [19] Romans 8:13–14.
[20] John 15:4, 5.   [21] John 6:57.
[22] This will be discussed in detail in Chapter XX.   [23] John 6:58.

from the Father, to receive from him an ever-increasing participation of his life so that no longer will any of our actions be from below, from the flesh, from the world, from pride, from Satan, but all our actions will begin in God and by him be divinely accomplished. Such is the supernatural life to which we are called.

In order to receive all from the Father, we must regularly report to him, coming into the divine presence as much as possible to ask: "Lord, begin all my actions by thy divine inspiration, and bring them to completion by thy assistance. Live in me!"

It is not enough hastily to ask this and then distractedly rush to our work. No, with great docility we should remain as much as possible in the divine presence, waiting to receive all things from God. We open our hearts with complete abandonment to his life-giving spirit, so that he can do with us what he will. Like Mary, we give ourselves completely and without reserve in perfect docility, saying: "Behold the handmaid of the Lord; be it done to me according to thy word." Thus we will receive from the Father the same Holy Spirit who came upon her, who will form in our souls the same Word Incarnate, so that everything in us, as in Christ, will be from the Father.

CHAPTER IX

"THE BRIGHTNESS OF HIS GLORY"

IN ORDER TO BE PERFECTLY CONFORMED to the image and likeness of God, we have to be like the eternal Word in every possible way. The Word gives glory to the Father, both eternally and in time. Therefore, we must strive to be like him in this, giving glory to God at all times, in everything we do.

But what is glory, and how do we give it to God? In the Bible, the expression "the glory of God" has three meanings, closely interrelated. First, the expression means the various manifestations of God, the shining forth of his majesty in his exterior works. Thus we read: "All the earth is full of his glory." [1] Obviously, therefore, the word "glory" means also that which is manifested in God's exterior works, namely, the very being of God, the infinite majesty in itself. "The heavens show forth the glory of God." [2] For this reason, God is referred to as Israel's glory. When the Israelites set up the golden calf, the psalmist remarks: "They changed their glory (i.e., their God) into the likeness of a calf that eats grass." [3]

But if everything created speaks of God's glory, his inner perfection, how much more should man; therefore, the psalmist says: "O ye spirits and souls of the just, bless the Lord; O ye holy and humble of heart, bless the Lord." [4] And so, the term, "glory of God" came to mean the praise given to him by his intellectual creatures. St. Augustine defines glory as "clear knowledge with praise." [5] When God's intellectual creatures really know him, whether through his manifestations of himself in his works or whether he directly reveals his inner glory to them, they are so delighted with him that they spontaneously break into praise of him. Theologians call this praise "the formal glory of God." The person who praises God sincerely does so because he is so in love with God, so delighted with him, that he wants to tell

---

[1] Isaias 6:3.   [3] Psalm 102:20.
[2] Psalm 18:1.   [4] Daniel 3:86.
[5] Quoted by St. Thomas in *Summa Theologiae*, Ia IIae, q. 2, a. 3.

the whole world about him. He wants to manifest God's glory to all.

This is what is meant by giving glory to God—manifesting God's perfection, his lovableness, so that everybody will know and love and praise him. When we do this, we are like the eternal Word. The Word glorifies God not only in time, not only in his life in human flesh, but indeed from all eternity.

To glorify God is to make him known. But that is precisely the Word's eternal function within the divinity; he manifests God to God. God knows himself in the Word, who eternally is the "brightness," that is, the shining forth, "of his glory, the image of his substance." [6] God, contemplating his infinite lovableness in the Word, spontaneously loves himself with the eternal, infinite love which is the living Holy Spirit, and is enraptured with infinite delight.

But such infinite bliss is too wonderful to be hoarded, too rapturous for God to keep it to himself, so, in infinite love, he wills to share it with other intelligent beings.

Therefore, the Word is given a new function: the Father sends him on a mission to manifest his glory to creatures. But the creatures first have to be created; and the very making of them is a manifestation of the divine glory. So, the Word begins the mission of glorifying God in the sight of creatures by creating them. For, says St. John about the Word, "all things were made through him, and without him was made nothing that has been made." [7] The making of them is a manifestation of divine glory, for all things are lesser likenesses of God, patterned on the Word who is the infinite image of God; therefore, all things resemble the Word in his function of glorifying, manifesting God. As the Word manifests God to God eternally, so in time, he

[6] Hebrews 1:3.   [7] John 1:3.

manifests God to creatures through creatures, all of which resemble him in greater or lesser degree.

The resemblance of the Word is in all things, but there had to be creatures capable of seeing this resemblance, and in it, of seeing God himself. Hence, God created beings endowed with intelligence to whom he manifests himself through these resemblances. This power of intelligence is itself a much higher participation in the Word, a more perfect sharing in his likeness, than the mere resemblance of the Word found in lower creatures. The light of reason by which man is able to know God's likeness in creatures, and eventually God himself, is a sharing in the eternal Light, the Word himself. "In him was life, and the life was the light of men." [8]

But none of this was enough. All that creatures could do was to reflect the inner glory of God to man. By looking at them, no one could see God face to face. This reflected glory could only whet man's appetite to see the divine glory in itself. Moses, who had seen God's glory reflected in nature, in the burning bush, in the consuming fire on Mount Sinai, in God's great miracles on behalf of his chosen people (and all these exterior manifestations were referred to by the Israelites as "the glory"), seeing these various reflections, was unsatisfied, and said to God: "Do let me see your glory!" [9]

But the Lord God had to refuse him. For alas, in the sin of Adam, mankind had forfeited this privilege. Nevertheless, the Lord does let Moses see him "in an obscure manner." [10] "But my face you cannot see," he says to Moses, "for no man sees me and still lives. Here," continued the Lord, "is a place near me where you shall station yourself on the rock. When my glory passes, I will set you in the hollow of the rock and will cover you with my hand until I have passed by. Then I

[8] John 1:4.   [9] Exodus 33:18.   [10] I Corinthians 13:12.

will remove my hand so that you may see my back; but my face is not to be seen." [11]

All that Moses is permitted, then, is a contemplative experience of God, in the obscure light of faith. For Adam had forfeited for all his children the privilege of seeing God face to face. The gates of heaven were guarded by the cherubim with "the flaming sword which turned every way to guard the way to the tree of life." [12]

But since the Lord God had made man in such a way that he could never be happy, never satisfied, unless he saw God's glory face to face, God had mercy on mankind and sent the eternal Word on another mission.

This time, the Word himself was made flesh, and dwelt among us, and we saw his glory, glory of the Only-begotten of the Father, full of grace and truth. "We saw his glory," says St. John. Does this mean that he and his fellow apostles saw on earth what had been denied to Moses? No, John does not mean that, in seeing Christ, the apostles actually saw the inner glory of God face to face.

They saw exterior manifestations of the inner glory of the Word when they beheld the miracles he performed. As a consequence, with the light of faith, they saw him as true Son of God, the eternal Word made flesh. But even this was not enough; and they understood that it was only a preparation for still greater things.

But even in order to see Christ's glory in a dark manner through faith, the apostles had to receive the interior supernatural enlightenment from the Word. "No one knows the Father except the Son, and him to whom the Son chooses to reveal him." [13] Even those who hated Christ saw his sacred humanity and the wonderful miracles he wrought, but the only ones who saw his glory, glory of the Only-begotten of

[11] Exodus 33:20–23.   [12] Genesis 3:24.   [13] Matthew 11:27.

the Father, were those who believed in his name; and they believed only because the Word enlightened them interiorly by giving them the gift of faith, and then, sanctifying grace, its perfection. Sanctifying grace is a sharing in the inner glory of God, a participation in the divine nature, for "they who believe in his name" are "born of God." [14] When we receive sanctifying grace, we receive the immortal Word himself, who is spiritually begotten in us by the Father, so that the Word glorifies God in our soul by manifesting the Father to us. "Father," said Jesus at the Last Supper, "I have glorified thee on earth. . . . I have manifested thy name to the men thou hast given me out of the world." [15]

In the Preface for the Epiphany, the Feast of the Manifestation, we rejoice over these things, praising God, saying: "When thine only-begotten Son appeared in the substance of our mortal flesh, he restored us by the new light of his own immortality." We are interiorly enlightened by receiving God's own immortal divine light, and this is the Word himself, the very light of divinity, in which God knows himself. "In him was life, and the life was the light of men." [16]

The threefold manifestation of Christ commemorated in the Epiphany—at the coming of the Magi, at his baptism in the Jordan, and at the wedding of Cana—are sacramental mysteries which signify the grace of interior manifestation which should take place in souls. We miss the point of the feast, so well put in the Preface, if we do not see that we are celebrating the fact that the Word is interiorly enlightening us by faith through the grace of this mystery.

But even that is only a prelude. Grace and faith are only the "seed of glory." The fullness of glory comes in heaven, when God gives us the fullness of his own glory in the

[14] John 1:12–13.   [15] John 17:4–6.   [16] John 1:4.

beatific vision, so that his glory is ours, our glory is his. This is the eternal epiphany, or manifestation, of God's glory, and for it we pray in the Collect of the earthly Feast of Epiphany: "Mercifully grant that we who now know thee by faith, may be led to contemplate the splendor of thy majesty."

The Word himself is "the splendor of divine glory." [17] Just as he eternally manifests God to God, so he manifests God to the saints in heaven. For it is impossible to see God "face to face . . . just as he is," [18] except in the Word, the infinite "image of his substance." Any lesser image than this infinite one is inadequate for manifesting the infinite being of God. Therefore, in heaven, as the theologians put it, we see God "in the Word."

And what will be the consequence of the Word's marvelous manifestation of God's glory to us in heaven? The same thing will happen to us that eternally happens to God. When God eternally beholds himself in the word, he eternally loves himself with infinite love, and delights in himself with infinite happiness. So, too, when we see God face to face in the Word, there will spring forth from our souls perfect love of God in the Holy Spirit, with resulting ecstatic delight in the possession of the divine Majesty, and spontaneous, joyous praise. This praise is our wholehearted approval of God, our rejoicing that God is God. This is what is meant by formal glory of God: God's intellectual creatures clearly knowing him and with all their will loving him, approving of him, rejoicing in him, praising him; and they rejoice primarily not so much because God has been good to them, but because he is infinitely good and perfect in himself; they forget self and rejoice because God is what he is.

Even on earth this sort of thing happens to us to the

[17] Hebrews 1:3.　　[18] I John 3:3; I Corinthians 13.

extent that we are interiorly enlightened by the Word, and thus see the glory of God. True knowledge of God, real insight into what he is, necessarily produces love and joy and praise. If we lack spiritual joy and fail to glorify God with praise in word and in work, it must be because we lack insight into the glory of God; we are not experiencing it in prayer enlightened by the Word. True and sincere glorifying of God is really the overflowing of God's own glory within us; it results because Christ has glorified the Father in us, by manifesting him to us, thus giving God's own inner glory to us. It is only because we have seen God's glory to some extent that we are able to give God glory; that is, sincerely praise him for what he is. Giving glory to God would be false, insincere, if it were based upon total ignorance of him. That is why St. Augustine says that glory is "clear knowledge with praise."

However, in this life a great deal of the time we are in the dark about God's true inner glory, not merely because we live by faith, in which we see God only in a dark manner, but even more because we do not seek his glory ardently enough. Our love and joy in him tends to dwindle, fade away, unless we deliberately, steadfastly seek his glory, unless we look for him persistently. "Seek and you shall find," he says. But where look for him? Wherever he has manifested himself— in nature, in his saints, in his law, in every manifestation of his holy will, but above all, in the Word Incarnate.

Sometimes we have to seek his glory very doggedly. When we seem to be surrounded only by darkness, we reassure ourselves by a sheer act of faith that God is glorious not only in himself but also in all his dealings with us. In difficult circumstances, when we say, "For the glory of God I shall persevere in my duty, or in my trials," it may well mean this: "I cannot see the purpose of this trial or this obligation; it looks foolish to me. But since this is the will of God for me, it has to be glorious, though the glory is veiled from me at present. With great trust in divine providence, I shall muddle through, believing that in due time I shall see how all this was to God's glory; how it really does manifest his goodness, wisdom, power, mercy; how all the while it was really preparing me to receive from him a greater inpouring of his glory into my soul in the beatific vision."

Or, again, when we strive for purity of intention by saying, "All for the glory of God," we are really removing the obstacles that stand in the way of his revealing his glory to us. For when we seek anything other than God in our actions, when we seek only our own glory, or riches, or power, or pleasure, we are narrowing our soul, blinding it so that the manifestation of God's glory to our soul is prevented. Therefore, we have the obligation to purify ourselves of other motives, the obligation to do all for the glory of God, precisely because we were made by God to receive his own glory into our soul.

What a blessed obligation! To seek the glory of God and thereby receive it! True giving of glory to God is the spontaneous result of seeing God's glory; it is true recognition of God's excellence, sincere acknowledgment of it, delighted testimony to it.

The Word glorifies the Father by manifesting him to us; the best way for us to glorify the Father is by receiving that light from Christ, letting him give to us the Father's own inner glory. If we have ever truly glorified God from our hearts, it was only because we have received some spiritual enlightenment from the Word—we saw, we loved, we approved, we were glad that God is what he is, we rejoiced and wanted to tell the world about it. A true apostolate of manifesting God's glory can spring only from such contemplation of God's glory.

For this reason, the Divine Office for the Epiphany repeats to us again and again the words of Isaias: "Arise, Jerusalem, be enlightened! For thy light has come and the glory of the Lord is risen upon thee." [19] The glory of God is present to us in Christ; it is up to us to let it shine into our souls. So arise, be enlightened! Let Christ, the Word, do his work of glorifying the Father in us, by manifesting the inner divine glory more fully to our souls.

Moses was not permitted to see God face to face, and the veil he wore on his face when speaking to Israel was a symbol of this. But "we all, with faces unveiled" (looking on "the glory of God shining on the face of Christ Jesus") ourselves "reflecting as in a mirror the glory of the Lord, are being transformed into his very image, from glory to glory, as through the Spirit of the Lord." [20]

[19] Isaias 60.   [20] II Corinthians 3:18 and 4:6.

CHAPTER X

"FATHER, I AM COMING TO THEE!"

EVERYTHING THE SON OF GOD has, in time and in eternity, he receives from the Father. We have to be like him in this, by beginning all our actions in God, letting God live and act in everything we do. Although the Word of God comes from the Father, he remains ever with the Father; and we, begotten by the Father in baptism, must learn to live, like the Word, ever in the Father's presence.

But the Word not only comes from the Father, he not only receives all things from the Father, but he returns to the Father and takes all things back to him. It is this return of the Word to the Father which we celebrate in the season of the Ascension and in the second glorious mystery of the Rosary. Therefore, in the Mass of the Sunday before the Ascension, to prepare us for the feast, the Church reads to us words of our Lord, whose mystery should be reproduced in our souls by the grace of the feast: "I came forth from the Father, and have come into the world. Again, I leave the world, and go to the Father." [1] The grace of this mystery will effectively take us, also, to the Father. For we have seen that the Word Incarnate is a living sign and the mysteries of his life contain divine power to reproduce themselves in our souls.

Everything that the Word of God did in his human nature signifies to us what he does eternally in his divine nature, and by their grace, his mysteries reproduce in our souls the very things that take place eternally in the Trinity; for Christ forms the life of the Trinity in our souls.

The things the Word does as Man, then, reflect the things he does eternally as God. Not only in his humanity, but also eternally in his divinity, the Word comes from the Father, and returns to the Father.

From all eternity, the Father begets the Son; the Son proceeds from the Father. But the begotten Son instantaneously goes back to the Father in that eternal impulse of love which is the living Holy Spirit.

In the fullness of time, God sends his Son the Word into the world on a mission: the salvation of mankind and the bringing back of all things to the Father. For all things originally came from the Father through the Word and they

[1] John 16:28.

must return to him through the Word. "All things were made through him, and without him was made nothing that has been made." [2] Therefore, it was the Father's "good pleasure," says St. Paul, "to re-establish all things in Christ, both those in the heavens and those on the earth." [3] And elsewhere, the same Apostle writes: "There is only one God, the Father, from whom are all things, and we unto him, and one Lord Jesus Christ, through whom are all things, and we through him." [4]

No sooner does the Word come from the Father into the world than he begins his return to the Father. In the very instant of his conception in the womb of the Virgin Mary, by an act of his human will, he goes back to the Father in an act of love, a love which resembles that eternal act of love which is the living Holy Spirit. This first return of Christ to the Father in love is a loving dedication of himself to the accomplishment of the Father's will. As St. Paul writes: "In coming into the world, he says . . . 'Behold, I come . . . to do thy will, O God.'" [5]

Love takes one out of himself and into the beloved. Christ's every act of love for the Father is thus a return to the Father from whom he came forth. Each action of his life that he performs according to the will of the Father is a step back to the Father.

But his return is complete only when his work on earth is fully accomplished. At the end of his life, he prays to the Father for the final perfection of his return, saying: "Father, the hour has come! Glorify thy Son that thy Son may glorify thee. . . . I have glorified thee on earth; I have accomplished the work that thou hast given me to do. And now, do thou, Father, glorify me with thyself, with the glory that I

[2] John 1:3.   [3] Ephesians 1:10.
[4] I Corinthians 8:6.   [5] Hebrews 10:5f.

had with thee before the world existed. . . . I am no longer
in the world . . . and I am coming to thee." [6]

The Word does not return to the Father empty-handed. St.
John writes that Jesus knew "that the Father had given all
things into his hands, and that he had come forth from God
and was going to God." [7] He prayed to the Father, saying:
"Father, thou hast given (thy Son) power over all flesh, in
order that to all thou hast given him he may give life
everlasting." [8] That is, the Word-made-flesh has power to
bring men back with himself to the Father; he brings them
into life everlasting; that is, into God's own life. On his
return to the Father, he takes his brethren with him: "I
ascend to my Father and your Father, to my God and your
God." [9] "I go to prepare a place for you. And if I go and
prepare a place for you, I am coming again, and I will take
you to myself; that where I am, there you also may be." [10]

Isaias the Prophet had foretold this when he spoke thus in
the name of God: "As the rain and the snow come down
from heaven, and return no more thither, but soak the earth
and water it, and make it to spring, and give seed to the
sower and bread to the eater, so shall my Word be, which
shall go forth from my mouth. It shall not return to me void,
but it shall do whatsoever I please, and shall prosper in the
things for which I sent it." [11]

In a sense, the ascension of the body of Christ into heaven
is but the outward sign of that return of Jesus to his Father
which took place in every single act of his life on earth, for
his every act was an act of love of the Father, taking him out
of himself and into the Father.

Since the Ascension is the outward sign of the continual

[6] John 17.   [7] John 13:3.
[8] John 13:3; 17:2.   [9] John 20:17.
[10] John 14:3.   [11] Isaias 55:10–11.

return of Christ's soul to the Father in love, the special grace which this mystery should produce in our souls, whether during the Ascension season or anytime we meditate on it, is a more perfect return of our souls to God in love, in all the actions of our life.

All of us came forth from the creative power of God without our willing it, but we can go back to God only by willing it, only by giving our will to him in love, in the same way that Jesus gave his human will to the Father in love and obedience.

But we can make this return to the Father only in Christ, only in the Word of God who does not return to God empty-handed. For he said: "I am the way, and the truth, and the life. No one comes to the Father but through me." [12] And in Christ we can return to God only by reproducing his acts; or better still, we should say that he must reproduce his acts in us. The sacramental power of the actions of his own life must produce in us by grace the same kind of actions which will take us to the Father in love and devotion. Unless Christ so acts in us, we cannot go to the Father. "Without me, you can do nothing," he says.[13]

It is very important, then, that we keep ourselves in the presence of Christ so that he can do these things in us, so that we can do them in him. If we meditate properly on the mysteries of his life, the grace he bestows upon us in the sacraments will reproduce these mysteries in us.

The Word of God, eternally proceeding from the Father, simultaneously and eternally returns to the Father in that living impulse of love, the Holy Spirit. And when the Word comes into this world as man, he returns to the Father in that same Holy Spirit. For in everything he did, the Scriptures tell us, Jesus was led by the Holy Spirit, and above all, on

[12] John 14:6.   [13] John 15:5.

Calvary, "through the Holy Spirit, he offered himself unblemished unto God." [14]

Only in that same Holy Spirit of love can we return in Christ to the Father. We can go to God only by the steps of love; not any kind of love, but only the divine love of charity, poured forth into our hearts by the Holy Spirit. During the Ascension season, or whenever we meditate on this mystery, when we see Jesus ascend to his Father, we fervently beseech him to send his Holy Spirit to us from the Father. "Show me the way in which I should walk, for to you I lift up my soul. . . . Teach me to do your will, for you are my God. May your good Spirit guide me on level ground." [15]

The whole of Christ's life has to be reproduced in us. So that the sacramental power of the mysteries can work more freely in us, here is a little plan for re-living the whole of our Lord's life in the course of each day.

At the instant we awake each morning, by our very first conscious act we should go to the Father, saying as Christ did on entering the world: "Behold, I come to do thy will, O God."

At the Offertory of the Mass, again we should go to the Father, presenting ourselves to him in Christ, on the paten and in the chalice, saying: *"Suscipe, Sancta Trinitas:* Receive, O Holy Trinity, this oblation." Again, in the closing words of the Canon, when Jesus in person is on the altar under the forms of bread and wine, we present him to the Father and go with him, saying: *"Per ipsum, et cum ipso et in ipso:* through him, and with him, and in him."

Thus, at Mass we ascend in spirit with Jesus to the right hand of the Father, renewing our determination to "seek only the things that are above, where Christ is seated at the right hand of God." [16]

[14] Hebrews 9:14.   [15] Psalm 142:8f.   [16] Colossians 3:1.

In the course of the day, when we sit down to refresh ourselves with food and drink, we should say, just as Jesus did when, weary from his journey, he refreshed himself at the well of Jacob: "My food is to do the will of him who sent me, that I may accomplish his work." [17] Thus again, neither food nor drink nor any of the things of the world will ever delay us on our journey to the Father. Nor will they turn us aside from him, for the material things we use will become sacramental reminders of spiritual things and will thereby speed us on our journey to the Father, because they are sanctified by the blessing of Christ, who sanctified them by using them himself. Eating of our earthly food should especially remind us of our Eucharistic food.

And whenever, during the day, the work assigned to us by the Father becomes very difficult and laborious, again we say, like Jesus: "Father, if it be possible, let this chalice pass from me. Nevertheless, not my will, but thy will be done." [18] Thus we come closer to the accomplishment of our mission, closer to the final return to the Father.

And at last, when our day's work is done and we retire for the night, with Jesus we say: "Father, I have accomplished the work that thou hast given me to do." [19] And then, with Jesus on the cross, we say: "It is finished." [20] Having said this, Jesus next said: "Father, into thy hands I commend my spirit," [21] thus giving back, in a supreme act of love, his whole being to the Father from whom he had received it. We should do the same in our last conscious thought before we fall asleep, surrendering ourselves to the Father's providence. "Father, I am coming to thee." [22] "Father, into thy hands I commend my spirit."

[17] John 4:34.   [18] Matthew 26:39.
[19] John 17:4.   [20] John 19:30.
[21] Luke 23:46.   [22] John 17:11.

PART THREE

How to Live With God,
Like the Word

CHAPTER XI

ADORING THE DIVINE PRESENCE

LIFE IN THE PRESENCE of God is for every Christian; it is not beyond the reach of any one of us. Like the Word, we can be with God, because living in the divine presence is the maturity of the life of grace and faith, hope and charity. Pope Pius XII has told us that if we wish to gain insights into the mystery of the divine indwelling, we must consider it in the light of the final goal to which it is directed—the life of the beatific vision in heaven,[1] for the dwelling of God in the soul by grace is heaven already begun. Grace is the seed of glory.

Lest we be discouraged by the thought that perhaps we are failing to live in the divine presence, let us show how we may have been doing so rather well, without even realizing it. The fact that, in the midst of aridity and great trials, we do not taste his sweetness does not prove that we have not been living in his presence. The tasting of sweetness is a by-product of something more fundamental, which can be had with or without the sweetness.

In this life, living in the presence of God involves three operations, three ways of being with God and living in him. First, by actually adoring him as present in the soul, with a lively consciousness that he is with us. And this may be with or without sweetness. Secondly, by doing all things for God with pure intention. When a person in the state of grace acts for supernatural motives, God lives and acts in him, and he lives in God, since living by pure intentions is living by faith

[1] Encyclical *Mystici Corporis* (Washington, D.C.: N.C.W.C., 1943), p. 50.

and charity; and active faith and charity always put us in direct contact with God. When we live by pure intention, the soul is not necessarily conscious of God at all times, though it should strive to be so. Thirdly, we live in the presence of God when we see the presence of God's love and providence in every detail of our life, being convinced by strong faith that in absolutely every trial and frustration, in everything that befalls us, God's love for us is at work, turning these things to our advantage through our love for him. "For those who love God, all things work together unto good." [2] Our love for him, convinced of his love and care for us even in the most severe trials, sees his presence in all the circumstances of life. Bitter trials and aridity may take away the sweetness of his presence, but nonetheless, in sheer faith, we are convinced that he is with us and working in us; and we abandon ourselves to this providence. Thus, we live in him, and he in us.

Let us consider the first way of living in God's presence— actually adoring him, present in the soul. Adoration is primarily an acknowledgment of the divine majesty, a recognition of his infinite perfections, with a consequent rejoicing that God is God. This delight in the fact that God is infinite goodness and perfection breaks forth in praise and gratitude. "We give thee thanks for thy great glory," we sing in the *Gloria* of the Mass.

All this infinite perfection of the divine majesty is present to us in our soul. There is no human act more noble than adoration, when it is inspired by charity; no act more perfect than this testifying to the infinite perfections of God. For this were we all created, "to contribute to the praise of his glory." [3] For all eternity, the angels and saints in heaven will give this testimony to God's majesty, with all the fervor of

[2] Romans 8:28. [3] Ephesians 1:12.

their being; their whole attitude of soul is a continuous hymn of praise: "They do not rest day and night, saying: 'Holy, holy, holy, the Lord God almighty, who was, and who is, and who is coming.' " [4] The intense happiness of the saints in heaven consists in their irrepressible delight in the fact that God is God, and that he is infinitely perfect and happy. Such delight in God is the fruit of charity, for we rejoice in the goodness and happiness of our Beloved.

Mature adoration, therefore, is more than a mere recognition that God is the supreme being, and that we are subject to him and must serve him; that is the minimum element of adoration. The fullness of adoration is a spontaneous, loving recognition of God's perfections, expressed in praise and joy and thanksgiving that God is what he is.

This praise and joy is the fruit of the Holy Spirit. "Be filled with the Spirit, speaking to one another in psalms and hymns and spiritual songs, singing and making melody in your hearts to the Lord, giving thanks always for all things in the name of our Lord Jesus Christ, to God the Father." [5] It is in the music of the sacred liturgy that this spiritual joy and praise should find its most perfect expression on earth.

In the preface of the Mass, we are called upon by the Church to join the angels and saints in heaven in their eternal "*sanctus.*" And while we pray to God to join our voices to those of the heavenly choir, we strive with all our might to duplicate on earth, as well as we can, the perfect adoration and praise of heaven.

The chief and most significant name of the Mass is "the Eucharist," which means "the thanksgiving." The whole spirit of the Mass is summed up in the opening words of the Preface, where we declare: "It is truly meet and just, right and salutary, that we should always and in all places give

[4] Apocalypse 4:8; cf. Isaias 6:3.   [5] Ephesians 5:19.

thanks to thee, O Lord, holy Father almighty, eternal God."
This praise and thanksgiving is the full flowering of adoration. In the Mass we join Christ our Lord in his perfect
adoration of the Father, so that "through him and with him
and in him" we may give "to thee, God the Father almighty,
in the unity of the Holy Spirit, all honor and glory." [6]

Above all else, we thank God because he is God: "We give
thee thanks for thy great glory." But we thank him also
because he has manifested this glory to us through his
beloved Son. We thank him because, through our redemption in his beloved Son, once gain we are able to find our
true and perfect happiness in loving God and in giving
expression to the rapture of this love in the eternal adoration
and praise of heaven. The *Sanctus* of the Mass is our daily
choir practice in which we rehearse the eternal hymn of
glory. Each day our hearts should sing it better.

Since such adoration is the ceaseless activity of heaven, it
is eminently worthwhile on earth. Time spent in adoration is
never a waste of time. No one may ever say, "I have more
important things to do; I am too busy for adoration." Since,
as Pope Pius XII has said, we are to understand the divine
indwelling in the soul in the light of the goal of heaven, we
can conclude that, just as heaven is the eternal adoration of
the divine majesty, so too, God has made our soul a little
heaven so that this adoration can begin even here on earth.
The most perfect form of living in the presence of God in this
life is adoration of the Trinity dwelling in the soul.

It is God's will that every Christian should have at least a
minimum amount of free time in which to engage in this
most noble of human occupations, the adoration of God.
That is the precise reason for the law of Sunday rest. God

---

[6] These are the closing words of the Canon, while the Preface is its
beginning.

wills that on one day a week the Christian be free of the work
which restricts his freedom to adore.

Certainly, therefore, on Sundays we can, with a clear
conscience, devote more time than on other days to the
adoration of God, even if it means putting aside other
pressing work which we claim must be done.

It was precisely for that adoration of God that baptism
consecrated our souls as temples of the living God. We are
temples in which God is to be worshipped. That is the
significance of the ceremony which immediately followed
our baptism; we were anointed on the crown of the head with
holy chrism and thus consecrated to God as his temple. This
ceremony is an outward sign of the interior consecration of
the soul by the baptismal character. This character alone
gives us the power to join in the offering of the Holy
Sacrifice of the Mass; it admits us to the privilege of singing
the *Sanctus* of the Mass in company with the heavenly
choirs. At Mass, we join in singing the *Sanctus* publicly in
the Church, but all day long we continue to make that
melody in our hearts to the Lord, in the inner temple of the
soul. Since our soul has been consecrated as a temple of God,
we strive to live ever more perfectly the life of heaven by
becoming ever more aware of the adorable God within us.

The Blessed Virgin Mary is a model of the continuous
adoration of God-within-us. As she carried her divine Son
with her in her womb, like any other mother, she was aware
by the sense of touch of his presence within her. Not by
touch, not by feeling, but by faith, she was aware that this
Child is the immortal God himself, and so, by faith, she lived
in continual adoration of him. Every physical movement of
the divine Infant within her would be enough to bring forth
from her soul an act of love and adoration of him.

So, too, the physical presence of the body of Christ in the

Holy Eucharist occasions similar acts of adoration in our souls, especially when, with our senses, we see and feel the Sacred Host. But this physical contact with the Holy Eucharist is only a means, an aid toward the more important contact of faith which inspires the act of adoration. The sense contact at time of Holy Communion, or the physical presence in the tabernacle on the altar, is for the sake of the contact of faith, the spiritual contact with God permanently dwelling in the temple of the soul. For Christ is present in the Eucharist so that he may be present permanently in the soul.

This real contact of faith may be with or without sensible sweetness. We must not judge our success in living in the presence of God by the amount of sweetness we experience. Sensible sweetness, though it is a gift of God and should be gratefully accepted, can be dangerous, for it may deceive us into thinking that we are holier than we really are and that our union with God is absolutely perfect. Since the true bond of union is faith, God often withdraws the sweetness to strengthen faith.

Therefore, in times of aridity, when in no way can we feel the presence of God in a sensible way, it is of extreme importance that we seek him and contact him in sheer faith. We must put ourselves in his presence by an act of faith, saying: "I know, Lord, that thou art with me, for I have received you today in worthy Holy Communion. When you come in Holy Communion in a physical way, you come to stay; you remain in a spiritual way in my soul, together with the Father and the Holy Spirit. I know, then, by faith that you are with me; I adore you."

Then, remaining in his presence by faith, we carry on our conversation with him, our mental prayer, remembering that he is truly in us. And although we should talk over our problems and needs with him, and make petitions to him, we do not let our prayer be exclusively this, but we strive also for sheer adoration: "Lord, it is good for me to be here in your presence, to rejoice that you are God." Prayer of petition is also good, because even that is basically adoration, since petition testifies to the fact that God is infinite goodness, the source of all benefits. The most perfect type of adoration, of course, looks upon God not so much as the source of the benefits he has given us, but as infinitely good and perfect in himself, worthy of all praise and love, and a source of all rejoicing.

Even if we think that perhaps we have lost God from our soul by sin, we are still able to put ourselves into his presence, for a fervent spiritual communion is enough to bring him back to us. A perfect spiritual communion is enough to restore a person to the state of grace, for it includes an act of perfect contrition. So, if there are times when we cannot seem to be aware of God's presence, when we cannot seem to contact him, then, in sheer faith, we make our spiritual communion: we fervently desire the body of Christ, which suffered for our sins, and Christ comes to us spiritually; then, in pure faith, we adore his presence. Such adoration in faith is eminently worthwhile; it is not a waste of time; it is carrying out in the dark manner of faith the perfect adoration of heaven.

Let us say, in the words of Jeremias, as we do each night in the *capitulum* of Compline: "Thou art in us, O Lord, and thy Holy Name is invoked over us; do not abandon us, O Lord." [7] And then, let us abandon ourselves to the care of the God who lives in us. "Into thy hands I commend my spirit" [8]—I give myself over to thee totally, so that you will live your life in me and I in thee.

---

[7] Jeremias 14:9.   [8] Luke 23:46.

CHAPTER XII

ADORATION: REPORTING FOR DUTY

ADORATION IS BEARING WITNESS to the divine majesty, testifying to God's excellence. The most perfect form of adoration takes place in heaven, where we declare the infinite perfection of God in an undying hymn of joyful praise and thanksgiving, rejoicing that God is what he is. But on earth, testimony to God's excellence usually takes a more fundamental form. Though at times even here this testimony consists in hymns of praise, more often it is expressed as eager willingness to serve God. Like the Lord, we sing: "My food is to do the will of him who sent me." Adoration is a reporting to God for duty, for on earth our most fundamental way of testifying to the divine majesty is by serving him. By service, we bear witness to God's excellence as Lord and Master of all, as our first beginning and our last end.

Though we would love to spend all our time like the saints in heaven in the presence of God, contemplating his infinite perfections and finding exquisite delight and happiness in singing his praises, God does not will it so, as long as we are still on earth. When we do come into his presence to enjoy him, when we do say like St. Peter on Mount Tabor, "Lord, it is good for us to be here in the presence of thy glory," very soon his majesty sends us out again on a mission. He gives us a task to accomplish for his glory, just as he sent his divine Son, so that by fidelity to his service we can merit to return to his presence, for the uninterrupted enjoyment and praise of his glory in heaven. Although to sit in the presence of his majesty, like Mary, is the better part, he requires most of us, most of the time, to play the role of

Martha. So we must learn to make even our labors a hymn of praise, a continual adoration. We must learn to work in his presence and thereby testify to his glory in everything we do. When the eternal Word went forth from the Father on his mission into the world, he did not leave the Father's side. *"Verbum supernum prodiens:* the heavenly Word proceeding forth, yet leaving not the Father's side," sings St. Thomas Aquinas in the Vespers hymn he composed for Corpus Christi. When we are sent by the Father to our work, we too must remain in the divine presence by continual recollection.

One way of remaining ever in the divine presence as we go about our work is by right intention. We must take care not only to begin all our labors with a right intention, but also to preserve that right intention to the very end.

Right intention necessarily begins with an act of adoration; that is, with an acknowledgment of the divine Majesty and his right to our service, and a declaration of willingness and determination to live for him. In adoration, we report for duty, seeking to know the will of God so that we may carry it out in testimony to his glory. We come into the presence of God for our instructions. We are good servants, standing in the presence of our Master. "Behold, as the eyes of the servants are on the hands of their masters, as the eyes of a maid are on the hands of her mistress, so are our eyes on the Lord our God," eager to anticipate his slightest will.

Every time we have a free moment, as soon as we have finished a task he has given us, we rush back to his presence to report, "Mission accomplished!" And we remain in his presence as long as possible, enjoying his company, but always ready to go forth again on his work when he sees fit to send us. The more time we spend in the divine presence, meditating upon his perfections, the more eager to serve we will be, and the more lasting our right intentions will be. Awareness of the divine perfections springs into devotion, which is defined as eager readiness to do the will of God. Consciousness of the divine majesty results in joyful eagerness to serve him. At times of trial, when life's sorrows seem to swallow up the joy of serving, then true devotion shows itself as a firm determination of the will to live for God, no matter how difficult it may be.

Experience shows that even though we are sincere enough in declaring our good intentions in the morning offering, very frequently these intentions deteriorate in the press of the day's activities. Every single sin is a departure from right intention and therefore a departure from the presence of God. In spite of good intentions at the beginning of the day or at the beginning of a particular task, bad motives easily slip in. If we are not on our guard, pride creeps even into our good works; we begin to act for motives of vanity or ambition, and thus we depart from the divine presence. God has been forgotten, we live only for self; we work no longer for the praise of his glory, but for our own glory.

Or again, perhaps it is discouragement which spoils our right intention. We stop the work which we began with such good motives, because it has become difficult, and we are not courageous enough to bear the burden. Again we have forgotten God, we have departed from his presence, for we fail to remember that God works with us; it is his work that we are doing, so he will not abandon us if we persevere in doing it. Even if the work fails exteriorly, our efforts are not a failure if, by persevering right intention, we work in God and he in us.

Sometimes it is sheer laziness or negligence which destroys our right intention; the intention was there at first,

but it bore no fruit. We failed because we forgot the presence
of God from whom nothing can be hid and to whom we must
give an accounting for every idle moment.

Therefore, since good intentions so easily deteriorate
because of human weaknesses, it is obvious that the mere
making of a morning offering does not automatically sanctify the whole day, but is only an excellent start in that
direction. The whole day would have been sanctified by that
morning offering if the original right intention it contained
had persevered. Therefore, special steps must be taken
throughout the day to preserve right intention, and we shall
speak of these steps shortly.

Furthermore, a good work is not necessarily sanctified by
saying, "All for Jesus." For the only works we can truly
sanctify are the ones which God wills that we should do.
Obviously, no sinful action can be sanctified by a sign of the
cross or the morning offering. But even some actions which
are good, or even very excellent in themselves, do not
sanctify us when we do them, though we do declare we are
doing them for God. This is the case when it is God's will that
we be engaged in some other activity at the time. It is only
the duty of the moment which can be truly sanctified. For
example, cultivating the mind by reading good literature is a
good work, but we cannot sanctify the reading of good books
if this reading prevents us from fulfilling the duty of prayer,
or the preparation of class work, or the doing of a household
charge. We are sanctified only by what God wants us to do
at this particular time.

The right intention of doing all things for the honor and
glory of God cannot lead us to do things contrary to the duty
of the moment; we can glorify God only by doing his will,
thereby testifying to his supreme rights over all our activity.
If, then, we engage in other works, no matter how good they

are in themselves, which interfere with doing what God wills we should do, it is because our right intention has deteriorated. We do these other works for motives of human respect, or pleasure, or vanity, or ambition, or laziness, or some such motive. And we talk our conscience into thinking we have done right by telling ourselves: "What I have done is a very good work; it has improved my mind, or it has brought glory to my community, or it has helped the needy, or it has refreshed me, etc."

One practical aid, therefore, for preserving our right intention is to examine our conscience, not only to find out whether we have done any bad works, but also to look at our good deeds, to see why we have done them. When we did them, was it really God's will that we do them? A true examination of conscience is made in God's presence; we put ourself in his presence, asking the Holy Spirit to show us as we really are; we look at self with his eyes, as he sees us.

Even when we carry out a work assigned to us in obedience, we are not necessarily sanctified in doing it, for if the wrong motives creep in, we are no longer serving Christ our King in doing it, but we are serving self. "The greatest treason," says T. S. Eliot, "is to do the right thing for the wrong reasons." For example, in obedience we are told to go to teach a class, and we accept the work in obedience. But the way we carry it out can totally spoil it. We must keep clearly in mind what God wills that we should be accomplishing in this particular class, and regularly examining ourselves in his light to see whether we are working toward those results he expects. This will save us from negligence in preparation, it will save us from seeking our own glory in our work, it will also spare us from wasting a lot of energy. For if we undertake a work in obedience, but then proceed to do it wholly on our own, rarely consulting God for guidance and help, the work is bound to deteriorate into the heresy of action; that is, into wasted activity, for after a time it will no longer be God's work we are doing, but a fruitless activity which produces no permanent supernatural results.

Many truly gifted persons fall into fruitless natural activity. Their work may indeed produce temporal results; the world may even sit up and take notice of them because they seem to be good teachers or wise administrators. But the judgment of God may reveal that they have built only of straw or wood or hay, instead of with gold and silver and precious stones.[1] Their motives had become purely natural; they had not examined their motives carefully each day from the point of view of God's will. We must daily put self into the presence of God and look at self with him. Truly to live and work in the presence of God, we must do the right thing at the right time, in the right way, and for the right reason.

It is because our right intentions can so easily deteriorate that St. Paul warns us: "See to it, brethren, that you walk with care: not as unwise, but as wise, making the most of your time, because the days are evil. Therefore, do not become foolish, but understand what the will of the Lord is."[2]

Understand what the will of the Lord is! This is the work of prudence. Right intention is formed and preserved by the virtue of prudence. Prudence is the servant of charity and the guide of devotion. What good is it lovingly and eagerly to declare that we will do God's will in all things, but then neglect to understand what the will of God is? Therefore, prudence requires meditation on the perfections of God to inspire devotion, meditation of what is his will in one's own case so that we can carry it out in devotion and examination of conscience to check on our motives.

[1] I Corinthians 3:14.   [2] Ephesians 5:15.

Let us therefore summarize a list of practical acts of prudence which will enable us to make and preserve right intention.

First, we should never begin any activity without an act of adoration of God present with us. Adoration is coming into the divine presence to report for duty, a standing at the divine throne to acknowledge that he alone has a right to our service.

Secondly, when his Majesty sends us out on our task, we should ask him to come with us; after all, it is his work we are doing, and we cannot do it without him. This reporting for duty and this asking God to come with us as we do it are beautifully expressed in the liturgy of the Mass: "Precede our actions with thy inspirations, we pray thee, O Lord, and follow them with thy assistance, so that all we do may begin from thee, and through thee being begun may be finished." Put us to work by thy inspirations, work with us by thy help.

It is especially at Mass that we report for duty. At the Offertory we present ourselves, our day, our plans and all the souls in our charge to his Majesty. At the Consecration we bow in profound adoration of our King. At the Communion we receive him so that he will go forth with us as we do our day's work.

Thirdly, often during the course of a task, we must return to the divine Majesty, present within us, for further consultation. It is an act of prudence to seek advice. The divine life we are living, the divine work we are doing, cannot be done with human light alone. Frequent consultation with God in prayer to learn his will opens our soul for the gift of counsel, by which the Holy Spirit will lead us to works fruitful for all eternity. It is only the Holy Spirit who can show us how to live in the presence of God even in the midst of the most exacting labors. This frequent return to the divine presence in the midst of our work prepares us for a permanent consciousness of God, which is possible only by the interior workings of the Holy Spirit.

Fourthly, in the presence of God, we must frequently examine our motives, asking the Holy Spirit to give us the light to see self as God sees us. Ask him: "Lord, am I doing your work or mine, for your reasons or for mine, in your way or in mine?"

Fifthly, we must have a healthy fear of our human limitations. The most successful and wise accomplishments, if they are purely human, are as straw in the light of eternity. We must enter the divine presence frequently, asking light to see true values, to see things in God.

Lastly, in every free moment we have, when no other duty calls, we should rush to the divine presence, enter our soul to stand in the presence of God to adore him in joyous praise and gratitude, saying: "Lord, it is good for me to be here in thy presence." Such silent adoration of his majesty is never a waste of time; it is a foretaste of the eternal adoration of heaven. Moreover, it guarantees that when his Majesty does send us forth, it will be his work we are doing; for the moments in his presence, meditating on his perfections, have given us new fervor of devotion, increased eagerness to do his will. Consequently, our right intentions will be more lasting and more fruitful and will guarantee that when we go out from his presence, we will truly do his will.

Thus, by striving for a right and pure intention, we really succeed in living in the presence of God. For only a frequent return to his presence, only frequent consultation with him in prayer and meditation, only frequent examination of conscience in his presence can preserve and strengthen right intention. For whatever is done with a right intention truly becomes adoration of the divine majesty, praise of his glory, testimony to the divine excellence. It is our way of meriting the privilege of entering the divine presence permanently in heaven, there to testify eternally to his divine majesty in an undying hymn of joyous praise and thanksgiving. In the evening of life, like Christ Jesus, we will be able to say: "Father, I have glorified thee on earth; I have accomplished the work that thou hast given me to do. . . . Glorify thy Son that thy Son may glorify thee." [3]

[3] John 17:1,4.

CHAPTER XIII

LIVING UNDER DIVINE PROVIDENCE

WHEN THE SON OF GOD went forth to his mission on earth, he did not depart from the Father in heaven. We too, as we walk the earth, can be with the Father in heaven; we too can live in the presence of God.

And though on earth we do not have the beatific vision that Christ enjoyed, still at times God does give us a kind of foretaste of this. In prayer we are able to taste and see that the Lord is sweet; we truly experience his presence with us, and in our delight we cry out with St. Peter on Mount Tabor: "It is good for us to be here!" [1]

But just as Christ himself was sent by the Father on a mission, so he also sends us. As we go about this work, in some way we must remain in the divine presence, in imitation of Christ, our model. We do this by living according to a right intention, guided by faith and inspired by charity. We know that these words which Jesus spoke of

[1] Matthew 17:4.

himself are true of us also: "He who sent me is with me; he has not left me alone, because I do always the things that are pleasing to him." [2]

When we sincerely strive to do the will of God, God works in us; we are not alone; we work in the presence of God. And in this too we rejoice, just as we rejoice when we actually taste the sweetness of his presence in prayer. We are delighted to be "about the Father's business." [3] We are like Christ, who, "like a giant, joyfully runs his course." [4] So intent are we on doing the Father's will, so overjoyed are we that we can serve him, that like our Lord, we declare, "My food—my very life—is to do the will of him who sent me, that I may accomplish his work." [5]

But then, like Christ himself, we must go through a third stage. There comes a time when all the joy seems to go out of life; the sweetness of God's presence can no longer be tasted because of dryness in prayer; the doing of God's will seems unrewarding, for our labors seem to be fruitless and we seem to fail in everything we do. But here again, the Son of Man, who is in the bosom of the Father, is our model. Even he went through a phase in which it seemed that the Father had abandoned him; and in his anguish and desolation, he cried out: "My God, my God, why hast thou forsaken me?" [6] His human soul and body were overwhelmed with anguish; his work seemed an utter failure; those to whom he had done so much good returned only evil, hatred for love, blows and scourges for kindness and cures. The Father himself treated him as though he were guilty of all the sins of the world, and heaped upon him their full penalty. Frustration, bitterness, darkness were the portion of his soul.

[2] John 8:29.   [3] Luke 2:49.   [4] Psalm 18:6.
[5] John 4:34.   [6] Matthew 27:46.

But does this mean he had lost the divine presence? Had the Father really deserted him? Not at all! Jesus knew this, and in complete confidence that the Father was still with him, he abandoned himself wholly to the Father's loving providence. "Father, into thy hands I commend my spirit!" [7] Just before his Passion, at the Last Supper, when he told his apostles that they would "be scattered, each to his own house, and would leave him alone," he added, "but I am not alone, because the Father is with me!" [8]

By these words he reassures us. If we do always the things that are pleasing to the Father, the Father will never leave us alone. If we always seek the presence of God by a right intention, then even in the most terrible of trials, we will not be forsaken by God. In bitter sufferings and desolation we will still be able to say with confidence: "Father, into thy hands, I commend my spirit."

For if we love the Father and seek always to do the things that please him, then it is certain that his love and providence are caring for us, no matter how much a failure we seem to be, no matter how bitter our trials. For the Holy Spirit assures us through St. Paul that "for those who love God, all things work together unto good." [9] But note, it is only those who love God who can be certain that everything will turn out to their advantage. For God's providence leads us to the beatific vision only by the cooperation of our free will; his love draws us to our goal only through our love's response to his. For those who love God and live out this love by right intention, all things work together for good. For Jesus assigns the reason why the Father has not left him alone; it is "because I do always the things that are pleasing to him." [10] Fortunately for us, when we fail to love God and

[7] Luke 23:46.   [8] John 16:32.
[9] Romans 8:28.   [10] John 8:29.

do not do his will, if we repent and begin again to love him and to do his will, then his love can turn even our failures to our advantage. Even our past sins work together for our good, if we now love God.

Therefore, the third great way of living in the presence of God is by seeing the presence of God's loving providence in all the circumstances of life, seeing his will at work in everything that comes our way. To live in God's presence in this way requires great faith. It is easy enough to be aware of God's presence when all is going well; but to remain convinced that the Father is still with us in the midst of failures and frustrations is possible only to lively faith. When everything seems to say that he has abandoned us, or that he is not pleased with us, then we must summon all the power of our faith to be convinced of Christ's love which surpasses knowledge, a love which never abandons those who love him, a love which even seeks out sinners and is ever busy seeking to bring them back to the Father. With St. Paul, we say in lively faith: "I live in the faith of the Son of God, who loved me and gave himself up for me"; [11] or, with St. John: "We have come to know, and have believed, the love that God has in our behalf. God is love, and he who abides in love abides in God, and God in him." [12]

Therefore, no matter what trials or hardships we endure, faith in God's love so convinces us that he has not forsaken us that we cry out: "Who shall separate us from the love of Christ? Shall tribulation, or distress, or persecution, or hunger, or nakedness, or danger, or the sword? . . . For I am sure that neither death, nor life, nor angels, nor principalities, nor things present, nor things to come, nor powers, nor height, nor depths, nor any other creature will

[11] Galatians 2:20.   [12] I John 4:16.

be able to separate us from the love of God which is in Christ
Jesus our Lord." [13]

Living in the presence of God in the midst of tribulation is
really our love responding to his love, our love accepting this
trial as the work of his love, our love surrendering to his will.
If God wills it, it is enough for me! For his is the will of
a Father. The will of God in sending trials is never arbitrary
or capricious. It is never a cold, calculating will, uncon-
cerned about those who suffer because of it; it is always and
only a will overflowing with fatherly love. Even when he
chastises, he is a Father inspired with love. "God deals with
you as with sons; for what son is there whom his father does
not correct? But if you are without discipline, in which all
have had a share, then you are illegitimate children and not
sons." [14]

Therefore, wherever the will of God is at work, the love of
God is working, and wherever God's love works, so too does
the wisdom of his providence. Indeed, we live in the presence
of God when we see the hand of his loving providence in
every circumstance of life, when we see his will in every
single thing that comes our way. In fact, God's precise
purpose in sending tribulations is to make us aware of his
presence. For when we forget him and his goodness, and
become all wrapped up in self or in created things, then he
wakes us up by troubles.

During World War II, Pope Pius XII said that "if all the
painful calamities of this turbulent period, which cruelly
torture almost countless men, are accepted as from God's
hands, with calm and submissive spirit, they naturally lift
souls above the passing things of earth to those of heaven
that abide forever, and stimulate a certain unsuspected thirst

[13] Romans 8:35–39.   [14] Hebrews 12:7.

and keen desire for spiritual things. Thus, with the added grace of the divine Spirit, men are moved and, one might say, compelled to be more thoughtful in seeking the kingdom of God." [15] Note, then, how even in the horrible sufferings of war, God is present with his people, even as he chastises them.

So that we shall be able to see the presence of God even in the calamities of life, we should prepare ourselves in the following way: First, we must be convinced in advance that periods of trial are inevitable. Mount Tabor never lasts long; we are soon transferred to Mount Calvary. We must be present with God on Calvary before we can be with him in heaven.

Secondly, we must live always with a right intention. If we seek always to do the things that please the Father, if we consult regularly with him in prayer and by examination of conscience, and ask his help, then we shall never have any regrets if we fail in our undertakings. For we shall know that the Father did not leave us alone in our work, but worked with us, so that in reality we did not fail. Because of our love responding to his, our seeming failure worked to our advantage. Thus, even in frustrations, the soul is filled with the "peace of God which surpasses understanding." [16]

Thirdly, in times of aridity in prayer, we can be sure that God is present with us and we are present with him, if we keenly desire him. If it pains us that he seems to be absent, then we can be sure that he is not absent. As St. Gregory says: "He who sincerely desires God already has him whom he loves. For one cannot love God unless he already

[15] Pope Pius XII, *Mystici Corporis* (Washington, D.C.: N.C.W.C., 1943), pp. 4–5.
[16] Philippians 4:7.

possesses him whom he loves." [17] It is by active faith and charity that we contact God and possess him.

Fourthly, in times of severe temptations, the proof that God is truly with us is our hatred for sin, for we can hate sin strongly only because God is present in us; we are holding on to him by charity.

Fifthly, in times of real suffering, if we make an act of faith in his love for us, and respond to his love by accepting his will in love, then, by that love, we will possess him.

We have seen that the purpose of adoration is to testify to the divine excellence. The saints and angels in heaven do this by their undying hymn of praise, and we do the same on earth by carrying out the will of God in all our actions. But one of the most sincere forms of adoration of which we are capable on earth is to recognize all our severe trials as the will of God. This is indeed eloquent testimony to the excellence of God and the perfection of his will.

It is easy to say that God is wonderful when he is showering us with gifts and we are enjoying the sweetness of his presence. But if we continue to say the same thing even when things are black, when it looks as if he has abandoned us, then indeed our praise of him is meaningful and sincere. If an act of adoration is a declaration that we want only the will of God, we prove the sincerity of such a declaration when we eagerly accept as his will all our bitter trials and sufferings. What better praise of the excellence of his holy will could there be? It is a declaration that nothing could be better than the way God does things.

The saints in heaven praise God above all else because he is God, infinitely perfect in himself, and because his perfect will is always accomplished. Our praise of God on earth is eloquent indeed if in the midst of the blackness of trials,

[17] Homily for the Feast of Pentecost (Dominican Breviary).

when we seem to have nothing left, we continue to rejoice that God is God and his holy will is still being done.

This is indeed a mature way of living in the presence of God—to be able to see God's wise and loving providence in everything that happens, whether it be painful or joyful; to be able to rejoice always that his will is being done; to be able to praise him even in bitter trials, saying with holy Job: "The Lord has given, the Lord has taken away. Blessed be the name of the Lord!" [18]

Such an attitude is indeed the very height of sanctity; it is the attitude of Christ himself in his Passion: "Father, not my will, but thy will be done." [19] "Father, into the hands of thy wise and loving providence, I commend my spirit." [20] This was the most supremely perfect act of adoration of all time, the world's most eloquent testimony to the excellence of God and his holy will.

[18] Job 1:21.   [19] Matthew 26:29.   [20] Luke 23:46.

CHAPTER XIV

DOGMA AND MORAL FIBER

THE EPISTLE TO THE HEBREWS is one of the most marvelous documents about Christ ever written. We will appreciate it all the more if we keep in mind that St. Paul wrote it to a discouraged people, a people so discouraged that they were on the verge of apostasy from the faith. Their moral fiber had become dangerously weak.

This is clear from the two strong warnings against apostasy contained in the letter and from the many earnest exhortations sprinkled throughout it. There are numerous phrases like these: "Brace up the hands that hang down and the tottering knees"; [1] "Take heed lest anyone be wanting in the grace of God"; [2] "Do not lose your confidence." [3]

But the Apostle is not content just to give warnings and exhortations. He gives positive remedies for discouragement and shows why their moral fiber is so weak. It is because they have failed to meditate on the great dogmas of Christianity. "You have grown dull of hearing," he says. "For whereas by this time you ought to be masters, you need to be taught again the rudiments of the words of God; and you have become such as have need of milk and not of solid food. For everyone who is fed on milk is unskilled in the word of justice; he is but a child. But solid food is for the mature, for those who by practice have their faculties trained to discern good and evil." [4]

We see, then, that by meditation on the words of God we train our spiritual faculties so that we acquire a deep insight into divine things. Only thus do we become spiritual rather than sensual men, who "do not perceive the things that are of the Spirit of God." [5] We gather from the epistle that Christ should be the chief object of our meditation, for the epistle's main theme is the deeper truths about Christ. This is the solid food which will dispel the discouragement of the Hebrews and give them the moral strength they need.

Throughout the epistle, St. Paul gives wonderful insights into the divinity of Christ, and into his humanity, into his weakness in suffering, and into the great power of his priesthood. Christ, he says, is "the brightness of God's glory, the image of his substance." [6] At the same time, Christ is also made in our image, for he is like us "in all things except

---

[1] Hebrews 12:12.   [2] *Ibid.*, 12:15.   [3] Hebrews 10:35.
[4] Hebrews 5:11f.   [5] I Corinthians 2:14.   [6] Hebrews 1:3.

sin," [7] one who "learned obedience from the things that he suffered." [8] And again, "he has an everlasting priesthood; therefore he is able at all times to save those who come to God through him, since he lives always to make intercession for them." [9] But it was by obedient suffering that "he became to all who obey him the cause of eternal salvation." [10]

And the Apostle reminds us emphatically of the greatness of Christ's message. In the past, at many times and in various ways, God had spoken by the prophets, but last of all, in these days, he has spoken to us by his own Son. "Therefore ought we the more earnestly to observe the things that we have heard, lest perhaps we drift away. . . . How shall we escape if we neglect so great a salvation?" [11]

We note, then, that St. Paul draws his moral conclusions from the great dogmatic truths about Christ. He summarizes his whole theme, saying: "Let us run with patience to the fight set before us; looking toward the author and finisher of faith, Jesus, who for the joy set before him, endured a cross, despising shame, and sits at the right hand of the throne of God. So that you may not grow weary and lose heart, consider him who endured such opposition from sinners against himself." [12]

In other words, to have a strong, courageous moral life, keep Christ before your minds, pondering his divinity and his humanity, his suffering weakness and his powerful priesthood. Dogma is the greatest source of true moral strength. Mature Christian morality must be solidly based upon Christian dogma. Christian morality is so different from that of the world precisely because it is based upon the great truths about Christ. Without a lively insight into the

[7] *Ibid.*, 4:16.   [8] Hebrews 5:8.   [9] Hebrews 7:25.
[10] *Ibid.*, 5:10.   [11] Hebrews 2:1–3.   [12] *Ibid.*, 12:1f.

dogmas of faith, our morality will degenerate into a mere natural morality, our prudence will turn into a mere worldly prudence. Supernatural motivation will disappear. But a deep and loving knowledge of God, a deep insight into Christ and a loving imitation of him, will refashion our moral life and bring it to a superhuman perfection, giving it a courage and fortitude and heroism impossible to human nature by itself. As a result of such knowledge and love of Christ, discouragement and weakness will be replaced by joy and strength in doing great things for God.

During the past few centuries, one of the greatest weaknesses in the teaching of religion has been the overemphasis of morals and the neglect of dogma. And even in moral theology, there has been too much of the negative approach —"Don't do this, don't do that." Much has been made of the commandments, but too little of the great dogmas, such as the indwelling of the Trinity in souls, the mystery of sanctifying grace, the sacramental life of the Mystical Body, the mystery that Christ is in you.

Even to this day, the purely negative approach is still too common. The discouraging effect that this negative approach has upon young people was well expressed by the high school girl who was overheard to say: "Everything I want to do is either illegal, immoral, or fattening!"

The teaching of dogma is neglected because it is so much more difficult than teaching morals. The teachers who will not make the required extra effort excuse themselves, saying: "These mysteries are too far above the heads of the students. I will only confuse them if I try to teach dogma." If Christ did not want these things taught, he would not have revealed them. We must never forget that the Holy Spirit dwells in the soul of the innocent baptized child and enlightens him from within even while we teach him by word.

Preaching the great mysteries of the faith has always been the special vocation of the Dominican Order. In its early days the Order was unique in this; it was a real innovation, something previously unheard of in the history of the Church. For the first time in history, the preaching and teaching authority of the bishops was shared by a religious order. The bishops are *ex officio* the doctors or teachers of the Church. Their teaching is primarily doctrinal, the exposition and explanation of the truths of the faith. This type of preaching and teaching was committed to the Dominican Order.

The Franciscan Order, on the other hand, was not given this commission. "The ministry of St. Francis and his first companions was not preaching, properly so called, but rather exhortation." They simply invited their hearers, "particularly by example and plain encouraging precepts, to love God and do penance." Exhortation to penance, not doctrinal preaching, was the end indicated for the Franciscans by Pope Innocent III, in approving the manner of life of St. Francis.[13]

When we take care of the positive side of our spiritual life by acquiring a deep knowledge of the Word Incarnate, resulting in a flaming love of God, the negative side of the spiritual life almost takes care of itself. That is, when we are strongly attached to God in burning love, attachment to sin and the world is burned out of us. For love of God, we eagerly put aside whatever stands between him and us, we willingly undertake the mortifications necessary to remove

[13] E. Cachia, *The Apostolic Ideal of the Early Friars Preachers* (Rabat, Malta: The Dominican Bookshop, 1956), p. 25.

the obstacles, we courageously run to the battle of life, shouldering our burdens joyfully for his sake. There is no room for sadness and discouragement in a heart bursting with love of God.

In order to have this positive approach which so strengthens our moral fiber and so effectively kills evil inclinations, it is necessary to keep our eyes persistently on Christ, endeavoring to reproduce in ourselves his attitudes of soul. We should remember that Christ lives in our souls; but in order that he may live his life to the full in us, we must cooperate by reproducing his virtues in ourselves, all the while trying to be conscious that he himself is living them in us.

But the cross is the great symbol of our Lord's life, and every phase of his life is marked by it. The self-denial of the cross appears already in the poverty and humility of the stable at Bethlehem, in the obedience of the divine Child at Nazareth, in the self-sacrifice of the Good Shepherd as he goes about Galilee healing the sick and preaching the gospel to the poor.

But what is the precise cause of this total detachment of Jesus from the riches and display and self-indulgence which so characterizes the world? It is his strong, unshakable attachment to his heavenly Father. So zealous is he for the Father's glory that his disciples remark that he is eaten up with zeal for the Father's house; so concerned about his Father's business that he does not hesitate to go about it, even though this causes great sorrow to his beloved Mary and Joseph. So intent is he upon his Father's work that he says it is his very life, his meat and drink, to do the will of him who sent him, that he may accomplish his work. So submissive to his Father's will that he is obedient even unto death. In short, he is totally dedicated to the Father, he belongs entirely to him, he is at his complete disposal.

Only such zealous attachment to God can produce perfect detachment from the world. That is why Christ came to us poor, with no place to lay his head, no room for him in the inn—it was because his heart and his home are with the Father in heaven. That is why he was so truly humble and self-effacing, never seeking the praise and applause of men, avoiding all worldly display of riches and power, hiding away in a manger—his heart was set only on the glory of the Father. That is why he gave up his very life—he loved the honor of the Father more than his life, he sacrificed his life to repair the glory of God, outraged by sin. That is why he was so forgetful of self—he was so in love with souls, so eager to bring them to the Father, that it was no effort for him to forget self.

Let us, therefore, adopt this positive approach of Christ our Savior, so attach ourselves to God in love that detachment from the world becomes comparatively effortless. Once we truly love God, we will have the desire and the courage to humble ourselves, to deny ourselves to whatever extent is necessary for perfect love. In love, we will be able to endure the most severe of trials, our moral fiber will become daily stronger.

But such love, such unwavering attachment to God, such courage in detachment, can come only from persistent recollection, remembering that Christ dwells in our souls in order to give us his own attitudes toward the Father and toward the world. Christ should be the chief object of our meditation; whatever virtue we consider, we should try to see how it is exemplified in Christ. But meditation is not merely watching Christ in his various virtues; meditation is never complete until it has borne fruit in the imitation of Christ. Meditation's fruit is most perfect when we are conscious that in us Christ himself is living his life and virtues which we have meditated. If the mysteries of Christ are truly alive in our own souls through such meditation, we shall have no difficulty in fulfilling our vocation to form Christ in other souls.

We have noted how St. Dominic loved to meditate on Christ. "Let us meditate on the Savior," he would say to his travelling companions, sending them ahead so that each could walk in silence.[14] And his Order has ever loved to preach these mysteries of Christ and to teach everyone how to meditate upon them and live them. The most manifest proof of this is the fact that the Order has alway preached our Lady's Rosary and is chiefly responsible for its spread throughout the world.

The fruit of such meditation on the mysteries of Christ is the source of moral strength. It is written of St. Dominic that nothing ever disturbed the even temper of his soul. No trials or afflictions or persecutions could shake his marvelous equilibrium. He is justly praised each night in Dominican Compline as "Rose of Patience." Very probably this marvelous moral perfection was due to his faithful fulfillment of St. Paul's directions to the Hebrews: "Looking toward the author and finisher of faith, Jesus, run with patience to the fight set before us." [15] With his eyes ever on Christ in meditation on the great dogmas concerning him, St. Dominic brought his moral fiber to the supreme heights of fortitude as he lived in ever keener awareness of the Christ living within him.

If we too live in a vital awareness of Christ present in our souls, discouragement will melt away from us like the morning mist before the rising sun. The darkness of sin and the shadows of worldly attachment will be dispelled from us by Christ, the Sun of Justice, the true center of our lives. The

[14] *Dominicana*, XLII, p. 239.   [15] Hebrews 12:1–2.

fickleness and wavering caused by fear and discouragement will be replaced by a firm confidence, resulting from our conviction that "Jesus Christ is the same, yesterday and today, yes, and forever." [16] To him alone we attach ourselves.

[16] *Ibid.*, 13:8.

CHAPTER XV

THE PRAYER OF RECOLLECTION

WE HAVE ALREADY SPOKEN of the indwelling of God in the soul and we have shown how man can live in the awareness of this presence. Let us take up this subject again, describing St. Teresa's technique for living in perpetual adoration of the God in us, by the prayer of recollection.

Prayer is "something which needs no bodily strength," [1] says St. Teresa, but only love and the formation of a habit. Neither weariness nor sickness is an obstacle to prayer; we can and should pray in spite of them. Love can do it! Jesus promised that we would find rest in prayer: "Come to me, all you who labor and are burdened, and I will give you rest." [2]

There is a way of praying which is exhausting and a way of praying which gives rest. There is an old Dominican Sister who, when she is exhausted, goes into the chapel and sits down, and says: "Lord, just let me rest a while with you." And turning within herself, she thinks of Jesus, who dwells within her soul, sitting there, crowned with thorns, utterly exhausted. (And we can imagine how exhausted he really was, if we remember that he had had a hard day's

[1] St. Teresa, *The Life*, Chap. VII.   [2] Matthew 11:29.

work teaching in the Temple. Then he had instructed his
disciples for several hours at the Last Supper. After that, in
agony, he prayed in the Garden of Olives. Next, he was
dragged and pushed to the high priest Annas, and from there
to Caiphas, all the while receiving all kinds of abuse. All
night long he had been on his feet. Now they push him on a
seat, not that he might rest, but that they might crown him
with thorns and make sport of him.) This is how the old
Sister recalls him—sitting there completely exhausted. And
she says to him in the words of the *Dies Irae: "Quaerens me,
sedisti lassus"*; "Lord, seeking me, thou didst sit exhausted."
And just sitting for some moments in the presence of the
weary Jesus, she soon finds herself so greatly refreshed that
she has no trouble continuing mental prayer, enjoying the
sweetness of his presence.

It is this sort of prayer we shall consider, this relaxing in
the presence of God. This is the kind of prayer which needs
no bodily strength and is so refreshing.

But first, a word or two about the kind of prayer which is
tiring, which is very difficult at times when one is already
weary. This is the prayer in which you use your intellectual
power, thinking things out, and then wearying your mind
trying to put across your idea to the Lord in many words.
But if your mind is already worn out from work, you have no
energy left to concentrate on many words and thoughts. You
are so tired you cannot control your thoughts; they are
distracted in every direction. Therefore, withdraw your
attention from everything; turn within yourself to find that
God is within you. Relax in him. All you have to do to rest
in him is to remember that he is in you; you don't have to
go looking for him with exhausting thoughts, reasonings,
words, imaginings; just turn within, and you will find him.

St. Paul says: "He is not far from any one of us. For in

him we live and move and have our being." [3] God's presence in us differs in a marvelous way from his presence in other creatures. He is present in everything by his power, because his power holds all things in existence. But in our case, his power is benevolent love, a love greatly concerned about us, a love which preserves us for himself and seeks our company and desires that we taste the sweetness of his presence. "Cast all your anxiety upon him because he cares for you." [4]

The whole purpose of his loving care for you is to lead you to enjoy intimacy with him. Therefore, by the divine indwelling through sanctifying grace, he is in you in a very special way, giving you the power to contact him directly, to be sweetly aware of his presence. So relax in the sustaining power of the love and care of him who so earnestly desires conversation with you. St. Teresa gives that as the reason why it is so easy to be in the presence of God: because you are so convinced that he loves you and desires conversation with you. As St. James puts it: "Draw near to God, and he will draw near to you." [5] Those are among the most consoling words in all the Bible; it is as easy as that: if you turn to him, he will turn to you. St. John of the Cross says that "if a soul is seeking God, its Beloved is seeking it much more." [6] St. Gregory the Great says: "He who desires God with a sincere mind, already has him whom he loves." [7]

The whole method for putting yourself in the presence of God and relaxing in his presence can be summed up in one word: *Remember*. The prayer of recollection is the prayer of remembering: reminding yourself that God is in you. Webster's dictionary, comparing the words "remember" and "recollect" says that recollect implies a conscious effort to

---

[3] Acts 17.   [4] I Peter 5:7.   [5] James 4:8.

[6] St. John of the Cross, *The Living Flame*, Stanza III.

[7] St. Gregory, *Hom. 30 in Evang.*

remember. Therefore, the prayer of recollection requires this conscious effort. As St. Teresa puts it: "Be careful to remember who is really the Guest of your soul." [8]

But St. Teresa makes an added point: this kind of prayer is not merely making an act of faith in the truth of the divine indwelling; it is "endeavoring to realize it by experience." [9] We remind ourselves that God is in us so that we may actually experience the sweetness of his presence. "Taste and see that the Lord is sweet."

But is that *all* that is necessary—merely taking care to *recall* that he is with you? Again, Webster's dictionary comes to your help. The word "recollect," besides meaning "to make a conscious effort to remember," also means "to collect again something that has been scattered." To recollect, therefore, means to gather together the scattered attention of your faculties, which have gone out to the things of the world. To turn your attention to the remembrance of God, you have to withdraw your attention from everything else. As St. Teresa puts it: "It is called the prayer of recollection because in it the soul brings together all its faculties and enters into itself to be with God." [10] It is a withdrawing of the powers to the interior of the soul.

Thus, the prayer of recollection does require the mortification of the senses, turning them aside from idle talk, curious looking, eager listening; it means avoiding things which wildly stimulate the imagination. The two dictionary meanings of recollect—to gather together and to recall—are summed up by St. Teresa when she says that we ought to withdraw into the interior of our souls by reminding ourselves of him who keeps us company, and by forming the

---

[8] St. Teresa, *Way of Perfection*, Chap. XXVIII.
[9] *Ibid., loc. cit.*   [10] *Ibid.*, Chap. XXVIII.

habit of excluding exterior things and of fleeing the occasions of distractions from without.[11]

Keep your rule of silence; seek solitude whenever you possibly can. For, says St. Teresa, "the Lord always gives us an opportunity if we want one. I say always; for though there may be times when we are prevented by various hindrances, and even by illness, from spending much time alone, there are plenty of others when we are in sufficiently good health to do so." [12] In other words, never pass up any opportunity God gives you to pray.

Those who complain most about having no time to pray are the ones who *waste* most time when they do have a bit of God-given freedom; they, for example, are the ones who will pass an entire holiday or vacation without giving one extra moment to prayer. You acquire the habit of recollection in those God-given free moments which you must snatch here and there. Usually, in those odd moments you are tired; you say you need your relaxation and should not pray then. The answer is, relax in the presence of God like that old Dominican Sister. Prayer, says St. Teresa, "needs no bodily strength, but only love and the formation of a habit." [13] If you love him enough, you will make opportunities to seek him out; you will take every opportunity he gives you, and thus you will form a habit, so that at last, in a flash, any time and any place, you can quickly withdraw within yourself and enjoy the sweetness of his presence.

"Even though at first it may cause you some fatiguing effort," says St. Teresa, "for everything is difficult until one becomes accustomed to it, I can assure you that you will soon be consoled to realize that, without any fatiguing effort on

[11] *Ibid.*, Chap. XXIX.   [12] St. Teresa, *The Life*, Chap. VII.
[13] St. Teresa, *The Life*, Chap. VII.

your part, you will find within you the almighty Father to whom you pray." [14]

"Let the soul, in accustoming itself to recollection, disregard the initial fatigue. . . . If with serious diligence, you continue your efforts for several days, you will clearly perceive what benefit you will derive from your efforts." [15] St. Teresa explains that "no sooner does the soul manifest its desire for recollection, than the senses straightway obey and become submissive. They wander again, but it is a great gain that they are now inclined to obey. . . . If the will recalls them, the senses return with increasing alacrity." [16]

St. Teresa makes the important point that the prayer of recollection depends upon our own will, and we can attain it with the help of God. We can have it whenever our soul desires it, "whenever the soul closes the door to all worldly things and desires to enter into this paradise solely with its God." [17] In other words, this kind of prayer is not infused contemplation, but it is the highest kind of prayer we can acquire by our own efforts, and therefore it depends upon our will to be recollected. It is the preparation of the soul for infused contemplation.

In her commentary on the Our Father, St. Teresa teaches her sisters how to be recollected when they say their vocal prayers. Following her guidance, let us try to show how you can be refreshed in saying the Office or any other vocal prayer if you do so with a consciousness of the presence of God within you.

St. Teresa says that when we carry on a conversation of friendship with human beings, we turn in their direction and look at them, so that they will be truly in our presence and

[14] St. Teresa, *Way of Perfection*, Chap. XXVIII.
[15] *Way of Perfection, loc. cit.*   [16] *Ibid.*
[17] *The Way of Perfection*, Chap. XXVIII.

we in theirs. We do not turn our back on them to be occupied with something else which will interfere with our conversation. So too, when we carry on prayer, our friendly talk with God, with a little effort we can be aware that he is with us; we can remind ourselves of his loving, interested glance upon us; and we can return that glance consistently throughout the time of prayer.

And to accomplish this during your own vocal prayer, the surest method is silently to recollect yourself for a space of time before the beginning of prayer. For a few minutes, and especially if you are tired and tense, you should first sit silently and relax in his presence. This, of course, is done best if you come to chapel a little ahead of time for Office. And if that is impossible, at the very minimum, as soon as the bell sounds for prayer, at once shut out everything else and turn your attention inward to find him.

According to St. Teresa, the soul that is interiorly recollected in this way can meditate on the Passion, can represent God the Son to itself within itself, and can offer him to the heavenly Father without going out to seek him on Mount Calvary, or in the Garden, or at the pillar. When you turn within and find Jesus in your soul, you will find him making that everlasting offering of himself to the Father, and at once in union with his divine intention, you will be offering yourself in him and him in you.

Thus, throughout the recitation of your Office or other vocal prayers, with a little thoughtful effort you will be praying in him. Sometimes you will be aware that he, within you, is speaking to you the words of the Office; at other times, you will be addressing them to him. Or when you bow for the "Glory be to the Father," you will know that Jesus within you is adoring the Father. Sometimes you will be praying in Christ for Christ; that is, for the suffering and

needy members of his body, the Church; sometimes it will be
in union with his intentions, for all those whom he desires to
help through your prayers. "In this way," says St. Teresa,
"we shall be able to recite our vocal prayers not only in
peace, but without weariness as well." You see, then, that the
recollected recitation of the Office can be relaxing and
refreshing, and especially if often during the day you rest a
moment in the God within you.

St. Teresa has something to say about those who give up
prayer on the plea that they are too sick, too busy, too tired.
She says, that to give up prayer in time of trials is to add
"more trials . . . and to shut the door upon God so that he
shall not give you the joy of praying. You do not find the
refreshment for your souls which he promises to those who
come to him in prayer when they labor and are heavily
burdened." Such people, St. Teresa says, "are serving God
at great cost to themselves; but when people practice the
prayer of recollection, the Lord himself bears the cost; in
exchange for a little labor on their part, he gives them such
consolation as will enable them to bear their trials." [18]

Elsewhere, she says: "And even despite illness, or other
hindrances, we can still engage in true prayer, when there is
love in the soul, by offering up that very impediment,
remembering him for whom we suffer it and being resigned
to it. . . . It is here that love comes in. . . . With a little
care, great blessings can be acquired at times when the Lord
deprives us of our hours of prayer by sending us trials." [19] It
is at times of sickness and trial that the method of resting in
the weary Jesus is most effective in putting you in his
presence.

All these things prove how wrong is the claim that the
modern religious cannot be expected to live a life of prayer

[18] St .Teresa. *The Life*. Chap. VIII.   [19] *Ibid.*, Chap. VII.

because she is overworked. The practice of prayer is an integral part of every religious vocation; that being so, no obstacle can hinder the grace which God will give to fulfill the vocation. The only thing which can interfere with that grace is the failure to mortify our senses, the failure to keep the silence and other mortifications which the rule prescribes. If we are not living lives of prayer, it is because we are not living our religious life. If we are living our religious life as prescribed, by God's grace that life will lead inevitably to success in prayer.

St. Teresa tells us that if we cultivate recollection, our Lord will prepare the way for perfect contemplation: "No one should be discouraged who wishes to arrive at this state of prayer of recollection, which I repeatedly insist is within our power. Accustom yourself to it, and gradually you will gain self-mastery. Instead of dissipating your powers in aimless distractions, strive for mastery over self by forcing your faculties to recollection in the interior of your soul. . . .

"If you apply yourself, I know that with the help of God, you will succeed after a year, or perhaps even after six months. Realize how short a time this is to acquire a grace so well suited to become a solid foundation for those exalted things to which our Lord perhaps will deign to call you. Thus, by the very fact that you were close to him in recollection, he will find in you excellent dispositions. May it please his Majesty never to permit you to withdraw from his presence." [20]

[20] St. Teresa, *Way of Perfection*, Chap. XX.

PART FOUR

Like the Word, Through
the Rosary

CHAPTER XVI

LIVING CHRIST'S LIFE
IN THE ROSARY

As a friar preacher, the great artist Fra Angelico had a vocation to preach Christ Jesus, and he fulfilled it more eloquently by his great paintings than many another preacher does by his words. Frequently in his pictures of the mysteries of our blessed Savior's life, Fra Angelico puts St. Dominic on the scene. Though Dominic lived thirteen centuries later than Christ, to look at these masterpieces one would think that he had walked the earth with Christ himself, like the twelve apostles, following him wherever he went on the highways and byways of Palestine, listening attentively to his words, going with him all the way to Calvary and beyond.

There is the painting, for example, of Jesus carrying his cross. The Mother of Jesus walks a step or two behind him, filled with compassion, experiencing with her divine Son everything that he is suffering. But St. Dominic is there too, kneeling in the road, meeting the two as they advance along the sorrowful way. We read in his face that he is suffering intensely with Jesus and Mary. He is truly living the mystery of the way of the cross in his soul, as truly as if he had actually walked to Calvary with Christ and his Mother many centuries before.

Likewise, in a painting of the crucifixion, Fra Angelico places St. Dominic at the foot of the cross, kneeling on the ground, his arms around the cross as if to draw its full meaning and value into his soul. His face, uplifted to the crucified Savior, expresses all the love and compassion and pain that he is experiencing. He seems to be asking the Lord what he can do to bring the benefits of his crucifixion to the world.

Dominic is also at the empty tomb of Jesus on the morning of the Resurrection, listening to the words of the angel as he tells the holy women: "He is risen, he is not here. Behold the place where they laid him. But go, tell his disciples." [1] At these words, Dominic receives the inspiration to go tell the whole world of these things.

By putting him on the scene in this way, Fra Angelico intends to teach us that it was St. Dominic's custom to re-live the great mysteries of our Lord's life, first in his meditations, and then in everything he did. Quite frequently, Dominic would say to his brethren: "Let us meditate on our Savior." In this way he became ever more perfectly like the Lord, who indeed lived his own life in Dominic.

Like Dominic, every Christian has to re-live the mysteries of Christ in his own life. For the mysteries of Christ are incomplete until they find their completion in the members of his Mystical Body. Christ exists as Head, full of grace and truth, so that he may live his own divine life in all his members. In a very real sense, Christ is incomplete until he lives his life in his members, who are his fulfillment. Christ, together with his members is "the whole Christ."

Therefore, as we have seen, his mysteries—the things he did as man—are like so many sacramental signs which contain divine grace to reproduce themselves in us. That is, his mysteries signify to us what Christ will do in our souls by his grace as he lives his divine life in us, and what we must do in order to live his life to the full.

Christ does not accomplish these wonders in us without

[1] Mark 16:6–7.

our cooperation. With the help of his grace, we must consciously imitate his life, endeavoring to reproduce his mysteries in ourselves. St. John says: "We may know that we are in him by the following test: He who says he abides in him ought to conduct himself just as he conducted himself." [2] Jesus came "full of grace and truth"; both grace and truth are necessary for forming the life of Christ in our souls. Grace makes us adopted sons of God, but only in conformity to the truth found in Christ, only in his likeness. When, for supernatural motives, we do what Christ did, Christ himself does these things in us, living again in us his own life.

Our imitation of Christ—our actions in conformity to his—take on a certain sacramental value, receiving power from the grace of his mysteries to form his life in us. By each mystery of his life on earth, Christ merited for us the grace that will reproduce this mystery in our life through the sacraments, and through our cooperation with the sacraments, by imitation of the mystery.

The mysteries of the life of Christ, then, have a personal meaning for every Christian. They contain the promise of what the grace of Christ will do for us if we imitate the truth we find in him. That is why in the prayer usually said at the end of the Rosary we ask God that through our calling to mind the mysteries of the life, death and resurrection of his only-begotten Son, we may be given the grace to imitate what these mysteries contain and so obtain what they promise. What they promise is that Christ will live his life in us in all its fullness, reproducing in us his own life in all its phases, from his infancy, through his sufferings, to his final glory in his ascension to his Father.

The more consciously and willingly we try to reproduce the mysteries of Christ's life in ourselves by imitation, the

[2] I John 2:5–6.

more freely the grace of the mysteries can accomplish them in us. In living the mysteries, we must imitate not only what Christ did, but also what Mary and the apostles and the other holy persons did in relationship to Christ, for these people are part of the mystery, just as we must be, and the part they played in it is a pattern for us.

To get the full benefit of the grace of Christ, which makes us sons of God in his image, we must keep in continual contact with Christ. The lives of the Gospel people, and especially the life of Mary, exemplify to us the ways of doing this. The things these persons of the Gospel did, the situations in which they found themselves, their ways of acting toward Jesus, the things Jesus did for them, are frequently to be repeated in our lives. Their lives present examples of what the grace of Christ will do for us if we act toward him as they did.

Therefore, when we live the mysteries of Christ's life as St. Dominic did, using a method like the one we shall explain, we put ourselves in the same relationships toward Jesus that we find exemplified in the lives of these people whom we see with Jesus in the mysteries. We act toward Jesus as they did, making the same kind of acts of faith, confidence, love, adoration, humility, obedience. At other times, in living the mystery we do what we see Jesus doing in it.

The following, therefore, is a method for re-living the mysteries of our Lord's life as we pray the Rosary, so that we will live the life of Christ in everything we do and will be truly, like St. Catherine of Siena, "another Himself." The method involves three steps, expressed by three words which are easy to remember: observe, judge, act.

Observe: With the help of the memory and imagination, look at the scene of the mystery to see what is going on. You are there. Put yourself, for example, at the scene of our Lord's birth at Bethlehem and watch what takes place.

Judge: See what personal meaning the event has for you. Judge how you fit into the mystery. Is there any person in the scene whose place you can take, whose part you can play?

Act: Play the part of the person whom you have chosen. Put yourself in his or her place—whether it be Jesus, Mary, Joseph, or someone else, such as the shepherds or Magi—and do as he or she did.

For example, in the first glorious mystery, you observe what is going on. You see how Jesus, risen from the dead, shows his glorious wounds to the doubting Thomas. Thomas, at last believing, now that he can put his fingers into the wounds in the hands of Jesus, falls on his knees before him in love and adoration and says: "My Lord and my God!" [3]

When you see these things, you judge that you belong in the place of Thomas. You know at once that what Jesus says to Thomas, he says to you as well: "Be not incredulous, but believing!" [4]

Spontaneously, you act as Thomas did. You fall on your knees and adore your risen God, saying: "My Lord and my God!"

This method brings faith, hope and charity into action, thus stirring up the divine life which is in us by grace. Faith, hope and charity put us into immediate contact and union with Christ who is God, so that by the activity of these virtues he lives his life in us. Our mental prayer has thus united us directly to God, so that here and now he is truly living in us.

Thus, observing the scene of the mystery will usually inspire an act of faith in the mystery. Judging the mystery's personal meaning in our own life will ordinarily give rise to hope of the fulfillment of the mystery in us. The third step, action, will usually be an act of love or of some other virtue inspired by love. Sometimes, faith, hope and charity will act

[3] John 20:28.   [4] John 20:27.

simultaneously; sometimes one will act more predominantly than the other. A few examples will bear this out.

In the first step we observe what takes place in the mystery as though we were actually there when it takes place. The memory recalls what we know of the Gospel story of the mystery and the imagination brings it to life. We watch what goes on, we listen to what is said. Usually it is enough to observe only a few details. In the third joyful mystery, for example, we see a young mother kneeling on the ground before her newborn Son. But at once faith gives new life, real life, to this picture of the imagination. Faith knows why this mother kneels before her own child with the most profound reverence. Her child is God. The mother must adore her God, even though he is also her son.

The second step comes spontaneously. We judge immediately what we must do: this Child is our God, too, so we must adore him with his mother.

We act at once. In our mind and heart as we do as Mary does. We adore her Son with all the intensity of our faith and love. We prolong this action of faith and love as long as possible, remaining thus in true living union with him whom we adore, receiving from him all the while the vital flow of his graces.

As we continue to observe the scene with this living faith, we make further judgments about its personal meaning for ourselves. This Son of Mary whom we are adoring with her was born of her for our sakes. He is living the life of men so that we can live the life of God. At once we act upon this thought: with living hope we cry out to him: "Lord, live in me! Make me a son of God in your own likeness." "Mary, give him to me, that I possess him as you do."

If faith, hope and charity seem to wane and the divine mystery begins to fade, perhaps the consideration of other details of the scene will bring it to life again. We find a child concealed in a manger, because his star in the east has betrayed his hiding place to us. At once we recognize the infant as Lord of the universe—the very stars obey him. Spontaneously we act, subjecting our will to him in love, so that we will not be outshone by the stars. For this child is:

> He who dismisses the light, and it departs,
>   calls it, and it obeys him trembling;
> Before whom the stars at their posts
>   shine and rejoice.
> When he calls them, they answer "Here we are!"
>   shining with joy for their Maker.[5]

Or we watch this little child, helpless in his swaddling clothes, though we hear his angels in the skies praise his mighty power: "Glory to God in the highest." [6] As we keep these details or others in our minds, our faith penetrates their deeper meaning, and with the shepherds we come over to Bethlehem and "understand the word which was spoken to them by the angel." [7] We penetrate ever more deeply into the mystery of God himself, understanding his gracious love for us. Our love cannot help responding to such love. Our meditation is fruitful and complete in our acts of love. Christ now lives in us more perfectly than before by faith, hope and charity. Because in meditation we have lived his life with him and he has lived it in us, he will live in us and we will live in him in everything we do. And with the Apostle, we will say in truth: "I live—yet no longer I, but Christ lives in me; and the life that I now live in the flesh, I live in the faith of the Son of God, who loved me and gave himself up for me." [8]

---

[5] Baruch 3:33–35.   [6] Luke 2:14.
[7] Luke 2:17.   [8] Galatians 2:20.

CHAPTER XVII

THE ROSARY: AN ENCOUNTER
WITH GOD

FRA ANGELICO HAS SHOWN us in his paintings that the mysteries of Christ's life were a "living presence" for St. Dominic. Those who knew Dominic well have made it clear that for him prayer was a face-to-face encounter with Christ, a lively conversation with him.[1]

All of us can achieve this same kind of prayer with the help of the Rosary. All the mysteries proposed for meditation in the Rosary are sacramental; that is, the things our Lord did during his life among us are sign and symbol of the real presence of God among us in Christ, Emmanuel. The deeds of Christ signify God's loving will to sanctify us; they make his sanctifying power present among us. The mysteries themselves, then, are truly a living presence of God among us in all his loving mercy, for our sanctification.

As signs or symbols, these mysteries call forth from us a living response to this living presence of God among us in Christ. For we ourselves have to be actively present to him in order to benefit from his presence.

Our living response to him in faith and charity is made possible and efficacious by the sacramental powers within us. Baptism has given us a permanent sacramental contact and union with Christ, for the character it impresses upon the soul is an incorporation into him and a lasting source of grace. It is a power for coming into living and efficacious contact with Christ through active faith, not only in the

---

[1] Cf. Bede Jarrett, O.P., *Life of St. Dominic*, pp. 108–114.

reception of the other sacraments and in the functions of the sacred liturgy, but in all of our living. The character is a power to be ever alert to the life-giving presence of Christ and God, thereby attaining a vital union with Christ through faith working by charity.

Our active presence to this life-giving presence of God is most perfect in Mass and Holy Communion and in the spiritual communion which is the continuation of sacramental Communion. We are speaking now of spiritual communion as the spiritual feeding upon Christ and God by active faith and charity.

This continuing spiritual communion is nothing else than a type of mental prayer. Mental prayer is a living presence with God or, as St. Teresa says, it is "nothing else, in my opinion, but being on terms of friendship with God, frequently conversing in secret with him who, as we know, loves us." [2]

Mental prayer is perfected by infused contemplation, which in this life is the ultimate fruit of the sacraments in our souls. The actual reception of a sacrament is a living encounter with God in Christ and it confers graces and a further invigoration of faith, hope and charity, to bring this encounter to the ultimate perfection possible in this life: the intimate experience of God in infused contemplation. The sacrament of baptism bestows on us the supernatural organism of the life of grace, including the infused virtues and the gifts. This is the equipment needed for living in the presence of God, and this same equipment is at work even in infused contemplation. All baptized Christians in the state of grace have the necessary powers, and therefore contemplation is possible to all. Moreover, we notice that in the lives of great mystics such as St. Teresa of Avila and St. Catherine of

[2] St. Teresa, *The Life*, Chap. VIII.

Siena, their encounter with God in mystical contemplation was usually most intense and perfect after Holy Communion; it was but a continuation of that sacramental encounter.

Mental prayer, therefore, as an awareness of the living presence with God, should be the normal outcome of our sacramental encounter with Christ in the Eucharist. It is the most precious fruit of the sacraments in our personal life, short of the beatific vision, which also is the fruit of communion with Christ: "He who eats my flesh and drinks my blood has life everlasting." [3] It is from the perfection of this contemplation that our action should flow. Like Moses coming down from Mount Sinai, we go forth from the divine presence (without leaving it) to bring God to men.

The method which we presented in the preceding chapter for re-living the mysteries of Christ's life in Rosary meditation can also dispose every Christian for the heights of contemplation (in conjunction, of course, with the sacraments and the required purgation). This method is not merely a meditation of a lower order, but a living in the presence of Christ, reacting to the presence of his sanctifying power and living his life as he lives in us. We explained that this method is the theological virtues actively at work to bring us into intimate union with Christ. Only through these virtues can we have a living encounter with God, because these virtues have God as their object. For example, by the act of faith we assent not to the mere words of a doctrinal formula, but to God as First Truth. Even in a sacrament there is no real encounter with God unless the reception of the sacrament is a living profession of this faith by which alone one can make contact with God.

When we meditate on the virtues of Christ for the purpose of imitating them ourselves, the fruit of our meditation

[3] John 6:55.

should not be merely a practical resolution, but rather an act of adoration of this virtue (that is, the Person whose virtue it is), an intense love of the virtue, a humble petition for it, an opening of self to Christ who is here and now present to us in our living faith, so that he will fashion it in us by the grace he merited for us.

This is a far more profitable way of growing in virtue than the meticulous examination of conscience and the detailed resolutions which we may soon break anyway in our human weakness. St. John of the Cross refers to it as a means of progress in virtue through "anagogical love," which is the humble admission of our helplessness to practice the virtue by ourselves, accompanied by love's confident cry to Christ to form it in us. We cry to him in our failures: "Lord, give me *your* patience, *your* charity, *your* humility, etc."

From our living presence with Christ in the first sorrowful mystery, we learn that "the weakness of God is stronger than men." [4] That is, the weakness of Christ, weighed down to the ground in the agony of the Garden by human sin and suffering, is our strength. The mystery of human weakness in Christ is the mystery containing his infinite divine power to take away our weakness. "The weak things of the world has God chosen to put to shame the strong." [5]

That is why in this mystery we hear Christ tell us to watch and pray in his presence: "Could you not watch one hour with me? The spirit indeed is willing, but the flesh is weak. Watch and pray, lest you enter into temptation." [6] His own human helplessness in his agony is the sacramental instrument of his divinity in taking away our weakness, forming in us his own virtues. We adore his helplessness in living faith, for it is the helplessness of God, and as we adore, we receive its strength.

[4] I Corinthians 1:25.   [5] I Corinthians 1:27.   [6] Matthew 26:40–41.

This form of meditation in the living presence of Christ attributes man's sanctification primarily to Christ present to us and in us, and only secondarily to our own efforts. All of our efforts have to be an engagement in the sacramental mysteries of Christ's own life, through the sacraments and meditation. Our very exercise of the virtues becomes a sacramental instrument of the sanctifying power of Christ who lives in us.

The right use of the Rosary combines, in a simple form, the best features of the various methods of meditation with the fully contemplative aspects of mental prayer. The hands are chained by the beads, to tame the restless body. The lips are put to work praising God in the words of the "Hail Mary," to keep the body further occupied with God, lest it distract the soul. The senses are withdrawn from attention to their normal objects by concentration upon definite scenes from our Lord's mysteries, vividly re-presented by the interior senses of memory and imagination. But since Christ is the object of the meditation, since it is he who is recalled and imagined, faith and charity, aroused by these scenes, quickly put us into his living presence so that all the sanctifying power of his life, death and resurrection can here and now flow into our whole being. The contact with Christ effected in us through the sacraments is thus stirred up into lasting action; our brief encounter with him at Mass and Holy Communion, or in some other sacrament, is lengthened and continued and perfected in the more lasting encounter of mental prayer and, perhaps, infused contemplation.

As the former Master General of the Dominicans, Archbishop Gillet, said in his encyclical letter on the Rosary: "Each mystery is a living 'presence' in which we go from Mary to Jesus, who leads us to God present in us, in the very depths of our souls, and gives us over to the inspirations of his Spirit." Then at last, like St. Paul, we can truly say, "I know nothing . . . except Jesus Christ, and him crucified." [7]

CHAPTER XVIII

PRESERVING THE FRUITS OF MEDITATION

IF WE TAKE CARE to meet the living Christ again and again in mental prayer, we will acquire the habit of centering our whole life of thought and love about his living Person. And the more we love, the more we will become like the one we love. All his virtues will grow in us.

Let us give a few examples to show how, in our living encounter with Christ in mental prayer as we re-live the mysteries of his life, many other virtues besides faith, hope and charity will come into action and will grow in us, as we find more and more ways in which we are part of our Lord's life.

It is meaningless for us, for example, to observe the bitter sufferings of Christ in the sorrowful mysteries, unless we judge the scene we watch, to find in what way we ourselves have part in the mystery of his suffering. Watching our Lord's sufferings is of no profit to us unless we realize and admit that we ourselves are the cause of these sufferings.

To illustrate this point, let us put ourselves on the scene of our Lord's scourging at the pillar. We observe the soldiers cruelly scourge him. We grow hot with anger over the

[7] I Corinthians 2:2; Gillet, *The Revivified Devotion and Apostolate of the Rosary* (Somerset: The Rosary Press), p. 17.

brutality we see; we are enraged at the soldiers. But just a minute! We judge that we ourselves are the ones who are scourging our Lord. Our own sins have done this to him. So we turn our anger from the soldiers to ourselves; we turn in hatred against our sins, detesting them, renouncing them. And thus the virtue of penance comes into action in our souls. Even as we re-live the scene, we are purifying our souls by contrition. Thenceforth, the mere thought of the scourging of Christ brings forth in us a spontaneous act of contrition, and our meditation bears continuing fruit.

Or again, we are on Calvary with Mary, watching as Jesus is nailed to the cross. We listen as he says: "Father, forgive them, for they know not what they do." At once we judge that we, too, like our Lord, must forgive our enemies and those who injure us in any way. Immediately we act; we do as Jesus does, and from the heart we forgive our enemies and resolve to be reconciled with them as soon as possible.

We remain on the scene of this mystery, and soon we hear the repentant thief as he says: "Lord, remember me when thou comest into thy kingdom." [1] At once we judge that we too have sinned against Christ like the thief, and like him we must ask for pardon. We act, saying: "Lord, remember me!" When Jesus responds to the thief and to us, saying, "This day thou shalt be with me in paradise," hope springs up in us, despite our sins. [2]

Or again, we watch, in the third sorrowful mystery, as the Son of God is crowned with thorns, mocked, spit upon, struck with the reed. When Fra Angelico painted this scene, he did not paint the bodies of the soldiers, but only their spitting lips and their striking hands. He kept the soldiers anonymous, as it were, to hint to us that we were the ones striking Jesus these blows, we were the ones spitting on

[1] Luke 23:42.   [2] Luke 23:43.

Christ. "Each single sin," wrote Pope Pius XI, "is to be considered as renewing in its way the passion of the Lord, crucifying again the Son of God and making him a mockery." [3]

When we watch the soldiers, then, as they spit upon Christ and beat the crown of thorns into his head with the reed, the bodies and faces of the soldiers fade away, and in their places we see our own. At once we act, asking his pardon, expressing sorrow for what we have done.

Or, as we watch the soldiers striking him, we are amazed at his patience with his tormentors, whom he could destroy with one angry word of his divine power. We judge at once that this patience with them is for our sake; then we will appreciate his patience with our sins, and will learn how to be patient in turn with our fellowman, "for the anger of man worketh not the justice of God." [4] Realizing how far short we fall of this example of our Lord, we act at once, crying out: "Jesus, meek and humble of heart, make our hearts like unto thine!" The very desire for this virtue is a disposition toward it.

Sometimes, as we re-live a mystery, we observe people who act in an evil way in regard to our Lord. Instead of putting ourselves in their places, we do just the opposite. Thus, in the third sorrowful mystery, we see Jesus crowned with thorns, and watch as Pilate takes him before the crowd, saying: "Behold your king!" The crowd rejects their king, crying: "We will have no king but Caesar!" [5]

We react at once, we accept the King whom they have rejected, bowing our knee before him in adoration. "Thy kingdom come!" is the sentiment of our hearts.

In the agony in the Garden, we watch Jesus, overwhelmed

---

[3] *Miserentissimus Redemptor*, May 8, 1928.   [4] James 1:20.
[5] John 19:15.

with sorrow, coming to Peter and James and John for
consolation. "My soul is sad, even unto death. Wait here,
and watch with me." [6] But we see how little consolation he
receives from these three. "Then he came to his disciples and
found them sleeping. And he said to Peter: 'Could you not
then watch one hour with me?' " [7] And we remember the
words of Jesus spoken through the prophet: "Reproach has
broken my heart, and I have become weak. And I looked for
someone to pity me, but there was none, and for someone to
comfort me, but I found none." [8]

At once we act, making up our minds to console him by
watching with him, at least as long as it takes to finish the
mysteries of our Rosary. And by our watching, we comfort
him by making reparation for the outrages committed
against him by those who persecute the members of his
Mystical Body.

Sometimes, as we re-live a mystery, we make an immediate act of the virtue we observe; sometimes our action is a
rehearsal for future action. For example, when we observe
Mary's eager readiness to do the will of God, expressed in
her words, "Behold the handmaid of the Lord," [9] at once we
do as she did. Using her own words, we make a similar act of
devotion, putting ourselves at the total service of God.

Or again, in the first sorrowful mystery, we observe Jesus
in agony, faced with the Father's will that he should die. The
will of the Father is so difficult to accomplish that Jesus
prays for its removal: "Father, if it be possible, let this
chalice pass from me." [10] But in his prompt readiness to do
the will of God at all costs, Jesus adds at once: "Nevertheless, not my will, but thy will be done." As we judge this
scene to find our part in the mystery, we realize that we too

---

[6] Matthew 26:38.   [7] Matthew 26:40.   [8] Psalm 68:21.
[9] Luke 1:38.   [10] Matthew 26:39.

are often faced with the difficult will of the Father. So that we will always be prompt in doing it, no matter what the cost, we put ourselves in the place of Jesus and say as he says: "Not my will but thine be done." [11] Thus we rehearse for future action, so that we will know how to act when the difficulties of life come. The very rehearsal is an act of the virtues we will need in the future, and a strengthening of them. Better still, by our contact with Jesus in this mystery, the grace of the mystery has strengthened his virtues in us.

By frequently re-living the mysteries in the Rosary or in other forms of mental prayer, we build up habits to be used in future meditations and in future living. We acquire a store of images in the memory—images concerning events in the life, sufferings and resurrection of our Lord, images which can be recalled at a moment's notice. But these images should not be mere beautiful pictures to admire. Rather, they should be images which will habitually evoke from us spontaneous acts: acts of love, adoration, humility or some other virtue.

For example, just to bring to mind the image of Jesus in the Garden of Olives, flat on the ground, adoring the holy will of the Father, should suffice to arouse our will to an act of submission to the will of the Father like that of Jesus. Thus, in a flash our meditation produces fruit—no need for long drawn-out reasoning; only a momentary thought of the obedience of Jesus, and our will produces a similar act patterned after the act of Jesus.

Or, just to picture the soldiers bending their knees to Jesus in mockery, as they crown him with thorns, is enough to send us to our knees in loving adoration and reparation.

Images such as these stored up in our memory sum up in capsule form, as it were, whole meditations. Perhaps in the

[11] Luke 22:42.

beginning, the threefold process of observing, judging, and then acting, will be gone through laboriously. But the meditation can be preserved for future use in the form of an image or picture which will promptly evoke from our heart an act of virtue as soon as it is called to mind.

The act of virtue inspired by the image is often expressed in the form of an ejaculation, such as the words of Thomas when he felt the wounds in the risen body of Jesus: "My Lord and my God!" or the words of Mary at the Annunciation: "Behold the handmaid of the Lord." In our meditations we have learned to make our very own the attitudes of soul expressed in these words, so that in life situations we find it easier spontaneously to react in the right way to our Blessed Lord.

In this way, meditation carries over into all of our living. And with the help of the ejaculations which summarize and express the fruit of a whole meditation, we are able to continue our prayer all day, reviving it at odd moments throughout the day by recalling the image or pronouncing the ejaculation. And since these images concern the mysteries of our Lord's life, with their help we live forever in his presence, meeting him anew each time we think of the mystery. Christ is indeed our Emmanuel, God with us in full reality.

PART FIVE

The Eucharist, the Interior Life and Christian Action

CHAPTER XIX

MAKING HOLY COMMUNION
PERMANENT

AFTER A FEW WEEKS, Jesus "came again to Cana of Galilee where he had made the water wine." [1] And a certain royal official, whose son was lying sick at Capharnaum, some eighteen miles away, came to him and besought him to come down and heal his son, for he was at the point of death. However, Jesus finds something imperfect about this official's faith, and says: "Unless you see signs and wonders, you do not believe."

What can be wrong with the man's faith? Obviously, he believes that Jesus has power to heal his son; otherwise he would not ask him to come down and heal him.

Jesus shows what is wrong with the man's faith by his way of dealing with the case. He refuses to go down to Capharnaum, but instead, heals the man's son from a distance, saying: "Go thy way, thy son lives!" Thus he teaches the man—and all of us—that his divine power is not limited to any one place; it is not restricted to the locality where he is physically present. The man's faith was imperfect because he had thought it necessary for Jesus to make the trip to Capharnaum in order to work the cure. But because Jesus is God as well as Man, his power to cure bodies and to sanctify souls is present *everywhere*.

We can apply this truth to the Holy Eucharist. The power of the Eucharist to make saints is not limited to the place where the Sacred Host is. When Jesus walked this earth,

[1] John 4:46.

"power went forth from him and healed all." [2] So, too, power goes forth from his Eucharistic presence. The sanctifying power of our Eucharistic Lord is as omnipresent as is God's creative power, which preserves all things in existence.

If this power of our Savior is present everywhere so that we can contact it by faith anytime, anywhere, then why is his body present in the Holy Eucharist in definite places? Or why does our Lord require us to have physical contact with his body in Holy Communion, if his sanctifying power is everywhere?

It is because he has compassion on the imperfection of our faith, and adapts the exercise of his divine power to our human weakness. When Jesus told the royal official that there was something imperfect about his faith, the man, in his pressing anxiety over his son, ignored our Lord's remark and said: "Lord, this is no time for theological discussion about the qualities of faith; one more moment and it may be too late; my son is at the brink of death." Jesus therefore does not wait till the man's faith is perfectly instructed, but mercifully works the cure at once. However, in so doing he thereby instructs the man's faith about the greatness of his power.

So, too, with us; though our Lord's power of sanctification is everywhere, so that if our faith is perfect we can contact it at will anywhere we happen to be, yet he mercifully adjusts his power to our weakness and "comes down" among us by the physical presence of his true body in the Holy Eucharist. At the same time, he would like us to realize that his power is not restricted to the tabernacle where the Host is reserved, nor is his power in us at an end when the Host we receive in Holy Communion has dissolved. The more we realize the omnipresence of the sanctifying power issuing forth from the

[2] Luke 6:19.

tabernacle, or from the Host we receive in Holy Communion, the more we will benefit from the Eucharist.

Our Lord has various reasons for commanding us to contact his body physically by receiving him in Holy Communion. First of all, our very nature as creatures, made of body and soul, requires an outward profession of the faith which is in our hearts. The use of the physical, bodily elements of the sacraments as outward signs gives an expression to, and intensifies, the faith which is in our hearts.

Furthermore, the sacramental ceremonies, and above all, those of the Eucharist, focus our faith. They direct our act of faith to very precise things which we must believe about Christ's power of sanctification. For example, Christ's divine power works in us only on account of his Passion, which merited our sanctification. Therefore, lest we forget our indebtedness to his Passion, Christ applies the fruits of the Passion to our souls in the Eucharist, through the same body which suffered and died for us. Thus, in the Mass, the physical presence of the body which suffered and the blood which was shed, makes his sacrifice of the Cross truly present to us to sanctify us.

Christ requires that in Holy Communion we be physically united with this humanity which suffered for us, not only to convince us that all the power of his Passion is here and now present to sanctify us, but also, so that in an act of humility we will profess our total dependence upon his Passion and will express our lasting gratitude to him. For although he is divinely eager to put that power of sanctification to work in us, it is necessary for us to remember that this power works not because we sinners deserve it, but because he has mercifully suffered and died to win it for us.

Furthermore, though his power is present everywhere and

he is always eager to sanctify us, lest in the weakness of our faith we doubt that it works in us, he gives us infallible signs that it does. These signs are the sacraments, which infallibly, efficaciously, apply his power to us. Thus, the physical contact which we have with Christ's body in the worthy reception of Holy Communion, infallibly brings the power of Christ's passion to our souls, so that we are certain that it works in us.

Thus, we again see the compassion of our Savior. Though perfect faith should be enough to put us in contact with his power, which is everywhere, in condescension to the weakness of our human nature, he permits us the direct touch of his body. And yet, the physical contact with his body is worthless without simultaneous spiritual contact with him by faith, for the power of sanctifying which goes forth from his body is a spiritual power and it must be contacted spiritually.

The physical contact with his body is for the sake of arousing and strengthening the spiritual contact of faith, a contact which should remain even after the physical contact is over. The physical contact with the Sacred Host is brief, but the spiritual contact can be, and should be, permanent, for the spiritual power of Christ is permanently present to us, even after Holy Communion, unless we impede it by sin.

In Holy Communion, Christ, through his bodily presence within us, touches our soul with his divinity, and that touch leaves a lasting mark. Though his body departs when the Host dissolves, the divine power of Holy Communion, which goes forth from that body, remains present to the soul. This is because the divine Jesus himself does not depart from the soul when his body does. The passing contact with his body has infallibly brought his divinity, which remains present to the soul, to sanctify it if only it will let him.

We should live in permanent spiritual contact with this sanctifying power, which indeed is identical with Christ's divinity. The lasting impression left on the soul by the touch of Christ's body in Holy Communion is a new sharing in his divine power, because it is a new sharing in his divine life. All that is required of us is that we activate this power by living the divine life which is in us.

We do this by letting Christ live in us; and we let him live in us when we put into action our faith and charity, which are indeed his power at work in us. Faith and charity as habits are supernatural powers which Christ constantly communicates to the soul as long as he is in it. But we must put his powers to work by active faith and charity.

Each Holy Communion incorporates us more perfectly into Christ our Head, uniting us to his physical body in order to bring us more perfectly into his Mystical Body, so that as our Head he can live his divine life in us and in all our actions. As the new Adam, the new Head of the human race, he gives us a new life—the divine life of the eternal God; for the new Adam is a "life-giving spirit." [3]

St. Thomas explains how our Head gives his life to his members: "Just as the members of the natural body derive sensation and movement from the head, so from their spiritual Head who is Christ, his members derive spiritual sensation, the knowledge of truth, and spiritual movement, by the inspiration of his grace." [4]

In other words, Christ, who lives in the essence of our soul by sanctifying grace, lives in our intellect by enlightening it with faith and in our will by inflaming it with love. Since each Holy Communion causes a still closer incorporation into Christ our Head, it brings Christ more perfectly into the essence of our soul by grace, and thereby increases the

[3] I Corinthians 15:45. [4] *Summa Theologiae*, IIIa, q. 69, a. 5.

power and vigor of our faith and charity. This divine power
in us is always ready to go into action, in lively faith and
burning charity, unless we impede it by venial sin. That is
why we say that in order to profit to the maximum from Holy
Communion, all we have to do is activate the divine power
within us by putting faith and charity into action throughout
the day; especially charity, for the chief effect of Holy
Communion is to give new vigor to our power to love God
and neighbor. It is up to us to use this power.

Let us strive, then, to be conscious always of these divine
powers which are in us through Holy Communion, lest we
neglect them through thoughtlessness or impede them by
venial sin. Better yet, let us be conscious of the presence of
the source of all these supernatural powers, the divine
Person, Christ our Head, who is living in our souls. Mindful
of his presence in us, let us surrender our intellects to him so
that he will enlighten them, our wills so that he will inflame
them, our emotions so that he will set them in order and use
them in his service. The surest guarantee that we will live a
totally supernatural life is to concentrate on this presence of
our Head within us; if we do so, enlightenment and love will
spontaneously follow. Of course, to succeed in all this, we
have to die more and more to self and to the world.

Since, then, the sanctifying power of Holy Communion is
not limited to the place where the Host is physically present,
nor to the moments after Holy Communion, let us remember
often during the day that we have received the body of Christ
in the morning, and that the touch of his body has left Jesus
himself permanently present spiritually in our souls, with all
the power of his divinity. With this truth in mind, we can
adore him any time just as fervently and profitably as in the
moments immediately after Holy Communion, for by the
conviction of our faith and the fervor of our love, we are in

true spiritual communion with him, and his divine power of sanctification is at work in us. In this way we prolong the effects of Holy Communion all day. In fact, the purpose of sacramental Holy Communion is to give us the power to carry on this continuing spiritual communion with our Lord, and through him and with him and in him, communion with the Holy Trinity.

However, even perfect faith in this lasting spiritual presence of Christ in our souls and in the omnipresence of his sanctifying power will not free us from the humble necessity of going frequently to the physical presence of his body in Holy Communion. We have already mentioned various reasons, but a predominant one is that a new touch of his body will incorporate us still more perfectly into him our Head, so that his divine life can flow to us more freely and fully.

Frequently, and especially at Mass, we should profess our faith in the fact that Christ lives in us and his power sanctifies us, because the body once nailed to the cross and the blood once shed on the cross have been made present to us on the altar and we have received them in Holy Communion.

When we fully realize these truths and live them, like St. Paul we will declare in full truth: "I have died to everything else that I may live to God. With Christ, I am nailed to the cross. It is no longer I that live, but Christ lives in me. And the life that I now live in the flesh, I live in the faith of the Son of God, who loved me, and gave himself up for me." [5]

[5] Galatians 2:20f.

CHAPTER XX

"PANIS ANGELICUS"

BEFORE THE Archangel Raphael departed from Tobias and his family, he said, "I seemed to eat and to drink with you, but I use an invisible food and drink which cannot be seen by men." [1] No doubt, St. Thomas Aquinas was thinking of these words of Raphael when he sang out with joy in the Matins hymn he composed for the feast of Corpus Christi: "*Panis angelicus fit panis hominum*—The bread of angels becomes the food of men!" For until Christ died on the cross, the food of angels, the beatific vision, was beyond the reach of men. But in the Eucharist, the angelic nourishment is made available to us. The bread of angels becomes the food of men!

We are speaking metaphorically, of course, when we speak of food of angels. We are speaking not of bodily eating, but of a spiritual eating, in which the angels feed upon God, the Bread of life, by making him the object of their thoughts and of their love. When we speak of food for thought, we mean truth. But the will also has its food—the good which it loves. The angels, therefore, feed upon God when, in the beatific vision, their intellects enjoy him who is infinite Truth, their wills find perfect fulfillment and happiness in loving him who is infinite Good.

Human beings yearn for this very same food. Our hungry souls cannot be satisfied until we too enjoy the beatific vision and love God perfectly. This is the bread we will receive in heaven. But even on earth, we can feed on that same Bread

[1] Tobias 12:19.

of life. Listen to what Jesus says: "I am the Bread of life. He who comes to me shall not hunger, and he who believes in me shall never thirst." [2] In this life we feed on God, not by the clear vision and perfect charity of heaven, but by faith and love. Notice that the first time Jesus said, "I am the Bread of life," he was referring not to the Holy Eucharist, but to this spiritual feeding upon him by faith and love, that is, occupying the mind and heart with God in prayer, lovingly thinking of him, speaking to him, walking in his presence, tasting that the Lord is sweet. This spiritual feeding is like that of the angels in heaven, who do not receive the Holy Eucharist sacramentally.

So that we might be able to do this, the Bread of life had to come down from heaven to be within our reach. "For the bread of God is that which comes down from heaven and gives life to the world." [3] It is only through Jesus Christ that human beings can enjoy the food of angels; only through faith in him do we feed upon God. "He who sees me sees the Father," said Jesus.[4] There is no other way for man to live in the presence of God; man can reach him only through Christ our Lord. "I am the way, and the truth, and the life. No one comes to the Father but through me." [5]

It was only after Christ had spoken of this spiritual feeding upon him through faith and charity that he went on to speak of feeding on him in the Holy Eucharist. "I am the living bread that came down from heaven. If anyone eat of this bread, he shall live forever; and the bread that I will give is my flesh for the life of the world." [6] The whole purpose of Holy Communion is to make it possible for us later on to feed upon God in the beatific vision in everlasting life, and to feed upon him *now* by faith and love. For, says St. Thomas

[2] John 6:35. [3] John 6:33. [4] John 14:9.
[5] John 14:6. [6] John 6:33.

Aquinas, "sacramental eating is for the purpose of spiritual eating." [7]

"The receiving of Christ in the Eucharist is ordained to the enjoyment of heaven in the same way as the angels enjoy it." [8] And again St. Thomas says: "The effect of this sacrament is to be spiritually united with Christ through faith and charity." [9] Thus, spiritual communion with God in faith and charity is the purpose of sacramental Communion. A sacramental Communion is in vain if it does not stir up in us more active faith and more fervent charity, because this increase in faith and charity is the special sacramental grace which Holy Communion produces. This really means that we receive Jesus sacramentally in the morning so that we may be with him all day long in a spiritual communion of lively faith and fervent charity. Such communion with Christ in faith and charity is mental prayer—living in his presence, feeding on him in the way the angels do. Any time our mind and heart are occupied with God, we are in spiritual communion with him; we are feeding upon him by faith and love.

Therefore, sacramental Holy Communion is our primary aid to mental prayer. Mental prayer, says St. Teresa of Avila, is nothing more than being on terms of intimate friendship with God, frequently conversing with him in secret, because we know that he loves us.[10] In this life such conversation is possible only through faith and charity. Mental prayer is faith and charity at work, bringing us into intimate, immediate contact with God. Since fervent Holy Communion is our chief source of active faith and fervent charity, it is the chief cause of success in mental prayer. Continual mental prayer can be achieved only by the grace

[7] *Summa Theologiae*, IIIa, q. 80, a. 1 ad 1.   [8] *Ibid.*, a. 2 ad 1.
[9] *Ibid.*, q. 80, a. 1.   [10] St. Teresa, *The Life*, Chap. VIII.

of God, and the particular graces necessary are given chiefly in Holy Communion.

One of the most fundamental requisites for success in mental prayer is humility, the humility to admit that, after all, this intimate conversation with God is his gracious gift. Although he is most eager to give it, he waits until we are humble enough for it. "God resists the proud, but gives grace to the humble." [11] He gives this gift through a sacrament to bring home to us that it really is a gift of his grace, something so far above our natural powers that it takes a sacrament to bring it easily within our reach. We should, therefore, begin our efforts at mental prayer by humbly going to the Bread of life, where he has come down to our level in the Holy Eucharist.

But if these graces of Holy Communion, which enable us to feed on Christ in the continual spiritual communion of prayer, are to take full effect, our cooperation is necessary. Especially at the time of Holy Communion, and immediately before and after, we must endeavor to activate our faith and charity, not necessarily by making acts of faith and love in words, but by concentrating our whole attention on the divine Jesus whom we receive, forgetting all else and enjoying the presence of his Majesty. Such recollection in him, begun in the morning at the time of Holy Communion by his grace and our efforts, can be maintained by the same grace and efforts. Holy Communion supplies us with power all day to make those efforts successful.

Of course, we must carry on a most persistent fight against all unnecessary distractions and against dissipation in any form; we must fight perseveringly to keep in touch with him. But the fact that the fight must be persistent does not mean that recollection is impossible. It is wrong to give up and say

[11] James 4:6.

that it is not for me. Anyone who wishes to achieve recollection must first be convinced that it is possible, and that it is Holy Communion which helps make it possible. The Eucharist, upon which all may feed, is the source of the most sublime favors of prayer and contemplation which the saints enjoyed. Since the sacrament is within the reach of all, no wonder we can say that mental prayer and sublime contemplation are within the reach of all. These are but the full flowering of the active faith and charity produced by fervent sacramental Communion.

Therefore, whoever desires continual mental prayer should hunger for Holy Communion. When we seem to be carrying on a losing battle against distractions, and all our recollection seems to be gone, a quick way to get back to the spiritual communion which is mental prayer is by making an act of spiritual communion; that is, by fervently desiring to receive Holy Communion, the source of all our spiritual feeding upon God. The very desire for him puts us into spiritual communion with him, brings our mind and heart into union with him, and gives us much the same graces as actual sacramental Communion. A spiritual reaching out to the tabernacle, a yearning for him, quickly brings him into the soul. He has been in the soul all the time, but faith and charity, which we have aroused by his grace, enable us to taste the sweetness of his presence.

Of course, at times it will be so hard to pray that all we can do is to make a series of seemingly desperate spiritual communions. Though we reach out for him, he seems to elude us. But our desires will not be in vain, for only love can stir up such longing for him, and love which fights in this way to reach him will grow stronger as it fights. As long as love desires him, it already possesses him. St. Gregory says: "He who desires God with a sincere mind, truly already has him whom he loves. For no one could love God if he did not have him whom he loves." [12] The fervent desire to pray is itself a prayer, a spiritual communion. When it seems to us that we cannot pray, if we keenly long to pray, then we are praying without knowing it.

By means of that charity, expressed in fervent desire, we are indeed with God, like the Word. For the Word eternally with the Father in an everlasting embrace of love in the Holy Spirit. Even when our minds cannot be with God in prayer, our hearts can be with him in charity. This is possible through the grace of Holy Communion, whose chief sacramental effect is the fervor of charity. By active charity we are with the Father, like the Son, in the unity of the Holy Spirit—even when it is necessary that our thoughts be elsewhere, provided they are "about the Father's business." [13]

If a spiritual communion—a turning to the Eucharist with desire—is our best weapon when we are fighting distractions and striving for recollection, there are other times when we are already recollected and can commune with the Bread of life without actually thinking of the sacrament. After all, it is the same Christ whom we reach, whether with the help of the crucifix, our Rosary, or a visit to the Blessed Sacrament. We are in spiritual communion with him, no matter what method we use in bringing our minds and hearts to him.

However, this recollection, this lasting spiritual communion of the mind and heart with him, by its very nature should bring forth desires to receive the sacrament more perfectly. For they who feed upon him, hunger still more: "He who eats of me will hunger still; he who drinks of me will thirst for more." [14]

---

[12] St. Gregory, Homily for the Feast of Pentecost, at Matins.
[13] Luke 2:49.   [14] Sirach 24:20.

The more we taste of the sweetness of God by faith and love, so much the more do we desire to taste him more perfectly still. That is why, when we are in spiritual communion with him in mental prayer, a flame of desire for closer union with him springs forth. Since we know that the sacrament of Holy Communion is the quickest, surest way to perfect union with Christ, we desire to receive it more perfectly than ever. That hungry desire is the best possible preparation of all for Holy Communion, since hunger is the best preparation for any kind of food.

In the midst of the necessary distractions of life and work, as we have seen, very often the intellect will have to be occupied with things other than Christ, but the will can be with him permanently, no matter what comes. Holy Communion produces the fervent charity which brings about this permanent union of will with Christ. But for this too we must struggle persistently, using the graces which Holy Communion puts at our disposal in such abundance.

For example, perhaps daily we meet difficulties in accepting the will of God as it is manifested to us in some duty, some sickness or frustration, or some friction we may have with our neighbor. When we find it hard to embrace Christ by embracing his will, manifest in these difficulties, then is the time we especially need a spiritual communion—a turning to the Blessed Sacrament to obtain that fervent charity which alone will bend our will to embrace his. Only when we have embraced his will in all things, in all the circumstances, duties and trials of life, only then will our spiritual communion with him in love be perfect and undisturbed. Holy Communion gives us the fervor to desire this and to strive for it.

The effect of Holy Communion, therefore, is to unite us spiritually with Christ through lively faith and fervent charity in this life, so that, in the next life, we may eat of him spiritually the way the angels do, by clear vision and perfect charity. God has decreed to give us this Bread of angels only through Jesus Christ and his Blessed Sacrament. Therefore, he who sincerely desires mental prayer, and he who is homesick for the beatific vision, fervently desires the Blessed Sacrament of the altar, the source of all our spiritual communion with God. It is the Holy Eucharist which makes available to us the *Panis angelicus,* the Bread of angels.

CHAPTER XXI

"PER IPSUM ET CUM IPSO ET IN IPSO"

IT IS AN UNFORTUNATE MISTAKE to think that the Holy Eucharist as a sacrament is really distinct from the Holy Eucharist as a sacrifice. The Eucharist is not sacrifice and sacrament successively, but simultaneously. By its very nature, Holy Communion is inseparable from the Mass; by its very nature, Communion is the eating of a sacrifice. Even when the Blessed Sacrament is received outside of Mass, the Communion should be seen as a participation in the sacrifice of the Mass. Moreover, for the perfect participation in the sacrifice of the Mass by the faithful, it should be terminated by the reception of Communion. Finally, the permanent presence of the Blessed Sacrament in the tabernacle is a lasting memorial of the sacrifice of the Mass, a continuing application of its fruits to souls.

In short, the Holy Eucharist is a sacrificial banquet. Just as the sacrifice of the paschal lamb in the Old Law was completed only by the eating of the lamb, so, too, in the Mass, Christ is sacrificed under the appearances of bread and wine rather than under some other form so that we can eat him in Holy Communion and thereby become one with him in his act of sacrificing himself. The primary purpose of Holy Communion is to identify us with Christ sacrificing and Christ sacrificed, by more closely incorporating us into his Mystical Body. In no other way can we achieve union with God, except in union with Christ.

At the Offertory of the Mass we present our gifts to God, bread and wine, which represent us, for the gifts are a symbol of the giver, a sign that he is giving himself to God.

However, our gift of self is unacceptable to God unless we have in some way been changed into Christ. For we are members of the sinful race of Adam, enemies of God, until we have been "re-created" in Christ, the New Adam, incorporated into him, and identified with him as members of his Mystical Body. Therefore, at the Consecration of the Mass, the gifts of bread and wine, which we presented at the Offertory as symbols of ourselves, are changed into Christ to symbolize how the power of his sacrifice on the cross changes us into himself when we eat the sacrificed Christ in Holy Communion. Jesus said to St. Augustine: "Eat me. Nor will you change me into yourself, as you do the food of your flesh, but you will be changed into me."

By changing us into Christ sacrificing and Christ sacrificed, Holy Communion makes us acceptable to God and unites us to him in Christ. There is no other way of reaching this union. "For unless you eat the flesh of the Son of Man and drink his blood, you shall not have life in you." [1] Therefore, at Mass, between the Consecration and the

[1] John 6:54.

Communion, the priest declares this truth in a striking ceremony. As he says the words, *"per Ipsum et cum Ipso et in Ipso, est tibi Deo Patri omnipotenti,"* he makes three signs of the cross with the Sacred Host, each time a little deeper into the chalice which contains the Precious Blood. The Host, consecrated from bread which was made of many grains of wheat, symbolizes the Mystical Body of Christ, made up of many human beings in union with Christ its Head. This Host is lowered ever more deeply into the chalice in order to show how, through repeated fervent Holy Communions, we enter ever more deeply into the sacrifice of the cross, becoming ever more perfectly identified with Christ sacrificing and Christ sacrificed.

In changing us into Christ crucified, Holy Communion reproduces his own life in us, the life which we can have only through his death, the life which we can live only by dying with him. "I have died . . . that I may live to God. With Christ I am nailed to the cross. It is no longer I that live, but Christ lives in me." [2]

By incorporating us into the sacrifice of Christ and giving us his life, Holy Communion reproduces in our souls the very same dispositions which were in the soul of Jesus as he sacrificed himself on the cross, so that our whole life becomes identically one sacrifice with his. The permanent dispositions of his soul, to which he gave expression in his sacrifice on the cross, become permanent dispositions of our soul, so that, like him, we live totally for God.

The offering of a sacrifice is a visible ceremony which gives outward expression to the invisible dispositions of the soul, such as adoration of God, submission to his will, eagerness to make reparation. The sacrifice of Jesus on the cross was the outward expression of his permanent, perfect

[2] Galatians 2:19f.

dispositions of soul toward the eternal Father. At every instant of his existence in human nature, the relationship of the soul of Jesus to God was absolutely perfect, permanently the same in its total dedication to the will of the Father in burning charity. "In coming into the world, he says: . . . 'Behold I come . . . to do thy will, O God.' " [3] Never did he waver in this steadfast dedication until he had consummated the will of God on Calvary. His total consecration of himself to the Father in unspeakable love proved itself by his perfect obedience even unto the death of the cross. His zeal for the will of the Father caused him to mourn over those who violate the Father's will, and induced him to offer himself as a sacrifice of reparation. These unchanging attitudes of Christ's soul throughout his life found their most perfect outward expression in the sacrifice of the cross.

Since Holy Communion unites us with Christ and identifies us with his sacrifice, it makes permanent in our souls the attitudes he expressed so beautifully on Calvary, provided that we cooperate with the grace of Communion by consciously imitating Christ's soul. Since Holy Communion is inseparable from the Eucharist as sacrifice, and its whole purpose is to reproduce Christ's sacrifice in our lives, the most fruitful way of receiving Holy Communion is to participate in the Mass in the most perfect way we possibly can, consciously trying to accomplish, in union with Christ, the four ends of sacrifice, so that when we go out from the Mass, we can, by the grace of Holy Communion, bring these four ends to perfection in our daily living.

By its visible ceremonies, the sacrifice of the Mass gives outward expression to Christ's attitudes of soul so that it can reproduce them in us by our participation in the sacrifice. The Mass ceremonies teach us how to do what Christ did,

[3] Hebrews 10:5–7, *passim.*

and the grace of the Eucharist gives us the power to accomplish this, so that it is truly Christ living in us who does these things in us.

For example, one of the four purposes for which Christ sacrificed himself was reparation for sin. Therefore, contrition for sin is suggested to us in many ways by the ceremonies of the Mass. For example, at the *Confiteor* we confess our sins in order to renounce them and be freed of them through the merits of Christ's sacrifice in which we are about to share. A *Confiteor* said with true contrition will reproduce in our soul Christ's own attitude toward sin—his uncompromising hatred for it, his zeal to repair the honor of God outraged by it. If we think of these things at the *Confiteor*, we will offer the Precious Blood in the Mass more fervently as a reparation for our own sins and those of others. The grace of Holy Communion will perfect and make permanent in our souls this spirit of reparation.

Another Mass ceremony which will inspire in us this spirit of contrition and reparation is the profound bow of the priest immediately after the Lavabo, as he says the words of Daniel: "In a spirit of humility and with a contrite heart, may we be received by Thee, O Lord." [4]

Another purpose of sacrifice is adoration, or acknowledgment of God's supreme dominion, with a consequent total submission to his will. But this submission is perfect only when it is like that of Jesus throughout his life and on Calvary, inspired by flaming love, a completely voluntary consecration of himself to the Father's will. Therefore, at the Offertory of the Mass, when we give our lives anew to God, consecrating ourselves to his holy will, saying: *"Suscipe, Sancta Trinitas;* Receive, O Holy Trinity," let us strive to surrender ourselves to him in union with Christ's total

[4] Daniel 3:39; Psalm 50:19.

abandonment to the Father: "Father, into thy hands I commend my spirit." [5]

The more perfectly we enter into the Offertory, the more abundantly the grace of Holy Communion will work in us to make this disposition of soul more permanent in us, so that throughout the day and throughout our whole life, no matter what the will of God demands of us, we shall always be able to say: "Not my will, but thy will be done." All our sufferings, accepted in this spirit, will become reparation in Christ. By bringing Christ into our soul in the way explained previously, Holy Communion will enable us to do this.

Another purpose of sacrifice is thanksgiving. Again and again in the Gospels Jesus is described as "giving thanks to the Father," but especially when he worked the miracle of feeding five thousand persons as a foreshadowing of the Holy Eucharist, and at the Last Supper when he instituted the Holy Eucharist. This emphasizes the fact that it is a sacrifice of thanksgiving. The very name "Eucharist" means "thanksgiving."

What reason did Jesus have for giving thanks? Did not all things belong to him eternally because he is God? Whom should he thank for what is eternally his own? It is as Man that our Lord gives thanks, and he is really giving thanks in the name of the whole Mystical Body. For whatever was given by the Father to the human nature of Christ our head was given to his members; all that he received was for our salvation. Therefore, as Man, he thanks the Father for the fullness of grace which enables him to sanctify his members; he thanks the Father for his own glory, which is really the glory of his Mystical Body.

More specifically, he thanks the Father for all the fruits of the Redemption, all the benefits of his sacrifice. Therefore, at the Consecration of the Mass, living in the priest and in the

[5] Luke 23:46.

people, who are offering his sacrifice, Christ again "with his eyes lifted up toward heaven, *giving thanks*," breaks the bread and gives it to us, saying: "Take and eat ye all of this, for this is my body."

Since Christ is thanking the Father for all the benefits of his sacrifice, we also, in union with him at Mass, joyously thank God, not only for past benefits, but also for the eternal life still to come to us through this Mass. Since Holy Communion unites us to Christ sacrificed, our eternal life is assured and we can joyously praise God for it, in the firm hope of receiving it. Fervent Holy Communion is its pledge. We sing all the hymns of the Mass in this same spirit of thanksgiving—the Introit, the Gradual and Alleluias, the *Gloria,* and above all, the Preface: "It is truly meet and just, right and salutary, that we should always and in all things give thanks to thee, O Lord, holy Father almighty, eternal God, *through Christ our Lord.*" Through Christ and with Christ and in Christ, we give thanks at Mass, and Christ, living permanently in our souls because of Holy Communion, continues this hymn of praise and thanks in us throughout the day.

Lastly, petition is one of the purposes of sacrifice. The Church presents her petitions many times in the course of the Mass—at the Collect, Secret, Postcommunion—always adding, "through Jesus Christ our Lord," praying with him, praying in him. But above all, and most intimately in Jesus, she makes her petitions at the *Pater Noster,* in his very own words. This is immediately after the impressive ceremony of the *"Per Ipsum."* The priest has just lowered all the people into Jesus Christ by the three descending signs of the cross with the Host over the Precious Blood. Then, all of us, living in Christ, pray to the Father in him and with him and through him: *"Pater Noster:* Our Father." He is our Father because he is the Father of Jesus, and we are one with him.

The words ring true because Jesus living in us is saying them in us: "Our Father, who art in heaven, hallowed be thy name. Thy kingdom come, thy will be done." Christ prays in us that his dispositions of soul will be perfected in us through the Holy Communion we are about to receive.

"Thy will be done." May all be as totally dedicated to the Father's will as Christ was in his obedience unto death. May God's kingdom come into their souls as Christ enters them in Holy Communion. As his perfect members, may he use them as instruments in advancing the kingdom.

"Give us this day our daily bread." Give us the Bread of life, Holy Communion, so that Christ will live in us and, living in us, will pray in us, sing thy praises, offer reparation through our sufferings, and do thy will with the perfect dedication of flaming love. Thus, through our Holy Communion, our whole life will be a living sacrifice, one with Christ sacrificing and Christ sacrificed. *"Per Ipsum et cum Ipso et in Ipso est tibi Deo Patri omnipotenti, in unitate Spiritus Sancti, omnis honor et gloria."*

CHAPTER XXII

THE EUCHARIST, CONTEMPLATION AND ACTION

> The heavenly Word proceeding forth,
> Yet leaving not the Father's side,
> And going to his work on earth
> Had reached at length life's eventide.[1]

IN THESE WORDS St. Thomas Aquinas tells us that when the Son of God became man, he still remained in heaven, living

---

[1] From the hymn for Lauds on the feast of Corpus Christi.

his divine life to the full, for the Incarnation in no way injured or lessened his divinity. When he was on earth, Jesus described himself to Nicodemus as "the Son of Man who is in heaven." [2] Nor was this true of him merely because he was God, but even his humanity was in heaven when it was on earth, in the sense that his human soul, at every instant of his life on earth, enjoyed the beatific vision. His human soul was full of the sanctifying grace which lifts man to a share in the divine life; his human intellect was always enlightened by the light of glory; his human will was ever inflamed by the divine charity of the Holy Spirit. Thus, everything human in Christ was raised to the supernatural level and was "with God," just as everything human in us can be super-naturalized, divinized, by the divine life of grace given to us through Christ.

Without leaving his Father's side, he went forth to his work on earth. And that work was to bring us to his Father's side, that we too might be in heaven—not only to enjoy the beatific vision with him later in glory, but even here on earth to be in heaven, in the sense that through grace we share in the divine life and the Trinity dwells in our souls.

Moreover, just as Jesus, when he went about his work on earth, did not leave the presence of the Father, we too, as we do the work given to us by God, can live in the presence of the Trinity. In the previous chapter we began to explain the role of Holy Communion in making this amazing thing possible. We spoke chiefly of the mind and heart being perpetually with God by faith and charity, in the spiritual communion caused by sacramental Communion. Now we shall see that as a consequence our work becomes the work of Christ and, like Christ, as we go to our work and his, we remain with the Father. It is only in Christ that we can be

[2] John 3:13.

always with the Father, only in him can all that we are and do be from the Father, and only in him can we be on our way back to the Father in every action of our life, for his greater glory. Only what Christ does in us is done with the Father, from the Father, and brings us to the Father.

But we can be totally in Christ and he in us only by fervent sacramental and spiritual communion. "He who eats my flesh and drinks my blood abides in me and I in him. As the living Father has sent me, and as I live because of the Father, so he who eats me, he also shall live because of me." [3] The words, "I live because of the Father," are true of Jesus in two ways.

First, he lives because of the Father even in his divine nature, because he is eternally begotten of him as his Son. The Father and Jesus live one same divine life together. The Father did not exist before him, yet he proceeds from the Father eternally as his Son.

Secondly, as man, he lives because of the Father, not only because God has created and preserves in existence his created human nature, but even more because God forms in his human soul that divine life of sanctifying grace which enables even his humanity to enjoy the beatific vision.

And as Christ the Man lives because of the Father, so he who eats Christ in the Eucharist shall live because of Christ, in the same way that Christ's humanity lives the divine life of grace. The humanity of Christ, his human soul, is "full of grace and truth" received from his divinity, so that from his humanity we might partake of his divinity. [4] "For in him dwells all the fullness of the godhead bodily, and in him . . . you have received of that fullness." [5]

Only union with his sacred humanity can give us our share in his divinity, and he has decreed that ordinarily such union

[3] John 6:57.   [4] John 1:14.   [5] Colossians 2:9.

be achieved through the sacraments. Baptism incorporates us into his humanity so that, living in Christ, we may live with him his divine life, and the Holy Eucharist brings that union and life to its fullest perfection.

Jesus said to St. Augustine: "I am the food of great souls; grow and eat. Nor shalt thou change me into thyself as food of thy flesh, but thou shalt be changed into me." [6] The change into Christ, brought about in us by Holy Communion, is twofold: as we share in his divinity more and more, we also become ever more like his humanity. In Holy Communion we are united to the whole Christ—to his divinity as well as to his humanity—for his body which we receive is hypostatically united to his divine Person. His divinity, working through his humanity into which we are incorporated, forms his divinity in us.

The most immediate effect of Holy Communion is an increase of the divine life in us, with a special invigoration of charity. We are, as a result, capable of more lively faith and charity by which we can here and now have immediate contact with the Trinity dwelling within us. By putting this new vigor of our faith and charity into action, like Jesus we live with the Father and by the Father, and our actions proceed from the Father.

And when we go forth from Holy Communion to our work, we do not leave the Father, as Jesus did not leave him when he came to earth. We take our heaven with us, for we carry the Trinity in our soul and we remain in spiritual communion with the Trinity.

Though this primary effect of Holy Communion takes place interiorly in our souls, the divine life overflows from the soul into our whole being. When we go forth from morning Mass to our work, as Jesus went forth from heaven

[6] St. Augustine, *Confessions*, Book 7.

to his, we can act more and more like him in all that we do because his life is more vigorous in our souls because of our fervent Communion. As his interior life grows in us, our work more and more merges into his work. All that we do becomes part of his own divine apostolate. We live less and less for self, more and more for him and his work of saving souls.

But this happens to our work only to the extent that we use the vigor of our faith and charity, given to us by Holy Communion, actively to unite ourselves more closely to Christ. By active faith and charity we more intimately enter into the divine life, contemplating the divinity with Christ, remaining in spiritual communion with God, keeping our thoughts and our hearts in the presence of God.

In this way we acquire the mind of Christ and we see everything from his point of view. We acquire the heart of Christ, a heart zealous for the glory of the Father and the salvation of souls, and there is no room left in us for selfishness. We live no longer for self, but only for God and for the work of Christ, the Church. All the human elements in our life come to be lived in the same way that Christ lived the human elements of his life; for God became man not only to give man his divine life, but also to show man how to live that divine life. If, then, we would receive the maximum benefits from Holy Communion, we must keep our eyes on Christ and do as he did. When we do what he did, for his motives, he does it in us, and thus his life within us overflows and transforms our whole being and all our work.

Thus, it is clear that Holy Communion is the fountainhead both of our contemplative and of our active life. First, of our interior life, enabling us to live in spiritual communion with the Father, like Jesus, so that when we go forth to our active apostolate, we do not leave God, but take him with us.

In fact, there is no such thing as an "active life" which does not flow from the divine life within a soul. The active Christian life is not just any kind of activity, but only supernatural activity, the exercise of supernatural virtues, flowing from the divine life within us. The contemplative life and the active life are but two different vital activities of one and the same divine life of charity. If it does not flow from within, from charity, our activity is not the true active life. It is not life at all; that is, it is not supernatural life, not the life of Christ. If it does not flow from the grace and charity within us, our activity is not the divine work of Christ, but only a human imitation which, on the surface, may look like the work of Christ. But it bears no divine fruits, for there is no divine life of charity inspiring it, to make it living and life-giving.

To bear fruit, we must abide in the vine. "As the branch cannot bear fruit of itself unless it remain on the vine, so neither can you unless you abide in me. I am the vine, you are the branches. (He who eats my flesh and drinks my blood abides in me and I in him.) He who abides in me and I in him, he bears much fruit; for without me, you can do nothing." [7]

An apostolate of the active Christian life is a supernatural mission. It is a supernatural work which can bear supernatural fruits for the salvation of souls only because the power of Christ works in the apostle. No matter how perfect one's human skills, one's ability as a teacher, preacher, nurse, cook or administrator, it remains true that his effects on souls, his power to bring them to heaven, is always in proportion to the greatness of his charity, and this is in proportion to the divine life of Christ within him, nourished by fervent Communion.

[7] John 15:45 and 6:56.

The carrying out of a true apostolate, one truly flowing from charity, in turn increases the divine life within the soul, because we work in Christ and he in us. Such an apostolate flows from him and leads to him. Zeal for souls, first inflamed by the Eucharist, leads us back to the Eucharist, the only source of success in the apostolate. The more we try to save souls, the more we realize how helpless we are by ourselves, and therefore the more we go back to the Eucharist to obtain the charity of Christ, the heart of Christ, which alone can convert souls. We ask Christ in Holy Communion to give us his Sacred Heart so that we can love as he loves; we ask him to live and love in us, knowing that the depth of our influence in the apostolate depends upon how actively Christ lives and loves and works in us.

How well the modern Catholic Actionists know this, how convinced they are that the Mass and Holy Communion are the source of their apostolate! Their active life keeps their time for prayer down to a minimum. That is why they are all the more intent upon making their Mass and Communion as perfect as possible. As St. Thomas Aquinas points out, the Mass is the chief act of the contemplative life.[8] The great leaders of the Catholic Action movement are convinced that the apostolate must flow from within; that is why they like to compare their life to an iceberg. An iceberg is seven-eighths under water, one eighth above. So, too, every apostolate must be seven-eighths interior sanctity—Christ living in the soul—and all activity must flow from him.

At Holy Communion we therefore remind him that, just as he went forth from the Father to his work without leaving the Father, so we want him to live so fully in us that, even as we do our work, we too will be able to contemplate the Father with him.

[8] *Summa Theologiae*, IIa IIae, q. 180.

This is entirely possible, for the Eucharist is the source both of the interior and of the active life. The same Jesus lives both these phases of his life in us. From the point of view of mere human nature, the apostolate and the interior life are equally impossible—for both are supernatural, above mere human power. If, then, Christ, living in us through the Eucharist, can give us a successful apostolate, he can also give us a successful interior life; indeed, he will not give us one without the other, if he has sent us on an apostolic mission.

Since Holy Communion conforms our whole life to the whole life of Christ, it forms his interior life as well as his active life in us. He lived the two phases simultaneously, "going to his work on earth, yet leaving not his Father's side." As we grow in the spiritual life, we shall approach more and more such a simultaneous living of the two phases.

The Word of God came to earth because the Father sent him. Each morning of our life, the instant we arise, let us hear the voice of God sending us on our mission. At once, as we start forth to our work, let us think of the "heavenly Word proceeding forth, yet leaving not the Father's side." Let us go forth with him, inviting him to go forth with us. If he is with us, then we will be with the Father, for he never leaves the Father's side. All that we do will be from the Father, and will take us back to the Father. When we say to Christ in Holy Communion, "Live thou in me!" let us make it a petition for the privilege of contemplating the Father with him, even as we continue his work of salvation with him. For the Eucharist is the one source of both the contemplative and the active phases of our spiritual life. "All these things are the work of one and the same Spirit." [9]

[9] I Corinthians 12:11.

CHAPTER XXIII

ACTION AS A HELP
TO CONTEMPLATION

THE MOST PERFECT FORM of Christian living is not the contemplative life alone, nor the active life alone, but a balanced blend of the two. No one's life can be exclusively contemplative or exclusively active. In each individual both ingredients must be present, prayer and action, but they must be mixed in different proportions in different individuals. The proportions of the mixture must be regulated by prudence, in accordance with one's temperament, degree of perfection, type of apostolate, tasks assigned in obedience, state of one's health, and so on.

One person will be inclined more to contemplation than to activity; another person will be content only with more activity than contemplation. But each of these persons must be careful that he does not go to extremes in following his particular bent. The person who is strongly inclined to prayer is in danger of offending by neglecting the active works of charity, becoming annoyed when the needs of others calling for his help seem to interfere with his prayer. The actively inclined person is in danger of getting so involved in feverish activity that his prayer life dies. Our spiritual life develops in keeping with our natural temperament, for grace always perfects nature, but that natural temperament must be controlled by mortification lest it takes us to extremes, upsetting the even balance of action and contemplation which is so necessary in every Christian life.

Therefore, though it is true that for some people there is more of one ingredient than the other in his life, so that we call him "active" or "contemplative," it is also true that the person in the cloister has active works, and the most active Christian must have contemplative elements in his life; otherwise, neither is any longer a complete Christian.

Consequently, no one member of a community is justified in accusing another of being too active or too contemplative. The active ones accuse the prayerful ones of being lazy, wasting their time sitting in prayer; the prayerful ones accuse the active ones of being worldly, lacking true religious spirit. The accusations may or may not be true, depending on whether or not the individual in question has prudently or imprudently blended the elements of prayer and action.

Likewise, since every life has to be a harmonious mixture of action and contemplation, there should be no need to make the complaint: "My work interferes with my prayer life; my active life hampers my contemplative life." Such a statement implies a lack of understanding of what Christian life really is. We must not think of prayer and action as though they were two totally distinct compartments of life, separated from one another as one room is totally cut off from another by a wall. Prayer and action are really one and the same Christian life, mutually interdependent, mutually intermingled—just as the various systems of the human body do not hamper one another, but are only so many different vital functions of one same life. The circulatory, respiratory, digestive and nervous systems are intimately interdependent. So too our active side and contemplative side are but different vital functions of the one same supernatural life of charity.

Above all else, the supernatural life is charity. Anything

that is not impregnated by charity is not Christian life. As the soul gives life to every single cell of the body, so must charity give supernatural life to every single act of our spiritual life. Therefore, the term "active life" as used in spiritual language does not mean just any kind of activity, but only that supernatural activity which is inspired and vitalized by charity. Any action which is not guided by faith and impelled by charity is mere natural action; it does not belong to the supernatural, active life; it is not really spiritual life.

The Christian life consists in the exercise of the supernatural theological and moral virtues by which we live the divine life of grace. But in this living we have relationships to God and relationships to neighbor. The first are regulated chiefly by the theological virtues, the second chiefly by the moral. The contemplative phases of our life consists chiefly in the exercise of faith, hope and charity, by which we lift our mind and heart to God in prayer, while the active life, under the motivation of charity, is primarily the exercise of the moral virtues, especially justice and mercy, which regulate our dealings with others. More briefly, in an over-simplification, the contemplative life is love of God; the active life is love of neighbor. Even the active phases of our life, since they are the exercise of supernatural virtues, definitely bring spiritual growth in holiness. More than that, the active phases are a distinct aid to contemplation, rather than being an interference.

The contemplative and active phases of our spiritual life are mutually helpful. One phase cannot get along without the other any more than the respiratory system could do without the blood stream. We speak so much of action flowing from contemplation, quoting the famous words of St. Thomas Aquinas, *"Contemplata aliis tradere,"* that we tend to forget that the right kind of action can be a preparation for contemplation. This fact is clearly explained by St. Thomas when he shows how the exercise of the moral virtues in the active life is a necessary preparation for contemplation, for two reasons: first, the moral virtues remove the obstacles to contemplation by bringing calm and serenity to the soul through the regulation of the emotions; secondly, the active life enkindles love of neighbor, from which the mind and heart easily rise to more fervent love of God.

God is permanently in residence in the just Christian's soul, and therefore we should be able to enjoy his presence at will. For God dwells in the soul precisely so that the soul can contact him and experience his presence by the exercise of faith and charity. But before the soul can contemplate the divine guest at will, it must remove by mortification all the obstacles to that contemplation. It must bring all its emotions into such control that they will no longer agitate it and distract it from God. This control of the emotions is the work of that phase of the active life which involves the various moral virtues. Meekness, patience, chastity, fortitude, justice save us from the agitation of soul caused by anger, sadness, concupiscence, fear, envy, greed and the like.

The exercise of each of these moral virtues involves self-denial of some kind or other, lest the particular power of passion regulated by that virtue run away with us. But even while the virtues withdraw the emotions from dissipation, they direct these God-given powers into the service of God, of self and of neighbor. The emotions are God-given equipment; it is the work of the moral virtues to see to it that these emotions are used for good ends.

The control of the emotional powers through self-denial and the positive use of these powers in doing good for others bring about the eventual mastery and calming of the emotions so that they no longer interfere greatly with one's prayer life. The emotions of the self-centered person are very easily agitated, so that he is never very successful in living a consistent prayer life. But the emotions of the selfless apostle are controlled instruments always in the service of God and neighbor. A fruitful apostolate, involving much self-denial, an active life in the service of others, is always therefore a distinct aid in mastering the emotions so that they give little interference to prayer life.

The mere fact that we have to live with other human beings gives continual occasion for the exercise of the virtues of the active life. Mere peaceful co-existence requires the self-control of patience and meekness, together with the positive assistance of kindness and mercy, to say nothing of constant justice to all in word and in deed. None of these virtues of the active life can be exercised without a certain amount of mortification of self, which results in dying to self so that we may live to God and neighbor. Such dying to self is necessary for success in the contemplative side of our life.

Of all the moral virtues of the active life, justice is the principal one. Temperance and fortitude have chiefly the task of controlling our emotions, so that we are at peace within ourselves, but justice brings peace and harmony to our associations with others. The active life, however, is not content with mere avoidance of friction, but overflows in zeal for the welfare of neighbor. It abounds in works of mercy, both corporal and spiritual.

The love of neighbor which expresses itself in these works of mercy naturally flames into prayer and contemplation. For one and the same virtue of charity makes us zealous for souls and fervent in love of God and, therefore, fervent in prayer. The flames of love of neighbor are the flames of love of God, so the fire of love is already burning when the time comes for prayer. Thus charity is nourished both by prayer and by action, provided the action is impelled by charity.

A very active apostolate, if it is sparked by genuine charity, by a passion for souls, brings real spiritual growth and spontaneously breaks into prayer and praise of God. If, inspired by faith and charity, we engage unselfishly and generously in the works of mercy, in teaching, preaching, nursing and the like, if we are truly intent on serving God by serving others, as soon as there is a slight respite in our work, the mind easily rises to God.

This is especially true if in our work we are keenly aware of the frightful spiritual needs of so many souls. When the labors of the active apostolate seem to be bearing little fruit for the salvation of others, when because of their hard hearts or great worldliness people seem to be callous to all our efforts to lift them to God, then especially do we turn to God in fervent charity, beseeching his grace to melt those hearts. Then especially do we cry out for the grace of charity that we ourselves may love God more fervently, in order to inflame others more efficaciously.

St. Catherine of Siena begins her *Dialogue* by telling us that the more aware she became of the neediness of souls, the more desirous she was of becoming perfect herself, so that she would be more powerful in helping others. The difficulties of the apostolate, the resistance of souls to our efforts to save them, make us turn ever more fervently to God and lead us to bind ourselves ever more closely to his Sacred Heart, so that working in Christ, we will be able to do more good.

Nor do we wait for the end of our work to pray. An apostolate which is truly inspired by charity is full of fervent prayer. Again and again during the day we lift our thoughts to God. Though such acts of faith and love are necessarily brief, often they are much more fervent and intense than prayers said in the leisure of the hour of meditation. It is not the length of a prayer or the external act that counts; it is the intensity of love. A mere sign of the cross as we begin our work can be a very fervent act of love and dedication.

When inspired by true charity, a zealous apostolate, no matter how busy and exacting it may be, is no real hindrance to the life of prayer, but rather a distinct aid to it. But the problem is, how are we to have such fervent charity in our daily labors? The answer is that fervor is kindled at times of prayer. But is not that a vicious circle? A man cannot pray well because he has no charity in his labors, and he cannot labor well because he has no fervor in his prayers.

If one really is in such a vicious circle, there must be a lack of balance between the prayer and action of that individual. The two are not blended in proper proportions. The works of one's active life should not be so numerous and so exhausting that they destroy all possibility of an interior life of prayer. It is far more fruitful to have a limited apostolate with a deep interior life, than an excessively active life with little or no interior life. Unless one has reached the consummate heights of perfection, whenever he is under pressure and tension he will find it difficult to be so calm emotionally that no obstacle to prayer arises. Our active works, then, should not be too numerous or too exhausting.

And yet, we must not seek the equilibrium of our life at the lowest possible level, by keeping both our prayer and our action at a minimum. Though we have to avoid an excessively exhausting active life, we must not forget that a very exacting and busy apostolate in true charity is a distinct aid in the life of prayer, as long as the elements of prayer and action are blended in the right proportions. The greater one's perfection and charity, and the more perfectly one has mastered his emotional energies with the aid of the moral virtues, the greater the apostolic burden he can carry with ease and the more it will contribute to his charity in prayer.

If we are in a vicious circle in which the lack of interior prayer life gives no nourishment to the charity of our labors, and the lack of charity in our action provides no fuel for fervor in prayer, then we must change the vicious circle into a virtuous one by starting again at the first sources of charity: the sacraments and prayer. At Mass and Holy Communion, at the crucifix and in the reading of the Scriptures, we must re-enkindle our charity, but then keep that charity aflame by seeing to it that we engage in no activity unless charity be its motive. Charity enkindled at prayer will quickly grow cold if one's activity is nothing but the self-seeking of ambition or vainglory. If one teaches or nurses or preaches or scrubs floors only for self-satisfaction, charity will grow cold in one's labors and will be re-kindled at time of meditation only with great difficulty. It is only the complete selflessness of an active life of genuine charity that will keep the fires burning, so that very quickly at the time of prayer or Holy Communion they will be brought to ever greater fervor. If we are utterly generous in love of neighbor, ready to aid anyone in need, our love will remain ever burning, ready to flame to new heights as soon as we are free to lift mind and heart to God.

Love of God and love of neighbor are one and the same thing. In charity, God is loved for his own sake, and self and neighbor are loved for the sake of God. Whether we are exercising love of God in prayer or love of neighbor in the apostolate, one same love is growing. Often the people who complain most that their work interferes with their prayer life are the ones who divide their spiritual life into rigid compartments, making a complete dichotomy between their active life and their prayer life. They will never pray outside the prescribed times of prayer, nor will they lift a finger to do a bit of work of charity apart from what has been assigned them in obedience. "My schedule is too heavy," they say, "no time to extend a helping hand, no time for an extra moment of silent prayer." Their spiritual life is so rigid and limited that it can hardly be called life. True life is dynamic and adaptable, not mechanical, not cut and dried. In the truly spiritual life, prayer and action mutually penetrate and nourish one another.

The contemplative life, we said, requires serenity of soul; and the moral virtues of the active life, by controlling the emotions, help bring this serenity. So serene was St. Dominic that almost every witness at his process of canonization alludes to his marvelous equanimity of character, his absolute evenness of temper whatever befell. "Nothing disturbed the even temper of his soul except his quick compassion for those in need," wrote Bede Jarrett.[1]

That is why St. Dominic was such a great contemplative and yet one of the most active of all the saints. In the calm of his soul he contemplated Christ crucified, and there he was inflamed with the charity which made him so quick to come to the aid of others. He was so adaptable, so available to all souls because, as he said, "I have made my chief study in the book of charity, which teaches everything." His ever-open book of charity was the crucifix. Gazing at it, or rather carrying on a face-to-face conversation with the one who hung upon it, his favorite petition, as Blessed Jordan

[1] Bede Jarrett, O.P., *Life of St. Dominic* (Westminster: Newman, 1955), p. 148.

tells us, was always the same: "That true charity might be his, to help effectively in the saving of souls, for only then did he consider himself a true member of Christ's Mystical Body, when he could spend himself and be spent for souls, as his divine Master had spent himself for him on the cross." [2]

[2] *Ibid.*, pp. 14–15.

PART SIX

Like Christ, in Prayer

CHAPTER XXIV

TWO PRAYERS OF JESUS

IN THE PROLOGUE of the Gospel according to St. John, there are two key sentences which summarize the whole Gospel: "In the beginning was the Word, and the Word was with God, and the Word was God," and "The Word was made flesh, and dwelt among us." These sentences, and the entire Gospel, present a paradox, a seeming contradiction. They tell us that all the eternal majesty and power of divinity is in a divine Person who at the same time is capable of human emotion and sufferings, and even of death. The Word who in the beginning was with God and who was God, by whom all things were made, and who is the source of life and enlightenment of every human being who has ever lived, this Person is made flesh; that is, he takes on human nature with all its weaknesses except sin and concupiscence, and feels human affection and tenderness and other emotions such as anger, sadness and even weeping.

St. John, even more than the other evangelists, brings out this contrast because, writing much later than the others, he was faced with the task of combatting two heresies which had sprung up at opposite extremes. First, the Docetists denied that Jesus was truly man. They claimed that he only seemed to be man, he had only the outward appearance of man, without the true reality. Therefore, in his Gospel we find St. John dwelling on the humanity of Jesus, focusing our attention upon his weariness as he sits exhausted at Jacob's well, his weeping at the tomb of Lazarus, his soul troubled with sadness as he foretells his betrayal by Judas.

The heretics at the other extreme were the Ebionites, who denied not the humanity of Jesus but his divinity. They claimed that the eternal Person of the Word dwelt in the humanity of Christ only for a brief period, during the time between his baptism in the Jordan and the beginning of his Passion. Therefore, in his Gospel, each time St. John focuses our attention upon Christ's humanity, he also shows us the glory of the divinity present in it. Each time he speaks of Christ's human emotions and weariness and sufferings, immediately he draws our attention to the divine power of the Savior. He shows us Jesus sitting utterly exhausted at Jacob's well, hungry and thirsty, and yet, by the power of his divinity, reading secrets of the heart, telling the Samaritan woman "all that she has ever done." [1] And at the tomb of Lazarus, even while the tears of his human weeping are still fresh on his cheeks, with divine majesty he commands: "Lazarus, come forth!" [2] And at once, he who was dead comes forth, bound hands and feet with bandages, and his face tied up with a cloth.

And on Palm Sunday, after the triumphant entry into Jerusalem, Jesus, speaking of his Passion, is suddenly filled with the emotion of fear and says: "Father, save me from this hour!" But quickly recovering himself, as we must always do when troubled, he says: "No, this is why I came to this hour; Father, glorify thy name!" [3] Immediately, after this show of human emotion, the divinity of Jesus is manifested by a voice from heaven: "I have both glorified it and I will glorify it again." Again, in the very instant that Jesus exercises divine knowledge by foretelling his betrayal by Judas, he is troubled with human emotion over the ingratitude of the one who will betray him." [4]

It is not St. John alone who presents Jesus in this way. In

[1] John 4:40.   [2] John 11:44.   [3] John 12:27.   [4] John 13:21.

the last chapter we noted how St. Paul, in the epistle to the Hebrews, gives contrasting insights into the divinity and the humanity, the weakness and the power of Christ. And St. Thomas writes: "Almost everywhere in the gospels, we read that in the doings of Jesus, human things are mixed with divine, and any time something human is stated about Christ, at once something divine is added. We read nothing weaker about Christ than his Passion; and yet, while he hangs on the cross, his divine deeds are evident, such as the darkening of the sun, the rending of the rocks, the rising of the dead bodies of the saints. Also, at his birth, while he lies a helpless infant in the manger, he sends forth a new star to shine in the heavens, an angel sings his praises in the skies, Magi from the East come to offer gifts." [5]

Then there is that striking incident when Jesus is so worn out with his day's work of teaching that he sleeps soundly right through the roaring of the winds and waves and the bouncing of the fragile boat in the tempest. And yet, when his disciples shake him awake, with severe majesty he commands: "Peace! Be still!" [6] And the winds and waves obey him.

St. John, the evangelist who most forcefully presents to us the eternal majesty of the Word, is also the one who gives us the most intimate details about the tender human affection of Christ. It is he who describes the truly human side of the friendship of Jesus for Mary and Martha and Lazarus. It is John who tells us of the weeping of Jesus and records the remark of the Jews: "See how he loved him!" [7] John himself, of course, had been a chief recipient of such affection from Jesus; it was he who had leaned on the bosom of Jesus at the Last Supper.

[5] St. Thomas Aquinas, *Commentary on John*, chap. 11.
[6] Mark 4:39.   [7] John 11:37.

And when John shows us Jesus dead on the cross, truly dead because he was true man, his human flesh really pierced by a lance, giving forth blood and water, in the next breath John gives evidence of his divinity, his divine mission, by showing how all of this was in fulfillment of prophecies, all foretold by God, all under the complete control of his providence.[8]

St. John does not record for us the agony and prayer of Jesus in the Garden of Olives, where the helplessness of the humanity of Jesus is so strikingly evident. John does not have to tell us about this; the other evangelists have told it clearly enough. So John rounds out their picture by giving some new details which emphasize the divinity of Jesus on that last night of his earthly life. The Jesus who, a few moments earlier, had been prostrate in a bloody sweat, is shown by John in all his majesty as his enemies fall flat to the ground by his mere word: "I am he—Jesus of Nazareth whom you seek." [9]

In contrast to the agonized, troubled prayer of Jesus in the Garden of Olives, St. John presents to us the sublime, majestic serenity of the prayer of Jesus after the Last Supper. And yet, in either case, it is Christ as Man who is praying, for only in his humanity does he pray, not in his divinity.

In these two prayers addressed to the Father by Jesus in his humanity, two different sides of this humanity are evident. In the Garden, it is the aspect of human helplessness which is in the foreground; but in the prayer just after the Supper, there shines forth strikingly all the serene majesty of the divine Person who prays in this human nature. But his whole humanity shares in the serenity. The contrast is especially evident in the words of the Garden: "Father, not

[8] Cf. John 19:33–38.   [9] John 18:6.

my will, but thy will be done," [10] and the words of the
Cenacle: "Father, I will that where I am, they also whom
thou hast given me may be with me, in order that they may
behold my glory." [11] In the one case, Christ humbly sacrifices
his human will in submission to the Father; in the other, he
tells the Father exactly what his human will wants, in the full
confidence that what he asks will be accomplished.

In the prayer in the Garden, Jesus manifests that the Word
truly was made flesh, a flesh that is capable of suffering, and
yet naturally draws back from it. Though his human will
naturally would have preferred not to suffer the Passion,
considering the eternal will of the Father, Christ's human
will fully accepts the sufferings because the divine will has
decreed them. In this prayer in the Garden, the emphasis is
on the suffering humanity of Christ. But in the other prayer,
the emphasis is on the fullness of divine authority, vested in
that humanity. In the prayer after the Supper, Jesus manifests that to him, Son of Man, the Father has given power
over all things. Later, after his resurrection, Jesus was to
say: "All power in heaven and on earth has been given to
me." [12] But even at the Last Supper, when he is about to die,
he presents himself as Lord of the world. He says to the
Father: "Thou hast given thy Son power over all flesh." [13]

Also, St. John observes at the beginning of his account of
the discourse at the Last Supper that Jesus, "knowing that
the Father had given all things into his hands," nevertheless
humbled himself to wash his disciples' feet.[14] Fully conscious of his divinity and his power over the universe, he
humbles himself in death that he might wash his followers in
his Precious Blood.

In the prayer just after the Supper, therefore, it is obvious

[10] Luke 22:42.   [11] John 17:24.   [12] Matthew 28:18.
[13] John 17:2.   [14] John 13:3.

that Jesus is fully aware that all things have been subjected by the Father to his human will, and when he prays, "Father, I will that where I am they also whom thou hast given me may be with me," [15] he is manifesting the fact that the Father always hears his prayers. With his human will, Jesus has but to will that a thing be done, and the power of divinity at once fulfills his desire. Jesus declares this fact in the beginning of his Last Supper prayer when he says to the Father: "Thou hast given thy Son power over all flesh, in order that to all thou hast given him he may give life everlasting." [16] And earlier in his public life, Jesus had declared that all things were subject to his human will, when he said: "For as the Father raises the dead and gives them life, even so the Son also gives life to whom he will." [17]

To show how all divine power is subject to the human will of Christ, let us recall for a moment how divine power is subject to the human will of every ordained priest. The very same divine power which created the world out of nothing and gave sight to the blind and raised Lazarus from the dead, that power is invoked every time a human priest wills to use it in changing the bread and wine into the body and blood of Christ. It is the infinite power of God, but it does not go into operation in producing this effect unless the priest at the altar, by an act of his human will, wills to use it. But the priest has the infinite power of God subject to his will for the working of only a few effects, such as the Consecration in the Mass, the forgiveness of sin, the expulsion of devils. However, the human will of Christ has the power of God at his disposal for working absolutely any divine effect he chooses. Christ as Man is King of the universe, and all things, especially all souls, are subject to his human will so that he can do with them what he will.

[15] John 17:24.   [16] John 17:2.   [17] John 5:21.

That is why in his prayer after the Supper Jesus makes bold to say: "Father, I will that where I am these also whom thou hast given me may be with me." [18] He does not stop to say: "Father, if it be possible; Father, if thou wilt." Conscious that the Father has given all things into his hands, Jesus is manifesting to us that the desires and prayers of his human will on our behalf are infallibly heard by the Father; Jesus has but to will, and what he wills is accomplished. But in the other prayer, in the Garden, Jesus is teaching us how the rest of us should pray, with humble submission to the will of God.

The human will of Jesus is always in perfect conformity with the divine will; that is a favorite theme in the Gospel according to St. John. "I have come down from heaven not to do my own will, but the will of him who sent me." [19] Jesus never wills or asks anything contrary to the will of the Father. His human will, which was so obedient to the Father, receives all things from the Father. He did his Father's will, so the Father does his will. Therefore, in his prayer at the Last Supper, after saying, "Father, I have accomplished the work that thou hast given me to do," with serene confidence Jesus presents his own will to the Father, knowing that the Father will do it. "Father, I will that where I am, they also whom thou hast given me may be with me; in order that they may behold my glory which thou hast given me because thou hast loved me before the creation of the world." [20]

[18] John 17:24.　　　[19] John 6:38.　　　[20] John 17:24f.

CHAPTER XXV

"ASK, THAT YOUR JOY MAY BE FULL"

"Amen, amen, I say to you, if you ask the Father anything in my name, he will give it to you." [1] In this one sentence, St. Thomas Aquinas finds the seven qualities of a perfect prayer of petition.[2] As a true son of St. Dominic, he teaches us how to pray as sons of God in the likeness of Christ, how to pray to the Father of Jesus who is also our Father.

First, in order to be heard, we must pray with filial affection, as children of the Father, adopted by divine grace and sharing in his own life. We must pray to God as to a Father who is loved, rather than to a master or an enemy who is feared. Therefore, Jesus says: "If you ask the *Father*." In the Lord's Prayer, he teaches us to begin our prayer by saying, "Our Father."

This means that we must pray with the love of charity, inspired by the Holy Spirit of adoption. "You have not received a spirit of bondage so as to be again in fear, but you have received a spirit of adoption as sons, by virtue of which we cry, 'Abba, Father!' The Spirit himself gives testimony to our spirit that we are sons of God." [3] The prayer of the child of God must proceed from love and cause greater love. If a person begins to pray without love of God because he is God's enemy through sin, then he must persevere in prayer until prayer has prepared him to love. To pray in the right way, then, one must strive, as he prays, to love God more and

---

[1] John 16:23. [2] St. Thomas Aquinas, *Commentary on John*, 16:23.
[3] Romans 8:15–16.

more perfectly as a Father. There is something wrong with our prayer if we do not love God more after we have prayed than before we did so. Union with God in love is the goal of all forms of prayer, whether of petition or adoration or thanksgiving or reparation.

Prayer with such love of the Father, we said, can come only from the Holy Spirit. "The love of God is poured forth in our hearts by the Holy Spirit who has been given to us." [4] "God has sent the Spirit of his Son into our hearts, crying, 'Abba, Father!' " [5] Therefore, says St. Paul, "pray at all times in the Spirit." [6]

We must ask the Spirit to help us pray well. "The Spirit also helps our weakness. For we do not know what we should pray for as we ought, but the Spirit himself pleads for us with unutterable groanings." [7] To teach us to pray to God as to a Father, Jesus says: "If one of you asks his father for a loaf, will he hand him a stone? . . . If you, evil as you are, know how to give good gifts to your children, how much more will your heavenly Father give the good Spirit to those who ask him." [8]

But in order to pray to God as to a Father, we must become as little children. We must pray with childlike humility and confidence and complete trust in the goodness and wisdom of our Father. This attitude is inspired in us by the Holy Spirit's gift of piety. Piety is the ideal relationship between father and child. A little child is very conscious of his need of his father and of his complete dependence upon him. Humility is the basic characteristic of the true child of God and is a necessary element of all true prayer. Every prayer is a humble declaration of dependence upon God, the fatherly source of all good things. As we pray, we must strive

[4] Romans 5:5.   [5] Galatians 4:6.   [6] Ephesians 6:18.
[7] Romans 8:26.   [8] Luke 11:11–13.

to humble ourselves ever more completely before God.

But precisely because he is so conscious of his weakness, a little child has confidence in the strength and wisdom, the goodness and love of his father. The heavenly Father in his infinite power *can* give all things, and in his infinite love he *wants* to give them, but in his wisdom he gives them only in an orderly way. No good father dispenses things to his children in a haphazard way, but only in consideration of the genuine needs rather than the whimsical desires of his children. Therefore, our hope of receiving things from the heavenly Father, while relying upon his power and goodness, must be tempered by faith in his wisdom and a conviction that his providence dispenses good things only in an orderly way. Prayer requires trust in providence, in the conviction that the Father knows best what is good for his children and that his love will give or withhold, as his infinite wisdom sees best.

Genuine prayer, therefore, must include a surrender of our will to the Father's will, in complete and loving trust. "Not my will, but thine be done."

Persevering prayer, therefore, forms us in childlike simplicity by exercising us in humility, confidence, faith, hope and charity. All these benefits result if we pray to God as to a Father. Divine providence, above all else, is concerned about giving us the good Spirit, who will lead us home to our Father.

In order to be heard by the Father, we must pray in the name of his beloved Son, Jesus. To ask in the name of Jesus is to have confidence of access to the Father only through Jesus. "No one comes to the Father but through me." [9] We are sons of the Father only in Christ. To pray in the name of Christ is to pray with humility, for one who prays must not

[9] John 16:6.

rely on his own merits, which do not even exist except in dependence upon the merits of Christ. Because of our own unworthiness, we may trust only in the merits of Jesus. It is only in Christ that we are not an enemy of God, and when we are in Christ we are the child of God. Praying in Jesus, then, is praying to the Father with childlike humility.

But praying in Jesus is also praying with love of neighbor. If a prayer is to be heard, it must be said in concord with neighbor. Since it has to be said in Christ, in his name, it has to be said in union with all his members. If asking the Father means asking with filial charity, asking through Jesus means asking with fraternal charity. "I say to you that if two of you shall agree on earth about anything at all for which they ask, it shall be done for them by my Father in heaven. For where two or three are gathered together for my sake, there am I in the midst of them." [10] "If thou art offering thy gift at the altar, and there rememberest that thy brother has anything against thee, leave thy gift before the altar, and go first to be reconciled to thy brother, and then come and offer thy gift." [11]

The necessity of having love for neighbor if we wish our prayers to be heard is shown by the fact that the Lord taught us to say, not "My Father," but "Our Father." We can have God for our Father and dare address him by that sweet name, only on condition that we love all his children and live in concord with them. Therefore, praying to God as to a Father, in the name of Jesus, means praying with a consciousness of our unity with all his children. Such prayer strengthens love of neighbor even as it increases love of the Father.

We cannot pray to God as to a Father, we cannot pray with true childlike respect for him, unless we pray in an

[10] Matthew 18:19-20.   [11] Matthew 5:23.

orderly way, that is, with due submission to the Father's will, since he gives his gifts only according to the right order of his providence. To desire and to ask anything contrary to the decrees of his loving providence would be an offense against filial love and trust in the fatherly goodness. Every true prayer must contain an act of loving submission to the Father's will.

When we pray in the name of Jesus, we do pray in an orderly way. For asking in the name of Jesus means asking the things pertaining to salvation. These only the Father wills to give; his providence leads his children to eternal life. The name Jesus means "Jahweh is salvation," and the only thing Jesus merited for us is salvation and the things which lead to it. He who prays in the name of Jesus does not want a thing if it will hinder his salvation, since, in his love of the Father, salvation—the possession of God—is the thing he wants above all else. He loves the Father more than he loves the gifts He bestows.

Therefore, he is willing to sacrifice anything for the sake of salvation and the glory of his Father, just as Jesus, in whose name he prays, sacrificed all to win him that salvation for the glory of the Father. For this reason, every time the Christian prays, he expresses his willingness to sacrifice the very thing he petitions, for he says, at least implicitly, in every prayer: "Not my will, but thine be done." Because of his filial love, the Father's will is always paramount.

And this is the will of God—your salvation! The necessity of saying in every prayer, "Not my will, but thy will be done," thus makes of every prayer a prayer for salvation. Furthermore, the willingness to sacrifice the very thing we request purifies us of undue affection for the things we petition and more firmly binds our will to that of the Father in affectionate love. Every true prayer, therefore, purifies and raises our hearts to higher things.

If we are to ask only things pertaining to salvation, why does Jesus say: "If you ask the Father *anything*, he will give it?" Jesus did not say, "anything," but "anything in my name." We may not take the word "anything" independently of the words, "in my name." For it is unlawful to ask anything contrary to our salvation. It is lawful to ask only what it is lawful to desire. But it is lawful to desire only in an orderly way; that is, we may desire things only if, in some way, they can be ordered as means to eternal life. When earthly, temporal things are sincerely asked in the name of Jesus, they are no longer merely temporal; for the fact that they have been asked rightly in his name means that they are either necessary, or at least useful, in obtaining eternal life. If the petition has been properly made in the name of Jesus, it contains implicitly a dedication of the things requested to the service of God; a thing has not really been asked in the name of Jesus unless the petitioner has at least implicitly determined to use it according to the will of God, in such a way that it will help him reach God. That is why St. Paul says: "Every creature of God is good, and nothing is to be rejected that is accepted with thanksgiving. For it is sanctified by the word of God and prayer." [12] Sanctified by prayer; that is, dedicated for use in God's service by the very prayer in which it is requested of God. In scriptural language, a thing is called "sanctified" or "holy to the Lord" when it has been dedicated to God's service and therefore belongs to him.

St. Thomas says that one of the conditions for a good prayer is that we ask for spiritual things; Jesus lays down this condition when he says: "If you ask anything in my name." "For whatever is entirely earthly, even though it be something in itself, by comparison to spiritual things it is nothing: 'I deemed riches nothing in comparison with

[12] I Timothy 4:4–5.

wisdom' (Wisd. 7:8). . . . But a temporal thing, asked in relationship to spiritual things, is now something." [13]

And so we may ask anything in the name of Jesus; for all things dedicated to God and his service in the name of Jesus are "something," while the entirely temporal is nothing. Therefore, says St. Thomas, if prayer is to be good, we must always ask spiritual things—either things totally spiritual or things which have been made spiritual by their dedication to God's service.

Consequently, whenever we petition God, we must always make a judgment: we must look at what we ask in the light of spiritual, eternal realities. The necessity of making this comparison lifts our thoughts and desires far above the particular thing we ask, and good prayer requires that we make an offering of this thing, a dedication of it and its use to God, a declaration of intention of using it well in reaching him.

This means that every true prayer requires that we love God above all things, because only if we do, will we be able to make the dedication of the thing requested to his service and offer the thing in sacrifice, in case it is his will that we do not have it. The dedication of the thing requested includes an act of love of God. That is one reason why we said that true prayer springs from love of God and strengthens that love, even while it purifies it of undue affection for the thing requested. Everything requested must be "sanctified," offered in sacrifice; that is, either it must be directed to the service of God even while it is being asked or it must be totally given up for his sake if it cannot be so used or if his providence does not require its use in this case. "Not my will, but thy will be done" is the formula of dedication and sacrifice in every prayer.

[13] St. Thomas Aquinas, *Commentary on John*, 16:23.

Since the prayer of petition produces all these wonderful effects in us, is it any wonder that Jesus practically begs us to ask things of the Father? "Ask, and it shall be given you; seek, and you shall find; knock, and it shall be opened to you." [14] Prayer of petition has a nobility all its own, and in our efforts to encourage the other kinds of prayer, we should be careful not to discourage petition. An enthusiastic liturgist, in his zeal for prayer of adoration and thanksgiving, once recommended to his hearers that an excellent Lenten penance would be to give up all prayer of petition. We see the lack of wisdom in this recommendation when we recall that our Lord practically pleads with us to ask things of the Father and when we consider all the virtues exercised and developed by the right kind of petition. St. Thomas points out how we definitely pay honor to God when we petition his favors. "Man shows reverence to God by praying, inasmuch as he subjects himself to Him and, by praying, confesses that he needs Him as the Author of his goods." [15] This is confirmed by the liturgy itself, which is a golden chain of petition, as well as of praise and thanksgiving.

All the wonderful benefits which result from good prayer of petition make it clear that the Lord's prayer itself is a school of perfection, for to pray to our Father means to pray with the filial affection of charity, in the Holy Spirit, in union with Christ, in concord with our fellow men, with true humility and trust in divine providence, with the dedication of ourselves and all of God's gifts to us to the divine service, in total surrender to the will of the Father. All this is a summation of Christian perfection.

"The Lord's prayer is most perfect because, as Augustine says, "If we pray rightly and fittingly, we can say nothing

[14] Matthew 7:7.   [15] *Summa Theologiae*, IIa IIae, q. 83, a. 3.

else but what is contained in this prayer of our Lord. . . .
In the Lord's prayer not only do we ask for all that we may
rightly desire, but also in the order wherein we ought to
desire them, so that this prayer not only teaches us to ask,
but also directs all our affections." [16]

If every prayer of petition implicitly contains a prayer for
salvation, it follows that the complete answer to every prayer
is salvation, eternal life, which gives the fullness of joy. "Ask
and you shall receive, that your joy may be full." [17] Everything granted through prayer, if it is used in the way we
declared we would use it when we asked for it, leads us closer
to that fullness of joy. Moreover, since every genuine prayer
is inspired by charity, every prayer merits eternal life. No
wonder Jesus says: "Ask, and you shall receive, that your
joy may be full." Prayer of petition leads to the possession of
God, and in the possession of him alone is the fullness of
joy.

[16] *Ibid.*, a. 9.   [17] John 16:24.

PART SEVEN

Like the Lord

CHAPTER XXVI

LIKE THE LORD CRUCIFIED

"ALL WE WHO HAVE BEEN BAPTIZED into Christ Jesus have been baptized into his death. For we were buried with him by means of baptism into death in order that . . . we may walk in newness of life." [1]

The sons of God can attain to maturity only by living in Christ. We have "been baptized into Christ Jesus" so that in him "we may walk in newness of life." This newness of life, the divine life of grace, is totally above our mere human powers; that is why we can live it only if we are in Christ. "As the branch cannot bear fruit of itself unless it remain on the vine, so neither can you unless you abide in me. I am the vine, you are the branches . . . without me, you can do nothing." [2]

The life that we live in Christ is the same life that Christ lives in the Father, a share in the life that the eternal Word lives with the Father from the beginning. "In that day you will know," said Jesus, "that I am in my Father, and you in me, and I in you." [3] Since this life in Christ is a share in his own divine life, it makes us like the Word, so that we too are with God, we too receive all things from the Father, we too glorify the Father, we too go to the Father.

But the life of grace makes us like the Word in the glory of his divinity only by making us like the Word in the humility and crucifixion of his humanity. "For if we have been united with him in the likeness of his death," says St. Paul, "we shall be so in the likeness of his resurrection also. . . . If

[1] Romans 6:3f.   [2] John 15:4–6.   [3] John 14:20.

we have died with Christ, we believe that we shall also live together with Christ." [4]

Till now we have been speaking primarily of how to be like the Word in his divinity, how to live with him in the presence of the Father. Let us now consider how to be like the Word in his suffering humanity, how to die with Christ, so that we may live with God.

Prayer should be as natural to the Christian as breathing is to the body; it should be the very breath of our spiritual life. But a life of continual prayer can be built only on the solid foundation of complete self-denial. Only by dying to self can we live to God. The purpose of baptismal grace is to enable us to live in the presence of God, to be at home with him as his children. But to make this possible, baptismal grace of necessity has to kill in us, with our cooperation, all that stands between us and God. Baptism gives us the obligation and the grace to mortify ourselves continually throughout our life on earth. Our Lord did not say to take up the cross only now and then, but daily.

"Thus do you consider yourselves also as dead to sin, but alive to God in Christ Jesus." [5] "Mind the things that are above, not the things that are on earth. For you have died, and your life is hidden with Christ in God. . . . Therefore, mortify your members which are on earth." [6] In the various texts, St. Paul is really telling us that the grace given to us in baptism crucifies us daily, so that it can give us divine life. "With Christ I am nailed to the cross. It is now no longer I that live, but Christ lives in me." [7] Baptism has a double effect: it gives grace to die and grace to live. "We have been baptized into his death . . . that we may walk in newness of life."

[4] Romans 6:5, 8.   [5] Romans 6:11.   [6] Colossians 3:2f.
[7] Galatians 2:20.

But it is one and the same sanctifying grace which produces both of these effects. For the grace of baptism configures us to Christ; simultaneously it makes us like Christ in his glorious divinity and in his suffering humanity. Baptism incorporates us into Christ the Head, making us members of his Mystical Body. But members of a body always have to be conformed to the head; it would be gruesome indeed if a human head had the body of a bird or of an elephant. The members have to be of the same kind as the head; they have to be like the head, so that they can live one same life with the head.

But Christ our Head lived a most astonishing life. He is but one Person, and yet he has two natures, divine and human. He is only one being, he is not divided; and yet, when he was on earth, although he was infinitely happy and glorious and perfect in his divine nature, in his human nature he was weak and all but overwhelmed by the most intense sufferings. Since the grace of baptism makes us like Christ our Head, the one same sanctifying grace we receive from him makes us like him in the divine life he lives with the Father and simultaneously crucifies us with him, conforming us to his death.

Therefore, in the sacrament of baptism the priest says: "I baptize thee in the name of the Father and of the Son and of the Holy Spirit," to signify that this baptism gives us the likeness of the Trinity, bestowing upon us the divine life which Christ lives with the Father and the Holy Spirit. But he pours the water in the form of the cross to signify that the same grace gives us the likeness of Christ crucified. Daily throughout our lives, whenever we make the sign of the cross in remembrance of our baptism, we signify both our divine life in the Trinity and the cross through which we receive this life and by which we live it.

To the extent that grace grows in us, giving us an ever-increasing share in the life of the Trinity, to that extent this grace produces in us the likeness of Christ crucified. The more we live with God, the more we die to the world. There is no other way but the cross for attaining the fullness of life with God. Baptismal grace in a soul can grow and develop only in one direction—the direction of Calvary. There is no spiritual progress except by way of the cross. Baptismal grace crucifies us.

Therefore, in the baptismal ceremonies the cross is put on the various senses to signify the necessity of mortification of the senses; it is put on the back between the shoulders to show that we must carry the cross; it is put on the chest to show that we must steadfastly, bravely advance toward Calvary. If grace increases in us, inevitably it carries us in that direction. If we are not living a mortified life, then we are not making spiritual progress. Love of the cross and living the cross is the only sure sign that grace in us is vigorous and dynamic. Suffering great things for the love of Christ is one of the surest signs that we have been predestined to eternal life with Christ in God. Not just any kind of suffering, but suffering in Christ and with him and for him is the sure sign of salvation, suffering which is inspired and directed and enlivened by faith and grace. The cross is our sign of salvation only when it is reproduced in our daily living. This is emphatically taught by Christ when he says, "You *cannot* be my disciple, unless you take up your cross *daily* and follow me." [8]

Only the cross forms us in the likeness of Christ's divine life; the cross is the only mold in which a Christian can be cast. Therefore, we Christians are "always bearing about in our body the dying of Jesus, so that the life also of Jesus may

[8] Luke 9:23.

be made manifest in our mortal frame. For we, the living, are constantly being handed over to death for Jesus' sake, that the life also of Jesus may be made manifest in our mortal flesh." [9]

With St. Paul, every Christian addresses almighty God in the words of Psalm 43: "You marked us out as sheep to be slaughtered. . . . For your sake, we are being slain all the day." [10]

In the Temple at Jerusalem, the Levites used to inspect carefully all the sheep which had been brought for sacrifice. Those which had any defects were rejected; only those which were perfect were accepted, and a special mark was put upon them to indicate that they were fit and destined for sacrifice.

So, too, almighty God puts a mark on every Christian, the baptismal character, which destines him to be a victim, a sacrifice in union with Christ. "You marked us out as sheep to be slaughtered." Only the perfect sheep were accepted for sacrifice; God makes us perfect by the cross. Sufferings should be looked upon as a sign of God's special love: "Whom the Lord loves, he chastises; and he scourges every son whom he receives." [11] Only in this way can he prepare us for the fullness of his divine life.

And yet, marvelous paradox, the cross is a cause of joy for the one who lives it truly. With St. Paul, "gladly do we glory in our infirmities," [12] because they make us like the one we love, they give us our way of expressing our love and gratitude to him who has loved us and suffered for us. "God forbid that I should glory save in the cross of our Lord Jesus Christ, through whom the world is crucified to me and I to the world." [13] "We exult in the hope of the glory of the sons of God (in the fact that grace gives us the likeness of God).

[9] II Corinthians 4:10–12.   [10] Psalm 43:12, 23; Romans 8:36.
[11] Hebrews 12:6.   [12] II Corinthians 12:9.   [13] Galatians 6:14.

Not only this, but we exult in tribulations also (in the fact that grace makes us like Christ crucified), knowing that tribulation works out endurance, and endurance tried virtue, and tried virtue hope. And hope does not disappoint, because the charity of God is poured forth in our hearts by the Holy Spirit who has been given to us." [14]

Therefore, it behooves us to examine ourselves, to see whether we really are living the cross. In Lent and Passiontide we re-live the mystery of Christ crucified, and the grace of that mystery reproduces the mortified Christ in us.

The Church gives us a preliminary lesson about this mystery in the Gospel for the Sunday before Ash Wednesday. She wants us to understand from the start that there is no other way but the cross. It is not an easy lesson to grasp. In the day's Gospel, when Jesus speaks of the necessity of the cross, the evangelist adds the comment that the apostles "understood none of these things and this saying was hidden from them." [15] And because the apostles were still like blind men on the question of the cross, Jesus worked a miracle, giving sight to the blind man of Jericho who cried out to him: "Lord, that I may see!" [16] Thus Jesus gently suggests that since we are so blind concerning the necessity of taking up the cross, we also should cry out to him: "Lord, that I may see!"

We very easily blind ourselves to the necessity of the daily carrying of the cross, because the cross is unpleasant. Daily, we talk ourselves out of it, finding all sorts of reasons why it is not necessary to mortify ourselves in this situation or that. But if we consistently talk ourselves out of our cross, we will take Christ out of our lives. Let us, then, cry out to our Lord, like the blind man of Jericho: "Lord, that I may see!" That I

[14] Romans 5:2f.   [15] Luke 18:34.   [16] Luke 18:42.

may see and accept those countless opportunities for self-denial that I have been missing each day. That I may see that my particular vocation offers the most thoroughgoing self-denial possible, if only I live it.

Lord, may I see that in every act of patience I am exercising valuable self-denial. Lord, teach me to deny my tendency to indulge my curiosity, which fills my mind with thoughts that distract from thee. Teach me to mortify my inclination to talk at every opportunity, lest by my idle words I drive thee from my neighbor's thoughts. Teach me to deny my tendency to feel sorry for myself over every little trial. Teach me to live in thy presence by seeing thy providence in every situation. Teach me to mortify my tendency to become lax in prayer as soon as prayer becomes difficult. Give me the courage to continue to seek thee perseveringly in my difficulties, denying my tendency to take it too easy. Teach me to mortify my self-will by humbly accepting every obedience imposed upon me. Teach me to mortify my pride, which rebels at some of the seemingly foolish things I am expected to do. Teach me to die to self, so that I may live to thee, to forget myself, so that I may think of thee, to despise myself that I may love thee, to rid myself of all else, so that I may possess only thee. Lord, that I may see that only by being like thee on the cross can I be like thee in thy presence with the Father.

CHAPTER XXVII

LIKE THE LORD, LED BY THE HOLY SPIRIT

"THE SPIRIT OF THE LORD is upon me; because he has anointed me." [1] These are words of Isaias which Jesus read aloud one day in the synagogue and then announced that they were fulfilled in himself. "The Spirit of the Lord is upon me." In all his human actions, in everything he did, as Man, Jesus was led by the Holy Spirit. The Scriptures use frequent phrases like this: "Jesus returned in the power of the Spirit into Galilee"; "Jesus, full of the Holy Spirit, returned from the Jordan, and was led about the desert by the Spirit for forty days"; [2] "Christ, through the Holy Spirit, offered himself unblemished unto God." [3]

We, the adopted children of God, must strive to be just like Christ in this, to be led by the Spirit in everything we do. "For whoever are led by the Spirit of God, they are the sons of God." [4]

Our aim is to be like the Word Incarnate, who receives everything he has and everything he does from the Father, so that he is totally from God. We pray for this daily in the Mass, saying: "O Lord, may all our actions begin from thee, and through thee, being begun, may they be finished."

But it is impossible for us to achieve this without a thorough mortification. Those actions of ours which are not from God are either from the devil or from the evil tendencies of our fallen nature. Only by putting to death

---

[1] Luke 4:18.   [2] Luke 4:14, 1.   [3] Hebrews 9:14.   [4] Romans 8:14.

these contrary tendencies can all our actions begin with
God.

Jesus was led by the Holy Spirit into the desert to fast. At
once we think of the words of St. Paul: "If by the Spirit you
put to death the deeds of the flesh, you will live." [5] The Spirit
led Jesus to fast; the same Spirit leads us to mortify
ourselves. All true mortification must begin with the Holy
Spirit, with trust in the help and guidance he gives us. And
the ultimate goal of all mortification is perfect docility to the
Holy Spirit, so that all our actions will begin with God and
none will begin with the evil spirit or with the flesh. And the
means to this goal is mistrust of everything else, so that we
can trust only in God. It is because we trust too much in self,
in material possessions, in bodily strength, that we fail to
abandon ourselves totally to the guidance of the Holy Spirit.
We are too attached to these things to abandon them so that
the Spirit can lead us into the great unknown of the Trinity.
The three temptations to which Christ submitted himself in
the desert show us that all temptations come from one or
other of these three sources: our body, the things of the
world about us or our own will. Therefore, each of these
three sources must be mortified so that we no longer trust in
these things, but only in God.

This, according to St. Augustine, is the purpose of
self-denial: to kill self-trust, so that we may trust only in God
and surrender ourselves totally to his Spirit. Commenting on
our Savior's words, "If anyone will come after me, let him
deny himself, take up his cross, and follow me," [6] St.
Augustine says: "What does it mean to deny self? It means
not to trust in self. It means to realize that you are but man
and to remember the words of the prophet: 'Cursed be the
man that trusteth in man.' Therefore, detach yourself from

[5] Romans 8:13.   [6] Matthew 16:24.

self, but not downwards; detach yourself from self so that you may attach yourself to God." [7]

The positive approach to self-denial, therefore, is to look upon it as an exercise in trusting in God, an exercise in attaching oneself firmly to him in faith, hope and charity. Self-denial is never purely for its own sake, never for the sake of displaying will power. It is like a two-sided coin. The negative side, the reverse side of the coin, is giving up something, detaching self from something. But the positive side, the obverse side of the coin, is giving self to God, firmly attaching self to him in prayerful faith, hope and charity. Self-denial is worthless, and sometimes even harmful, if this positive element is not uppermost. If we take good care of the positive side of our spirituality, the Holy Spirit will lead us into self-denial in the full measure that is necessary for us. In our desires for closer union with God, we cry out to him: "Lord, that I may see how to deny myself, and may I have the courage to do it!"

The right kind of self-denial, then, exercises us in trust in God. Before we dare cut loose from our own will, or our body, or our possessions in which we trust, we must first make an act of trust in God. St. Peter would not have dared step out of the boat to walk on the water if he had trusted only in poor human nature. Carrying the cross of self-denial is like walking on water; we are afraid to cut loose from our own will, our possessions, our bodily strength in which we trust, so we stay in the boat of self-trust and never get to Jesus who is across the water. But if we trust in God, we bravely leave the boat of self-trust, and walk the waves of self-denial in serene faith and confidence that God will care for us if we make sacrifices for him.

If, then, we are afraid to live to the full the life of religious

[7] St. Augustine, *Sermo 47 de diversis.*

poverty, it is because we still trust in possessions and not in God. If we are always worrying about our health and are afraid to mortify the body by giving up food and rest, it is because we still trust more in our health and in our physical strength than we do in God. If we will not surrender our own will in obedience, it is because we trust in self and in our own wisdom and not in the Holy Spirit, who can lead us to a superior wisdom.

Self-denial, therefore, presupposes trust in God and it strengthens that trust. For this reason, the Lenten liturgy, especially the Mass of the first Sunday in Lent, puts great emphasis on trust in God. Introit, Response, Tract, Offertory and Communion of this Mass—all are taken from Psalm 90, that magnificent hymn of trust in God: "He that dwelleth in the aid of the Most High, shall abide under the protection of the God of heaven. He shall say to the Lord: Thou art my protector and my refuge; my God, in him will I trust." [8]

Our Blessed Lord said these things in another way when he said: "Do not be anxious, saying, 'What shall we eat?' or 'What shall we drink?' or 'What are we to put on?' For your Father knows that you need all these things. But seek first the kingdom of God and his justice, and all these things shall be given you besides." [9] If we seek God first, if we are firmly attached to him, we need not worry about health or possessions or the success of our work, for God will take care of these things for us, because we trust in him and not in our own efforts and skills and powers.

Since Christ guarantees that he will take care of everything for us if only we seek him with all our heart, then if our projects are not prospering, if we seem to lack the material things we need, if our labors are not blessed more abundantly, could it not mean that we are not really seeking

[8] Psalm 90:1.   [9] Matthew 6:31f.

God first of all? Is there perhaps too much self-seeking in our lives? Are we too unmortified? Are we too worldly? In our work, are we looking for the approval of the world rather than that of God? Are we seeking to accomplish what the world seeks, rather than what Christ would have us work for? If we truly seek first the kingdom of God in all our efforts, all our undertakings will be abundantly blessed by God, both spiritually and materially; materially, of course, only to the extent that is necessary for truly doing his work, not the world's work. We must mortify our trust in worldly approval, worldly standards, worldly goals, and seek first the kingdom of God.

When we have this absolute trust in God which is our aim in self-denial, we are relieved of all worry, so that our minds are free for the things of God. That is the precise reason why God calls some to religious life. As St. Paul puts it: "I would have you free of care. He who is unmarried is concerned about the things of the Lord, how he may please God. . . . The virgin thinks about the things of the Lord, that she may be holy in body and in spirit." [10]

Our Lord said to St. Catherine of Siena: "Be concerned about me, and I will be concerned about you." We may paraphrase these words thus: "Be zealous for my glory, and I will take care of your worries. Forget self and self-seeking; be totally mine, and I will take care of your health, your apostolate, all your projects. And I will save you from wasting your energies on the wrong things."

It is the goal of self-denial to enable us to forget self and everything else, so that we may think only of the things of God. As long as we are still attached to our body, our possessions, our own will and its projects, we will worry about them, our mind will always come back to them, it will

[10] I Corinthians 7:32.

be enslaved by them. Some of our most common distractions in our prayer life are thoughts such as these: "Will my health hold out? Will this project be a success? Will I get my work finished? I wonder what others are thinking about me? I hope there is something really good for supper tonight!"

We must forget body and health, ambitious personal plans and material things. "Is that possible?" you will ask. It becomes more and more possible the more we trust only in God, seek only him. On the way to this perfect trust in him—and it is a long road—we must practice self-denial concerning our worries—deny them admission to our thoughts, courageously put them out of mind, leaving them to God. When we find ourselves thinking of our worries, we must say: "Here, Lord, take care of these things, and give me the grace to forget self and all else, that I may think only of thee." "Cast all your anxiety upon him," says St. Peter, "because he cares for you." [11]

We are to trust in the grace of God; God guarantees to everyone the grace to fulfill his state in life. This does not mean that from the mere fact that I am appointed to some position of responsibility or power that automatically I shall have full grace of office. No, the working of the grace of office is dependent upon our cooperation with it and upon our praying for it. "Ask whatever you will . . . that you may bear very much fruit," said our Lord to the apostles,[12] thus making the fruits of the apostolate dependent upon their asking for those fruits.

He did this because we are prone to say in words, "Yes, I have the grace of my office and I trust in it," but then promptly forget about God's grace, and trust only in our own abilities, as if we were infallible. This is especially true if

[11] I Peter 5:7.   [12] John 15:8.

we are highly gifted persons. Therefore, our Lord expects us to make frequent acts of self-denial concerning our own talents; and this we do by *praying* for the fruits of our labors. When we pray for the continual flow of the graces of our vocation—as our Lord requires us to do—we are thereby mortifying our self-trust and exercising trust in God. Grace of office and grace of state are at our disposal, but flow to us fully only if we consciously trust in them. We put an obstacle in the way of this grace if we ignore it by acting as though we trusted only in our own abilities. We see, then, that every prayer of petition is an act of self-denial, a detaching from self-trust that we may trust in God.

In all mortification, therefore, our goal is to detach ourselves from self so that we may be attached to God; to kill self-trust so that we may trust only in God; to resist the spirit of the world that we may be led by the Holy Spirit of God; to forget self so that we may attain to thinking only of God. This is indeed a heroic undertaking; it is impossible to mere human power. But if by the Holy Spirit we mortify ourselves, if we trust in him, we shall succeed more and more in this superhuman undertaking. More and more we shall forget self; God will take the place of self in our thoughts.

When at last we are completely mortified, nothing at all that happens to us will be able seriously to disturb our calm recollection. The perfectly mortified person is able quickly and serenely to adjust himself to every new situation, whether it be loss of health or failure in work, loss of popularity or difficulty in prayer; whatever it may be, after a comparatively brief struggle he is able to say: "The Lord's will be done." He trusts so entirely in God's ways of doing things, that whatever God sees fit to send him, he soon accepts, sacrificing his own plans in which he had trusted.

With holy Job, he says: "The Lord has given, the Lord has taken away; blessed be the name of the Lord." [13]

St. Dominic attained to the absolute serenity which only perfect mortification and complete trust in divine providence can bring. "Nothing disturbed the even temper of his soul except his quick compassion for every kind of suffering," says Blessed Jordan.[14] Paul of Venice says that "he never saw Dominic angry, upset or troubled, even when tired out by traveling. Dominic never gave way to passion, but was always calm, joyful in tribulations and patient in adversities." [15] He could be serene in hardships because of the perfection of his trust in providence. Stephen of Spain testifies: "In all the necessities such as the lack of food and clothing, which Brother Dominic and the brethren suffered at that time, Dominic was always joyful and happy." [16] Whenever the house ran short of bread, wine or any item of food, the procurator would go to Dominic and say: "We have no bread or wine." He would answer: "Go and pray, for the Lord will provide." And the Lord always did provide.[17] On one occasion Dominic's cheerful trust in providence was rewarded by the appearance of the angels in the refectory to feed the brethren.[18]

Dominic's perfect serenity of soul, achieved only by a lifetime of mortification, delivered him so perfectly to the movement of the Holy Spirit that even the greatest trials did not disturb his contemplation. "He was so faithfully intent when he prayed," says Paul of Venice, "that he was never distracted by any tumult or noise." [19] Once in Milan, Dominic was sick, and Brother Bonvisus took care of him.

---

[13] Job 1:21.   [14] Cf. Bede Jarrett, O.P., *Life of St. Dominic*, p. 148.
[15] *Dominicana*, XLIII, p. 239.   [16] *Ibid.*, p. 236.   [17] *Op. cit.*, p. 138.
[18] *Ibid.*, p. 37.   [19] *Op. cit.*, p. 240.

Bonvisus testifies: "When the violence of the fever attacked him, he did not complain about this illness; rather, it seemed that he was in prayer and contemplation. This seemed so from certain signs on his face, which the patient, when well, was accustomed to show whenever he was in prayer and contemplation, as the witness well knew. When the fever diminished, he spoke of God with the brethren, or read a book, or had something read to him. Since his custom was always to rejoice in trials rather than in good fortune, he praised God and was happy about his sickness." [20]

Most of us are not contemplatives because we are not sufficiently mortified. We lack the serenity which only total mortification can bring. Still trusting in our own health and strength, our own abilities and efforts, our possessions or our popularity, we are distracted from God by our undue concern for these things. Consequently, we are not sufficiently attentive to the Holy Spirit, not docile enough to the workings of his gifts which alone can lead us to divine contemplation.

St. Basil the Great says that we have reached perfect renunciation when we no longer trust in self, but trust God so implicitly that we are indifferent even to life or to death. [21] If God places us on the brink of death, we say like St. Paul: "Yes, we have been carrying within our very selves our death sentence, in order that we may not trust in ourselves, but in God who raises the dead." [22]

With absolute confidence in God, we say, as Jesus did when he was at death's door: "Father, into thy hands I commend my spirit." Daily, we should rehearse for that situation by surrendering ourselves to the guidance of the

[20] *Ibid.*, p. 37.

[21] Homily read on the Feast of St. Basil, Dominican Breviary.

[22] II Corinthians 1:9.

Holy Spirit, renouncing everything else in which we might trust, commending ourselves with docility to the Holy Spirit, so that like the Word Incarnate, we too will be led by the Spirit in every single thing we do. Only if we let him lead us into the desert of self-denial can he lead us into the fullness of the divine presence.

CHAPTER XXVIII

LIKE THE LORD, VICTIM OF LOVE

IN BAPTISM almighty God impressed upon us the mark of Christ. He made us like the Word both in the glory of his divinity and in the crucifixion of his humanity. Because baptism conforms us to the Word in his divine sonship, we cry out to God, "Abba, Father." But because it likens us also to Christ's crucifixion and destines us to be a victim of sacrifice with him, we often cry out to our Father in distress: "You marked us out as sheep to be slaughtered." [1] Yes, the Father has placed upon us the mark of Christ, the Victim of the cross.

But this victimhood, to which we are obliged by reason of baptism, can be accomplished only by charity. Every Christian has to be a victim of love, for only willing victims are acceptable to God. The character of baptism conforms us to Christ's priesthood as well as to his victimhood, and charity was the motivation of his priesthood. As priest, Jesus offered himself in sacrifice in burning love for God and for mankind.

Therefore, the grace of baptism leads us to crucifixion by

[1] Psalm 43:12.

enkindling in us flaming love of God and neighbor, which impels us to offer ourselves eagerly, totally, as victims to God. "The love of God is poured forth in our hearts by the Holy Spirit who has been given to us," [2] that same Spirit who causes us to cry out "Abba, Father." He makes us victims of love by causing us to love God with our whole heart and soul and mind and strength, and our neighbor as self.

But what is a victim? The word itself seems to derive from the Latin word "*vinctum*," meaning "bound." In order that a victim could be more easily slain on an altar, it was bound with ropes. But we must not let this etymology mislead us into thinking that victimhood implies unwillingness. The Christian victim is tied to God by bonds of love and therefore is most willing to be slain for his glory. Christ eagerly thirsted for the day when he could be crucified for the honor of the Father and for love of souls. Speaking of his crucifixion, he said: "I have a baptism to be baptized with, and how distressed I am until it is accomplished!" [3]

Burning love for the Father made him thirst to be a victim of reparation in order to repair the glory of the Father which was outraged by sin. The same love made him long to die for souls, to save them from the misery of their sin. To the extent that baptismal grace grows in us, it inspires the same sort of love and desire in us, so that, priests with Christ, we crucify ourselves as victims of love.

But being crucified is only secondary in victimhood; the primary element is the bond of love, the charity which unites us to God so that we belong totally to him. In the sacrifices of holocaust in the Old Law, the animal offered as victim was slain, to signify that the people who offered it belonged totally to God. The victim was destroyed by sword and fire to

[2] Romans 5:5.   [3] Luke 12:50.

show expressively that it no longer belonged to man but was now God's very own. By this destruction it was withdrawn from man's use, so that it could no longer be his beast of burden or his possession nor could its wool or skin be used as his clothing.

The ceremony performed on the animal signified that the people themselves belonged to God; they were consecrated to him; they became his very own and, consequently, had to be withdrawn from everything opposed to God. To belong to God, they had to slay, by mortification, whatever would take them from him, they had to die to self and to sin. We see, then, that the primary element in victimhood is belonging totally to God; the crucifixion of self is the consequence of this.

Let us, therefore, analyze what is meant by belonging to God in the way every Christian must belong to him. Each thing must belong to God in a way corresponding to its own nature. All things belong to God in the triple sense that he made them, they are subject to his power, and they cannot escape the governance of his providence. But creatures endowed with intellect and free will must belong to God in a superior way. Since in their freedom they possess themselves, and within the limits of their nature they are masters of themselves, they belong to God in the way most in keeping with their free nature only when they freely give themselves to him in eager love.

This they do primarily by giving their will to God. When the will has been perfectly given to him in love, then everything has been given, for the will is the motive power, the commanding power of all one's actions, and therefore of all one's life and the living of it. We belong perfectly to God when we live our life for him; we live our life for him when our will is in perfect conformity with the will of God. Therefore, we are totally God's, we are God's victim, when love of God has perfectly identified our will with his. We are bound to him in love, as his very own.

Thus we live our victimhood and thereby fulfill our baptismal consecration when every action of our life is in perfect conformity with the will of God. Only charity can bring this about, only charity can crucify us with Christ. To be a victim of love means to be delicately responsive to the slightest wish of the Beloved, to seek only his will at each instant, to do his will at all costs, dying to self-will to live to his will, to accept his will lovingly in all trials, no matter how painful this may be. The very essence of sanctity is union of our will with God's will, identity of will in love.

This necessarily involves the crucifixion of one's own will a thousand times a day. Victimhood is a two-sided coin: the victimhood of belonging totally to God cannot exist without the victimhood of crucifying self, any more than any coin can exist with only one side. But the upper side is love uniting us to God, the reverse or negative side is separation from self and all that is opposed to God.

Though the essence of victimhood consists in doing God's will in love, in order to guarantee that we will carry out God's will perfectly, an eagerness to deny self and to suffer for God is absolutely indispensable. We can belong to God and be united to him only to the extent that we kill our tendencies to pride and the other vices. There is no other way to belong to God but by way of this crucifixion.

To keep alive in ourselves this necessary eagerness to deny self with Christ, we have to meditate persistently on the Passion of Christ to find out what it was that made him so thirsty for sufferings. It was love that made him long for the cross, it was love that crucified him. "The fire of divine love was the fetter which held him fastened and nailed to the cross," says the Father to St. Catherine.[4]

Love cannot bear anything which is injurious to the beloved. In his love for the heavenly Father, the Sacred Heart could not bear to see the outrages committed against the divine majesty by sin. This anguish caused by sin was the greatest, the most crucifying cause of our Lord's suffering, more painful by far than the tortures of his body. In his zeal for the beloved Father, Jesus was eager to repel these outrages against the Father's honor, to erase these blots from the Father's glory. That is why he offered himself so eagerly as a victim of reparation.

To the extent that we love God and are one with him in love, to that extent we too will suffer from the outrages committed against him by sinners, feeling sin as though it were directed against ourselves; as indeed it is, if we are one with God, identified with him in love. Eagerness to make reparation for sin is, therefore, one of the surest signs that our love for God is great. If we are not eagerly looking for opportunities to make reparation, then we can be sure that our love for God leaves much to be desired, or else we are quite blind to the existence of sin in the world.

It is well, therefore, to meditate on sin in connection with the Passion, so that we may learn to hate it truly and to weep over it, not with exterior tears, but with interior anguish of soul. "Blessed are they that mourn," says our Lord; blessed, because charity is the cause of their mourning over sin. It is important, then, that we keep in mind the horrible outrages committed against the divine majesty daily. If we do this, we are sure to thirst for an opportunity to offer reparation to God.

[4] *Dialogue of St. Catherine of Siena* (Westminster: Newman, 1943). p. 68.

Love crucifies us, love suffers over everything that is injurious to the beloved. Just as the lover of God cannot bear the horror of sin which is so injurious to the glory of God, but seeks to destroy sin by reparation, so, too, as the lover of neighbor, he suffers over the miseries of neighbor. The greatest of all miseries is sin. The thought of the sins being committed all about him makes the lover of God eager to sacrifice himself in reparation for sinners, in order to snatch them from their misery.

Love of God and love of neighbor, therefore, necessarily make us victims of reparation. Baptismal grace, which works by charity, which makes us love God and neighbor, necessarily crucifies us as victims of love, in union with Jesus Christ. This love impels us to make all the little or great sacrifices necessary in helping neighbor in charity.

In our eagerness to be victims for souls, we long to take upon ourselves all the penance we can, and we are distressed because we are able to do so little. Perhaps we are too weak to fast, too helpless to do other physical penances. But the good Lord purposely makes it impossible for us to do all the penances we would like to do, lest we forget that the essence of victimhood is love, and acceptance of his will in love, thereby belonging totally to him. Little things done with great love, in perfect conformity with his will, are far more profitable than great penances done with little love. And great penances done in pride and self-sufficiency are of no value at all. The mere fact that we feel anguish over sinners is itself valuable reparation for them. For this anguish of spirit is caused by charity, and the greatness of our charity makes of this anguish a reparation far more acceptable to God than severe penances done with little or no charity.

Our great aim is victimhood, and therefore, charity: burning love of Christ, which makes us of one will with him,

the Victim of the cross, a charity which will joyfully deny
self continually at every turn, in all the little things, in order
to be one with him and in order to bring others to him. If
Jesus, nailed to a cross, crowned with thorns, pierced with a
lance, is in our thoughts, always, love of him will spontaneously make us a victim with him, thus bringing to perfection
in us his mark of victimhood, impressed upon us by the
baptismal character.

Because baptism consecrated us as victims with Christ, it
is our principal duty as Christians to offer ourselves with him
in the Mass; but we can perfectly live up to that offering only
to the extent that we are conscious that our whole life is
consecrated to the making of reparation. By incorporating
us into Christ, baptism gave Christ a full right to all our
works and sufferings; he has a right to suffer in us and to use
our sufferings as reparation in saving souls through us. We
are depriving him of what is rightfully his when we suffer our
troubles unwillingly. We live our victimhood to the full,
then, when we are always conscious that we are dedicated by
baptism to reparation, and therefore each particular act we
perform is dedicated to this. We should be conscious that
membership in Christ makes us one mystical person with
him, so that he can continue in us and through us his great
work of reparation to the Father, and thereby save souls. If
we live in this spirit, we will never overlook any opportunity
for self-denial. We will give the Sacred Heart that reparation
so badly needed if he is to save the world. If we live in
continual union with the love of the Sacred Heart and the
Immaculate Heart of Mary, even our little acts of self-
denial will have tremendous value for the salvation of a
miserable world. And especially valuable are the acts of
self-denial necessary for doing the will of God in fulfilling
the duty of each moment. Doing the will of God is the very

heart of victimhood; it makes us like the Word Incarnate in his outstanding characteristic: doing the will of Him who sent him.

CHAPTER XXIX

SAVIORS LIKE THE LORD

INEVITABLY, the sons of God suffer with Christ. One cannot be an adopted son of the Father, in the likeness of his eternal Son, without being in the likeness of this Son crucified. The more the soul is "with God," like the Word, the more it desires to be like the Word nailed to the cross.

The more God fills the soul with the grace of divine adoption, giving it an ever-increasing insight into the holiness of the Father, the more the soul suffers and mourns over sin. It desires to make reparation to its beloved Father and to rescue souls from sin's misery, bringing them to the Father's glory. Thus, as grace draws the soul ever more powerfully to the Father, simultaneously it draws it to the cross of Christ and his desolation and abandonment by the Father.

This is one of the main themes of the book, *The Cross of Jesus,* written by Louis Chardon, a seventeenth-century Dominican.[1] St. Catherine of Siena before him had taught the same thing in her *Dialogue.* For example, the heavenly Father tells her that souls which have raised themselves to him perseveringly in prayer conceive ever greater love of neighbor and find courage to go forth from the consolation

---

[1] Louis Chardon, O.P., *The Cross of Jesus* (St. Louis: B. Herder, 1957 and 1959).

of the divine presence in order to help their neighbor. They arrive at a state of perfection in which "they place none other before the eye of their intellect than Christ crucified; not the Father, as do they who are imperfect in love and do not wish to suffer pain, but only to have the delight which they find in me." [2] That is, the soul which has been with God, like the Word, learns to sacrifice the joy of this in order to suffer with Christ crucified, to make reparation for sin and to save souls for the Father's glory.

This is precisely what happened to St. Dominic, *par excellence* an adopted son of the Father. One of Dominic's outstanding characteristics was the gift of tears, mourning over sin, suffering intensely in his soul over the sins of his fellow man. Those who witnessed his nightly vigils testify that he used to groan aloud in this pain over sin and would cry out: "O Lord, have pity on this people! What is to become of sinners!" [3] Or on his knees he would cry out like St. Stephen: "Lord, lay not this sin to their charge." [4] Three times nightly he would scourge himself in reparation for sin. Only thus, by this reparation, could his soul find relief from his pain over sin's outrage against the holiness of his beloved Father.

Even as a youth, says Blessed Jordan of Dominic, "a special grace had been given him by God, that of being able to sorrow for sinners. . . . His custom it was, but rarely broken, to pass the night in prayer, behind shut doors, beseeching God in solemn love; and the strong cry and tears, the unspeakable groanings which he could in no way restrain, broke out audibly from him. But there was one

[2] *Dialogue of St. Catherine of Siena*, pp. 170–171.

[3] Vicaire, "St. Dominique," *Dictionnaire de Spiritualité*, III, col. 1530.

[4] Acts 7:59; *St. Dominic at Prayer* (Dublin: Irish Rosary, 1947), p. 10.

special petition that he often made to God: that a true love might be his to help effectively in the saving of men's souls, deeming himself only then a real member of Christ's Mystical Body, when he could spend his whole being in gaining men, as his Lord Jesus had spent himself for them on the cross." [5]

In her great vision of Dominic as resembling the Lord, St. Catherine sees him like Christ in zeal for souls, a zeal so great that, like Christ, Dominic sends out disciples to save souls. The Father speaks to Catherine: "As my natural Son sent out his disciples, so this adopted son sent out his friars. . . . As my natural Son devoted all his life and actions to the salvation of souls, so my adopted son Dominic directed all his efforts and powers to the task of freeing souls from the snares of vice and error. This was the main reason why he founded and developed his Order: zeal for souls." [6]

Dominic personally was responsible for the insertion of the following words in the Constitutions of the Friars Preachers: "Our Order is known to have been instituted from the beginning especially for preaching and the salvation of souls, and all our effort must be directed principally and ardently and to its full power toward this end, that we may be able to be of use to the souls of our neighbors."

The principal means for achieving this goal of usefulness to neighbor is study and the contemplation of divine truth. St. Catherine is told by the Father in her *Dialogue:*

> Now look at the ship of thy father Dominic, my beloved son. He ordered it most perfectly, wishing that his sons should apply themselves only to my honor and the salvation of souls, with the light of knowledge, which light he laid as his principal foundation. . . . At

[5] Jarrett, *Life of St. Dominic*, pp. 14–15.
[6] Raymond of Capua. *Life of St. Catherine of Siena*, p. 184.

what table does he feed his sons with the light of knowledge? At the table of the cross, which is the table of holy desire, when souls are eaten for my honor. Dominic does not wish his sons to apply themselves to anything, but remaining at this table, there to seek with the light of learning the glory and praise of my name alone, and the salvation of souls.[7]

In one of her letters, St. Catherine tells us how this makes them like the Lord:

I write you in his precious blood, with the desire of seeing you famished for souls, for the glory of God, imitating the supreme and sweet Truth, who had such hunger and thirst for our salvation that he died of it. It does not seem to me that this immolated Lamb can ever be satisfied. He cries on the cross, and gorged with opprobrium, he says that he has thirst, but it is certain that the holy desire for our salvation was his greatest thirst.

O inestimable and most sweet charity, it does not seem to you, when you submit yourself to such torments, that you have given enough. For your desire to give all for the salvation of souls persists, even greater than before. Love is the cause. I am not astonished, since your love was infinite, and your torments finite. That is why the cross of desire was heavier, even than the cross of the body.[8]

St. Catherine explains elsewhere, from her own experience of the irresistible attraction of the child of God to the cross, that Christ and the Christian desire to suffer the cross in order to find relief from the pain caused by sin, for only reparation can remove this pain. In the lines we have just

[7] *Dialogue*, pp. 298–299.

[8] Louis-Paul Guigues, *Le Sang, la croix, la verité* (Paris: Gallimard, 1940), p. 17.

quoted, she says that Christ's pain of desire persists even in the midst of his physical torments, for these are but finite, while his love and desire to make reparation are infinite.[9]

As perfect adopted son of God, St. Dominic had in all its intensity this attraction to the cross, this desire to be like Christ crucified. Father Vicaire writes:

> Perhaps there is no movement in the prayer of St. Dominic more important than prayer for sinners. Indeed, it is the pivot of his life and that of his brethren, the point where intense contemplation of Jesus crucified finds fulfillment in ardent desire to save souls. In this prayer, Dominic bestirs himself even to the point of those loud groanings spoken of by the witnesses of his life.[10]

In this burning desire for souls, Dominic went to the Pope, and asked that he and his brethren be sent forth for their salvation. He wanted to be sent by the Lord, who had said: "As the Father has sent me, I also send you." [11] Dominic knew that to be truly sent by Christ, he would have to be sent by Christ's vicar. The Order which he established has always been characterized, as Popes Benedict XV and John XXIII have reminded us, by outstanding loyalty to the Holy See which gave it its preaching mission.[12]

The Lord was sent by the Father to gather the dispersed sheep of God into one flock under the one Shepherd and his vicar. Dominicans from the beginning have looked upon

[9] Cf. P. Hinnebusch, "Christ's Tears and St. Catherine's," *Life of the Spirit*, Vol. 16, August–September, 1961.

[10] Vicaire, "St. Dominique," *Dictionnaire de Spiritualité*, III, col. 1530.

[11] John 20:21.

[12] Pope Benedict XV, encyclical on the seventh centenary of the death of St. Dominic, June 29, 1921; Pope John XXIII, discourse to the members of the General Chapter of the Order of Preachers, September 25, 1961.

themselves as good shepherds, feeding the flock with the word of God, laying down their lives for them, bringing them back from heresy into unity with the shepherd at Rome.

The Dominican's study, contemplation and apostolate of salvation are all one great movement of his charity. These are not separate, distinct compartments of his life, independent of one another, but are different manifestations or activities of his one life as a son of God, in the likeness of Christ. The Friar Preacher's adoption as son leads to the cross, and from the cross to the apostolate of preaching. The apostolate of saving souls by preaching is, as it were, an uninterrupted continuation of the study and prayer of the preacher. When he studies, with the Word he contemplates the Father as revealed in the Word. His study of the Word in the Sacred Scripture and in theology's explanation of Scripture develops without a break, in one movement of the soul, into the contemplation of Christ crucified and the desire to spend self and be spent with him for souls. This, in turn, leads to preaching. The whole process is one great surge of charity, the love spirated by the Word in the souls of the sons of God. One can see that St. Thomas did not betray the idea of the founder when he gave as the Order's theme: *"Contemplata aliis tradere:* To give to others the fruits of one's contemplation."[13]

Jesus came into the world, sent by the Father. And when his mission was accomplished, he said: "Again I leave the world, and go to the Father."[14] But he did not go back alone. He had sought out and found the scattered sheep, and led them back to the Father.

> For just as from the heavens
> the rain and snow come down

[13] *Summa Theologiae*, IIa IIae, q. 188, a. 7.   [14] John 16:28.

And do not return there
  till they have watered the earth,
Making it fertile and fruitful,
  Giving seed to him who sows
And bread to him who eats,
  so shall my Word be
  that goes forth from my mouth;
It shall not return to me void,
  but shall do my will,
  achieving the end for which I sent it.[15]

Christ said to St. Catherine of Siena: "Let my true servants arise and learn of me, the Word, how to place the lost sheep on their shoulders and carry them along through me who am the bridge." We can pass through Christ to the Father only by bringing souls with us on our shoulders, just as all of us were the cross on Christ's own shoulders. We must be saviors with him.

He is Savior because he laid down his life for his sheep. He tells us that we must do the same, if we would be his friends. "You are my friends, if you do the things I command you. . . . This is my commandment, that you love one another as I have loved you. Greater love than this no one has, that one lay down his life for his friends." [16]

Lest we think that Christ meant these words only for the original twelve apostles, St. John clearly applies them to all Christians when he says: "In this have we come to know his love, that he laid down his life for us; and we likewise ought to lay down our life for the brethren." [17] Every Christian is called to be an intimate friend of Christ, and therefore to lay down his life with him for his brethren and be a savior of souls, an apostle. Self-sacrifice for others, according to St. John, is the only true mark of a Christian. He writes: "We

[15] Isaias 55:10–11.   [16] John 15–14, 12.   [17] I John 3:16.

know that we have passed from death to life because we love
the brethren." [18] Only by that sign—self-sacrificing love for
the brethren—can we be sure that we have passed from
death to the life of grace. "He who does not love," St. John
continues, "abides in death."

All of this is implicit in the mark of Christ put upon our
souls at baptism, by which we are adopted as children of
God. According to St. Thomas, the sanctifying grace given
to our souls in baptism is the likeness of the Holy Trinity, by
which we are sons of God in the likeness of the Word, while
the character impressed on the soul in that same sacrament is
the likeness of Christ crucified, marking us as victim with
Christ.[19] That is why the baptismal grace of adoption as sons
of God, as it grows in us, develops in us a love of the cross,
drawing us to the Father by drawing us to the cross, forming
in us Christ's own self-sacrificing heart, his willingness to be
a victim for souls. If anyone does not have a zealous love for
souls and a willingness to sacrifice for them, his grace of
divine sonship has not matured. It has been hindered by
selfishness.

If, then, we really have grown in the likeness of the Word,
like him we go to the Father, but not alone. Blessed Jordan,
realizing that St. Dominic has not gone to heaven alone,
addresses him thus in his prayer:

> Not for thy own sake, but for the good of others also
> did the grace of God enrich thy soul with abundant
> blessings. God meant not only to raise thee to the rest
> and peace of heaven and the glory of the saints, but
> likewise to draw innumerable souls to the same blessed
> state by the example of thy wonderful life, to en-
> courage numberless souls by thy loving advice, to in-

---

[18] I John 3:14.   [19] Cf. *Summa Theologiae*, IIIa, q. 63, a. 3.

struct them by thy most sweet teaching, to inspire
them to good by thy fervent preaching.[20]

St. Catherine of Siena also fulfilled this ideal. Father
Laurence Bright has written of her: "The Church may have
canonized greater saints—it is not for us to judge—but very
few in whom the essence of Christian holiness, the transformation into a likeness of the Incarnate Word, has so visibly
and vividly appeared. And certainly, Dominican history
offers no clearer example of the Dominican ideal in action." [21]

That ideal—of entering into the presence of God in
contemplation and then going forth for the salvation of
mankind, in utter loyalty to the Church and its head—is
magnificently illustrated by Father Urban Mullaney, writing
of the three great phases of St. Catherine's life. We give brief
excerpts from his thought, which certainly do not do justice
to his beautiful treatise:

> The first phase. . . .
> This was the time when, completely alone, Catherine
> walked into the shattering presence of God. . . .
> The second phase. . . .
> She who had begun by walking alone into the
> presence of God returned now to men, bearing the
> presence of God within her, and by the power of his
> presence, by reason of his illumination, she saw God in
> every man. From Christ-in-Catherine, love—compas-
> sionate love—called out to Christ-in-every-man. . . .
> Christ in the countenance, the need, the loneliness, yes,
> even in the degradation of all men; for in all Christ is
> in need, Christ in loneliness, Christ degraded. . . .
> The third phase . . . of Catherine's life, the time

[20] Blessed Jordan's prayer to St. Dominic.
[21] Editorial, *The Life of the Spirit*, April, 1961.

of yearning service of the Church-universal, finds explanation in Christ's words, "You shall be witnesses to me . . . even to the uttermost parts of the earth."

For this is the fruit of holiness: that love, transcending the limits of all personal experience and personal limitations, shall become all-embracing, all-inclusive in imitation of the limitlessness of Christ's love. Death's proof of love Christ offered not merely for some, and not alone for those encompassed within the merciful apostolate even of a Catherine of Siena, but for the great body of mankind. In this last phase of Christian growth, love can no longer be measured by one's own limited environment, can no longer be confined to the number—however great—of those to whom one can commit oneself. Now is Christ's experience alone adequate to love's intensity, Christ's self-donation to his Mystical Body alone adequate to love's yearning to give of self. Always therefore souls who have reached this degree of love are marked by almost ecstatic devotion to the Church as such—and therefore to the Holy Father, in whose person, as it were, the Church lives; for only the entire Christ in *all* his members is direct and immediate object great enough for love so intense.

It is such love of the Church, such love of the Roman See, that consumed Catherine.[22]

St. Dominic, too, had achieved this universal, all-embracing love which can at the same time love all and each of the members of Christ. "In the person of St. Dominic," writes Father Clerissac, "the apostolic intention appears clothed with an infinite tenderness. You remember how, seeing a city afar off, he wept over it, and the breviary gives us the very words of the first chroniclers, when it says: 'He

[22] Urban Mullaney, O.P., "The Message of Catherine Benincasa," *The Torch*, October, 1961, pp. 20–23.

was grievously afflicted by the sins and miseries of mankind.'
In a mere man, universality of affection excludes, as a
general rule, such a degree of tenderness, but in St. Dominic,
the union of these two elements is a proof of his likeness to
the Lord." [23]

Father Mullaney summarizes the three phases of Dominican contemplation by saying: "The vision of self in God; of
God in my brother; of all things in God. This is the way unto
beatific vision." [24]

[23] *The Spirit of St. Dominic* (London: Burns, Oates, 1939), p. 28.
[24] Cf. Mullaney, *op. cit.*

PART EIGHT

Eucharistic Heart of God and Fire of the Holy Spirit

CHAPTER XXX

"CHRIST LOVED ME"

WHEN JESUS WAS HANGING on the cross, every single member of the human race who ever lived or ever will live was present in his thoughts and in his love, not in a vague, indistinct way, but each one as an individual person. He knew each of us perfectly. All the secrets of our hearts were clearly manifest to him—all the good and all the evil that we have ever thought, desired, or done, or ever will think, desire, or do.

In spite of his knowledge of our sins, or rather, precisely because of his knowledge of the misery caused by our sins, Christ's compassionate heart loved us, each one of us individually, and delivered himself up for us. With St. Paul then, each one of us can say with conviction: "Christ loved *me*, and delivered himself up for *me*." [1]

Nowhere is this truth more strikingly manifest than in the holy sacrifice of the Mass. Since the Mass presents to us the sacrifice of the Cross, it also makes actually present to us the love of Christ with which he offered himself up for us.

Scripture tells us that Christ's death in propitiation for our sins is the supreme manifestation of divine love for us. "God commends his charity toward us," says St. Paul, "because when as yet we were sinners, Christ died for us." [2] And our Lord says: "As Moses lifted up the serpent in the desert, even so must the Son of Man be lifted up. . . . For God so loved the world that he gave his only-begotten Son, that those who believe in him may not perish, but may have life

[1] Galatians 2:20.   [2] Romans 5:8.

everlasting." [3] St. John comments on this by saying: "In this has the love of God been shown in our case, that God has sent his only-begotten Son into the world that we may live through him. In this is the love, not that we have loved God, but that he has first loved us, and sent his Son a propitiation for our sins." [4]

The holy sacrifice of the Mass, the re-enactment in our presence of Calvary's sacrifice of love, is the most convincing sign that this divine love in the heart of God and in the heart of Jesus, was concerned with us personally. To convince us that he loved us individually as he hung on the cross of Calvary and gave himself up for us, in the Mass Jesus again takes bread and wine into his holy and venerable hands, and blessing them, he says to us: "Take and eat, for this is my body which was delivered up for *you*. Take and drink, for this is the chalice of my blood which was shed for *you*." And he extends this body and blood to us through the hands of his priest who says: "Behold the Lamb of God, who takes away the sins of the world."

We miss the whole point of the Holy Eucharist if we do not see it vividly as a re-enactment of the passion and death of Christ in our very presence; if we do not see it clearly as the love of Christ crucified, reaching out to embrace us, handing his very own self to us, so that by eating of his sacrificial death we may "have life, and have it more abundantly." In each Mass we must see the heart of Christ here and now actively loving us personally and delivering himself up for us.

If, in the copious, magnificent writings of St. Thomas Aquinas on the Eucharist there is any one thought that stands out above all others, and echoes again and again, it is that the Eucharist is a living reminder and representation of

[3] John 3:14f.   [4] I John 4:9f.

Christ's passion, a sacrificial banquet in which Christ himself is received, a banquet in which we partake of the sacrifice of the Cross as recipients of the divine love of Christ.

In the mind of St. Thomas, the passion of Christ above all else is love; it is not mere suffering, not mere death, but it is suffering and death eagerly sought, joyfully endured out of love, a love which alone gave these sufferings their value as expiation for our sins, an infinite love for us personally. This is how St. Thomas views the Eucharist—as the sacrament of divine love for us, immediately present to each one of us, a sacrament which efficaciously creates the same love in us, for the sacramental grace of the Eucharist is charity.

St. Albert the Great, the teacher of St. Thomas, calls the Eucharist the love-gift of the heart of God. For Albert, the Eucharist and the heart of Jesus are inseparable. Not only is the Eucharist the gift of that divine heart, but the heart is itself present in the Eucharist, here and now actively loving us. God so loved the world that he gave his only-begotten Son in sacrifice on Calvary; he so loves each individual one of us that he gives his only-begotten Son again for us in the sacrifice of the Eucharist, so that we may eat and have life from that love.

As the love-gift of the divine heart of God, the Eucharist is the result of an eternal plan. In the Apocalypse St. John calls Christ "the lamb who has been slain from the foundation of the world." [5] For even before God made anything at all, he foresaw the fall of mankind, but in undaunted, merciful love, he planned in advance the Savior in whom he would "restore all things." Such is the "mystery of his will," determined even "before the foundations of the world." [6]

In announcing this plan of his love through his prophets, almighty God says to us: "I have loved thee with an

[5] Apocalypse 13:8. [6] Ephesians 1:1–14.

everlasting love; therefore have I drawn thee, taking pity on thee." [7] It was a love bestowed on us from eternity, before we existed, and so we did not merit it. It is a love given in sheer mercy, a love which first drew us from the nothingness of non-existence, and then from the misery of sin into which we fell. It is a love which remains forever present to us to maintain us in divine favor, or to lift us again if we fall.

And this Lamb, slain for us in accordance with the eternal will of God, was to be eaten by the people for whom he was slain. This part of the eternal plan—the eating of Christ in the Eucharist—was prefigured by the eating of the paschal lamb of the Old Law. The paschal lamb was a memorial of the deliverance of the Israelites from the slavery of Egypt; and in the midst of the ritual prescribed for its eating, the children of each Hebrew family would ask the question: "What is the meaning of this service?" And the father would answer: "It is the victim of the passage of the Lord, when he passed over the houses of the children of Israel in Egypt, striking the Egyptians, and saving our houses." [8]

Lest we miss the point of the Holy Eucharist, daily at Mass we ought to ask ourselves that question: "What is the meaning of this service?" It is the eating of the victim of divine love; it is the love-gift of the heart of God; it is the living reminder of our passage from sin and slavery through the blood of the Lamb of God. For he said: "Do this in remembrance of me." But especially in remembrance of the everlasting love of my heart for you, the love which inspired me on Calvary to deliver myself up for you, the love which still burns in my heart, and is immediately present to you in this sacrament. "For as often as you shall eat this bread and drink the cup, you proclaim the death of the Lord, until he come." [9]

Without the Holy Eucharist, the death of the Lord is

[7] Jeremias 31–3.   [8] Exodus 12:26f.   [9] I Corinthians 11:26.

incomplete, for a sacrifice is not complete until those who offer it partake of it as a sign of their oneness with it. And so the eating of Christ in the Eucharist is an integral part of the eternal plan of redemption: "Unless you eat of the flesh of the Son of Man and drink his blood, you shall not have life in you." That is why St. Thomas says that the chief reason we are baptized is that we may eat of the sacrifice of Christ in the Holy Eucharist. And even baptism of desire includes Holy Communion in desire. Holy Communion is union—in mutual love—with the divine Victim of love. Without this union, we cannot have life.

Long before this marvelous plan of God's love had been fully manifest, the prophets and psalmists had begun to praise it without fully realizing what they were praising, for even the Old Testament preparations for the ultimate fulfillment of the plan were so wonderful that these men could not contain their joy. Sophonias cries out: "Be glad and rejoice with your whole heart, O daughter of Jerusalem. . . . The Lord your God is in the midst of you! He will rejoice over you with gladness, he will renew you in his love!" [10]

And a psalmist declares: "The counsel of the Lord stands forever, the plans of his heart throughout the ages. . . . Behold the eyes of the Lord are on them that fear him, and on them that hope in his mercy, to deliver their souls from death, and feed them in famine." [11] But, when the fullness of time comes, and at last this everlasting plan of the heart of God has been fully manifest, it turns out to be so unspeakably wonderful, so ineffably surpassing all the wildest dreams of the prophets and psalmists, that their imperfect knowledge of it seems like sheer ignorance in contrast with knowledge of the full reality.

That is why St. Paul refers to it as "the mystery which has

[10] Sophonias 3:14–18.   [11] Psalm 32:11–19.

been hidden from eternity in God," but now has been revealed to the apostles to be told to all the nations.[12] As a learned Pharisee, well-versed in all the teachings of the Old Law, St. Paul was so amazed at the way in which Christ, the fulfillment of the Law, surpassed all expectations, that again and again he comes back to the theme of the marvelous mystery of the eternal plan, now manifest to us.

It is of this that he rhapsodizes, when he tells us how "the grace of God our Savior has appeared to all men." [13] And he speaks of "the grace bestowed upon us in Christ Jesus eternal ages ago, but now manifest through the appearing ('the epiphany') of our Savior, Christ Jesus." [14]

If only we would share St. Paul's ever-fresh wonderment over this marvelous mystery! We take too much for granted that merciful grace and favor of the everlasting love of God for us. Who in the Old Testament would ever have dared dream that God planned to give his very own self to us as our Bread of life? But we take it as a matter of course.

If the birth of Christ is the epiphany or manifestation to the world of the mystery of the eternal purpose of God's mercy, the Holy Eucharist is the manifestation of God's purpose in regard to us personally, for when Christ in the Mass gives his own body to us as our food, we are convinced that indeed he loved us and delivered himself up for us. The everlasting, merciful love of God, which has no beginning and no end, and burned in the heart of Christ crucified on Calvary, that same undying love comes into immediate contact with us in the Holy Eucharist; it embraces us and will hold us eternally in its embrace if we respond to it.

This everlasting love embraces us in the Holy Eucharist to heal us, strengthen us, nourish us, comfort us and refresh us.

---

[12] Ephesians 3:9, and the whole Epistle.　　[13] Titus 2:11.
[14] II Timothy 1:8.

And because of the daily re-offering of Calvary's sacrifice of love in our presence in the Mass, that everlasting love of the Sacred Heart is always present to us all day long, not just during the Mass or at the moment of Holy Communion. It is an everlasting love, present everywhere, present to us; it is not restricted to time or to place; it is restricted only by the narrowness of our hearts, too indifferent, too selfish to open to receive it.

If, then, we are to remain forever in the embrace of this everlasting love which embraces us in Holy Communion, we must die to the self-love which puts obstacles in its way. Christ loved us and died for us that we might have life. But we can live with him only if we die with him. Our daily Holy Communion, a union with the Lamb who was slain, is a daily dying with him by our death to sin, by our mortification of self, by our sufferings borne in union with him; and it is a daily living with him, for he lives in us more and more perfectly as we grow in love for him through self-sacrifice and fervent Communions.

Conscious of these wonderful realities, we cry out in joy with St. Paul: "I died . . . that I might live to God. I have been crucified with Christ, but I live—yet no longer I, but Christ lives in me. And the life I now live in the flesh, I live in the faith of the Son of God, who loved me, and gave himself up for me." [15]

> O Sacred Banquet, in which Christ is received;
> the memory of his Passion is renewed; the soul
> is filled with grace; and the pledge of future
> glory is given us!

[15] Galatians 2:19–20.

CHAPTER XXXI

"A LAMB STANDING AS IF SLAIN"

IN HIS APOCALYPSE, St. John sees, before the throne of God, "a lamb, standing as if slain." [1] It is Christ, the true Paschal Lamb, immolated for the salvation of God's chosen people. The lamb is standing, to signify that he is risen from the dead, but he stands as if slain, for even after his ascension to the throne of God, he still bears in his body the glorious wounds of his Passion.

This is the same Lamb of whom John writes elsewhere in the Apocalypse that he "has been slain from the foundation of the world." [2] This means that God, "with an everlasting love," had decreed, even before the creation of the world, that Christ should die for us so that through his sacrifice God's love and mercy could once again flow to us.

The Lamb of God, risen from the dead and ascended to the Father forever, bears the glorious wounds of his passion, as if eternally to remind the Father that he has done his will, as if to say perpetually: "I have accomplished the work thou hast given me to do." [3] Therefore, let thy love and mercy pour forth upon my brethren, for whom I have laid down my life, "that they may have life, and have it more abundantly." [4]

He bears these wounds permanently, furthermore, as a reminder to us of the permanence of that love which from all eternity had decreed that he be slain. This love is still with us and forever will be, for the eternal God is changeless.

---

[1] Apocalypse 5:6.   [2] Apocalypse 13:8.
[3] John 17:4.   [4] John 10:10.

Christ's wounds, the marks of his love, are signs of his love's lasting will to give us life through his death.

These marks of love, forever remaining in his risen body in heaven, in a certain sense are visible to each one of us in the Eucharist. The doubting Thomas once saw these wounds with his bodily eyes and touched them with his hands; but we, with the eyes of faith, see these wounds daily in the holy sacrifice of the Mass. For the Eucharistic signs signify Christ's sufferings and death, endured for love of us; they are the signs which efficaciously make this love present to each of us through this sacrament.

Everything in the Eucharist speaks to us about the passion of Christ. "Do this in remembrance of me," he said. And St. Paul adds: "For as often as you eat this bread and drink the cup, you proclaim the death of Christ until he comes." [5] First of all, the twofold consecration in the Mass clearly signifies the sacrifice of the Cross. The body of Christ is consecrated separately from the blood of Christ, to signify how Christ's blood was separated from his body in the sacrifice of the Cross. By these Eucharistic signs, the sacrifice of the Cross is offered again in our presence, the Lamb of God is slain mystically, sacramentally, before our very eyes, and the love which burned in his heart on Calvary is made immediately present to us. The words of consecration also signify the death of Christ: "This is the chalice of my blood . . . which shall be shed for you."

We are further reminded that the Eucharist is a partaking of the sacrifice of the Cross by the words of the priest as he presents Holy Communion to us, saying: "Behold the Lamb of God." Holy Mother Church does not want us to forget for one instant that the Holy Eucharist is the re-enactment of our Lord's passion and death in infinite love for us.

[5] I Corinthians 1:24f.

The same message is cried out by the crushed grapes from which is made the wine which becomes the blood of the Lord and the ground-up wheat from which is made the bread that becomes the body of the Lord. In the sacrifice of the Cross, Jesus was crushed in the winepress of the divine wrath, so that we might escape that wrath. He was ground like grain in the mill that we might be ground and crushed in true contrition for our sins.

All the signs of the Eucharist thus signify the Lamb who is slain for us. These signs bring the same message as the wounds of love he still bears in his risen body. And just as in heaven he is standing risen, even though he is slain, so, too, the Eucharistic signs present the Lamb to us both slain and standing alive at the same time—mystically slain by the sacramental signs and yet gloriously living in his risen body, truly present under the appearance of bread. "For we know that Christ, having risen from the dead, dies now no more, death shall no longer have dominion over him." [6]

And lest we miss this point, immediately after the Consecration of the Mass, when the Church has repeated our Lord's words, "As often as you shall do these things, you shall do them in remembrance of me," she tells the Lord God that right now she *is* doing these things in remembrance of him: "Therefore, O Lord, we thy servants, as also thy holy people, calling to mind the blessed passion of the same Christ thy Son our Lord, and also his resurrection. . . ." The Eucharist is a remembrance simultaneously of his death and of his resurrection; in the Eucharist he is the Lamb slain and standing risen at the same time, risen from the dead that he may give us his resurrection through this sacrament.

St. Thomas Aquinas states all of this in that wonderful, succinct *Magnificat* Antiphon which he wrote for the Feast

[6] Romans 6:9.

of Corpus Christi: "O Sacred Banquet, in which Christ is received, the memory of his passion is renewed, the mind is filled with grace, and a pledge of future glory is given to us." We commemorate his death, mystically but truly present to us in the Mass, and we eat of it, so that it will give us the life of grace now and the life of future glory later.

But what is our response to these wounds of the Lamb, vividly visible to our faith in the signs of the Eucharist? The wounds in his body and the sacramental signs of the Eucharist are the marks of his everlasting love for us. In response to his love, we desire similar marks to express our love for him. And so, in the Mass, with him we are nailed to the cross. Through Holy Communion with Christ we become a living victim of love. The faith and love inflamed by this union causes us to consider all our pains and fatigues and hardships as so many wounds of love endured for him.

Our wounds become his wounds, our sufferings truly become his, for the Eucharist makes us one Mystical Body with him, one with him in love, so that, when we suffer for him and with him, he suffers in us. "For I live, yet no longer I, but Christ lives in me," and suffers in me. "What is lacking of the sufferings of Christ, I fill up in my flesh for the sake of his body, which is the Church." [7]

Moreover, if our faith and charity are truly great, all our sufferings become for us vivid signs of Christ's love for us. Not only the wounds in *his* flesh, but everything that we suffer in ourselves are the marks of his love for us. But let us hear St. Catherine of Siena on this point. After her famous mystical death with Christ, Catherine explained various lessons she had learned from this amazing experience.

First of all, she tells us that one of the chief reasons why

[7] Colossians 1:24.

Christ took upon himself his terrible sufferings was his desire "to exhibit to us the immensity of his love; and he could not prove it more effectually. Love, and not nails, fastened him to the cross." [8]

Catherine then tells how she herself was privileged to experience his passion with him, and by suffering what he suffered, she truly experienced "how deeply the Savior loved *her* personally, and all mankind." [9] "This share of pain that he condescended to impart to me," she said, "made known to me more distinctly and perfectly my Creator's love." [10] This experience tremendously increased her love for him and inflamed her desire to suffer ever more for him in his Mystical Body.

In other words, for Catherine, her own sufferings were a perpetual reminder to her of what Christ had endured for her. She appreciated what he had suffered for her, for she was experiencing day after day his own sufferings in herself. She looked upon her pains as wounds which his love deliberately inflicted upon her so that she would fully understand his love for her.

This is the way every Christian who *really* "lives in the faith of the Son of God" sees his sufferings. Christians of truly lively faith spontaneously think of the cross of Christ in their hardships and endeavor to endure them in love, believing firmly that all trials are inflicted by God only in love. Our faith is weak or inactive if we do not look upon our trials in this way. All trials are meant by God to be an education in his love for us, as something to be endured joyfully, as a reminder and as an experience of what he endured for us. "Endure suffering as a discipline," says St. Paul.[11] The primary meaning of the word "discipline" is instruction, teaching, education.

---

[8] Blessed Raymond of Capua. *Life of St. Catherine*, p. 148.
[9] *Ibid.*, p. 149.   [10] *Ibid.*, p. 150.   [11] Hebrews 12:7.

When, through sufferings, we have been educated in Christ's love for us, we will love in return and eagerly suffer all that we can as the marks of our love for him. If daily at Mass we let the Eucharistic signs vividly remind us of the Lamb, standing as if slain, bearing in his body the glorious wounds received for love of us, we shall learn to see our own wounds as marks that his love has been directed to us personally. We shall die daily with him in our hardships with greater patience and generosity, and thus will experience the truth expressed by St. Paul, "as dying, yet behold! we are alive!" [12]

But again with St. Paul, we shall declare: "I have been crucified with Christ; but I live!—yet no longer I, but Christ lives in me; and the life I now live in the flesh, I live in the faith of the Son of God, who loved me, and gave himself up for me." [13]

CHAPTER XXXII

"ABIDE IN MY LOVE"

OUR BLESSED LORD SAID: "Abide in me, and I in you." Then he repeats this thought more impressively, saying: "Abide in my love." Unless we abide in him and he in us, we have no life; we wither up like a branch cut off from the vine and are fit only to be burned. Unless we abide in him, we can bring forth no fruit.[1]

But we abide in him by abiding in his love. "Abide in my love!" Let my love give you life, let my love bring forth fruit in you. "Without me, you can do nothing." You can do

12 II Corinthians 6:9.   13 Galatians 2:19f.   1 John 15.

nothing unless my love for you is actively at work in you, giving you life, giving you power to produce fruit. My love is the only source of your life and of your fruits. My continuing love for you is the continuing and only cause of all that is good in you. So abide in my love, be receptive to it, open your hearts to receive it.

But you can receive my love, you can abide in it, only by responding to it with your love; you can live in my love only by your love for me. But unless I first love you, you cannot love me. My love for you is the source of your love for me. So abide in my love; receive my love so that you can give love; for without me you can do nothing. If you do love me, it is only because I have first loved you. If you are seeking me, it is only because I am seeking you still more.

Abide in my love; rest secure in my love which is seeking you, which desires you, which is eager to give you all things. "If you abide in me, and if my words abide in you, ask whatever you will and it shall be done to you." Rest secure in my love, be nourished by it, respond to my love.

But, Lord, how shall we respond to thy love, how can we be receptive to it, how do we rest secure in it?

"If you keep my commandments you will abide in my love, as I also have kept my Father's commandments and abide in his love." [2] This is the command I have received from my Father: that I lay down my life for my sheep.[3] My command to you is just like that. "This is my commandment—a new commandment [4]—that you love one another as I have loved you. Greater love than this no one has, that one lay down his life for his friends." [5]

Yes, Lord, that is indeed a new commandment! Moses told us to love our neighbor only as we love ourselves.[6] But

[2] John 15:10.   [3] John 10:16, 18.   [4] John 13:34.   [5] John 15:12.
[6] Leviticus 19:18.

you tell us to love one another even as you have loved us! Truly you set high standards for us. For we love ourselves because we desire something for ourselves. But that is not how you loved us. Lord, you desired nothing for yourself in loving us; your love was entirely gratuitous. You loved only to give, never to get. You loved us in the only way that God can love; God loves only to give. Lord, is that how you would have us love one another?

Lord, you so loved us that you gave your very life for us. But even that does not tell the whole story. Whom was it that you loved in that way? Was it your friends? No, Lord, it was your enemies. Had you given your life only for your friends, we might have said that your love was not entirely gratuitous. But you gave your life for sinners, for your enemies.

St. Paul, your apostle, has said: "God commends his charity toward us, because when as yet we were sinners, Christ died for us." [7]

Why, then, Lord did you say: "Greater love than this no man has, that one lay down his life for his friends?" Is it not still greater love to lay down one's life for one's enemies?

No, the Lord replies, it is the same love; for by laying down my life for my enemies, I have made them my friends. Abide in this love. Respond to this love with love just like it, and you shall be my friends. "You are my friends if you do the things I command you," if you love one another as I have loved you, if you lay down your lives to transform my enemies into my friends.

Such is the fruit you shall bear by abiding in my love, by loving one another as gratuitously as I have loved you. I did not love you because I needed you; your love for me adds nothing to my infinite perfection. Because you can do me no

[7] Romans 5:8.

profit, be of profit to your neighbor, for love of me. Because, as I told my beloved daughter, St. Catherine of Siena: "I have placed you in the midst of your fellows that you may do for them what you cannot do for me, that is to say, that you may love your neighbor gratuitously without expecting any return from him,"—just as I have loved you gratuitously— and "what you do to him I count as done to me." [8]

Lord, that is indeed a high standard you have set for our love! To love neighbor as self is no longer enough; we must love one another as you have loved us.

But, Lord, is such love possible to poor creatures such as we? Is that not a wholly divine love possible only to God? Can we love with divine love?

Yes, little children, I have made such love possible for you. Without me, you can do nothing, but in me you can do all things. Abide in me, abide in my love. "He who eats my flesh and drinks my blood abides in me and I in him." [9] Abide in my love, made present to you in the Blessed Sacrament. Daily, through my priest at the altar, I take bread into my holy and venerable hands, and say to you: "Take and eat; this is my body which has been delivered up for you." Can you say, then, that you cannot lay down your lives for one another, when daily I give you the body that has been crucified for you? Daily, I take the chalice into my hands and say to you: "All of you drink of this, this is my blood which has been shed for you." Can you not then shed your blood for me, can you not die for one another? The real mystery is not how can you die for one another, but how can you be so cold and indifferent to one another, how can you be so impatient and unkind to one another, and offended with one another, after receiving my body and my blood? That is the real mystery!

[8] *Dialogue* of St. Catherine of Siena.   [9] John 6:57.

Abide, then, in the love I bestow on you in this Blessed Sacrament, and then you can love even as I love. When, by the power of the Eucharist, you love others even as I have loved you, your love is not merely patterned upon mine, you could never measure up to this divine pattern unless I were living in you, loving in you, loving others through you. In the Eucharist, I am the Vine; my life and my love course through you, my branches.

In the Eucharist, all the divine love with which I laid down my life for you on the cross, is present to you to inflame you. Abide in this love. The infinite eternal love of God became incarnate in my Sacred Heart when I became man, and is always present to you in my Sacred Heart so that you may abide in it. That infinite love is incarnate also in the Holy Eucharist, where my flaming Sacred Heart is always present. It is the very same love which burned in my heart when I was lifted upon the cross to cast fire upon the earth and to draw all hearts to myself. The Eucharist makes that living love present to you; abide in that love.

If you love others as I have loved you, you will abide in that love. Let my divine love be made present to all men through your hearts, bring my love, in your hearts, to everyone, by loving them as I have loved you. As my divine love became incarnate in my human heart when I became man, as my divine love is permanently incarnate in the Holy Eucharist, so let it be incarnate in your hearts, so that from your hearts I may cast the fire of divine charity upon the earth. If you do not abide in my love, if my love does not abide in you, the world you live in will remain dark and cold. But if you abide in my love, your heart, like mine, will be a chalice of compassion into which you will receive all sinners to sanctify them; your heart will be an altar on which you will offer these souls to me, and on which you will lay down your life for their salvation. The flames of that holocaust will ignite the world.

Therefore, abide in my love, receive my love in the Holy Eucharist, my life-giving love, and no more will you be impatient with one another, no more will you bear grudges or complain of one another, or speak sharply. Rather, you will spend yourselves and be spent for souls. You will no longer be able to think of me without thinking of souls to be saved, souls for whom you are eager to give your very lives, souls whom you embrace in your compassion and mine.

Only thus can you abide in my love and remain the object of my love. Only such a response to my love will keep you in my love. If you do not love in this way, you will fall away from my love, you will cut yourself off from it like a branch cut off from the vine. It is only to those who have not loved one another as I have loved you that I shall say: "Depart from me, ye cursed, into everlasting fire. For I was hungry and you did not give me to eat, thirsty and you gave me not to drink, naked and you clothed me not." [10] "Judgment is without mercy to him who has not shown mercy." [11] Abide, then, in my love; live in my love, by loving one another as I have loved you. Learn this lesson at the table of my Cross, the table of the Eucharist, where my sacrifice of the Cross is renewed daily for you.

"These things I have spoken to you that my joy may be in you, and that your joy may be made full." [12] My joy is the joy I experience eternally in the possession of my divinity, together with the Father and the Holy Spirit. If you abide in my love, if my love abides in you, if you love one another as I have loved you, my joy will be in you, your joy will be made full, in the possession of the Father and me and the Holy Spirit, eternally!

[10] Matthew 25.   [11] James 2:13.   [12] James 15:11.

Abide, then, in my love, my love manifested to you by the wound in my heart. My love ever present to you in the Holy Eucharist, my love ever eager to give you my joy!

CHAPTER XXXIII

THE FIRE OF SANCTITY

"COME, O SANCTIFIER, all-powerful and eternal God, and bless this sacrifice, prepared for the glory of thy name!" [1]

In this closing prayer of the Offertory of the Mass, the Church implores the Holy Spirit to come and change the bread and wine just offered to God into the body and blood of Christ. Similarly, in a prayer said by the priest before Mass, referring to the fire which fell from heaven to consume the sacrifices offered by Moses and Solomon and Elias, the Church prays: "May the invisible and incomprehensible majesty of the Holy Spirit descend upon our offerings, as formerly it descended upon the holocausts of the fathers, so that he will change our offerings into thy body and blood." [2]

In these prayers, why does the Church attribute to the Holy Spirit the miracle of the consecration of our Lord's body and blood, when it is a work of omnipotence, common to all three divine Persons? For the same reason that the angel Gabriel attributes the miracle of Mary's virginal conception to the Holy Spirit, though this too is a work of the omnipotence of the Holy Trinity: "The power of the Most High shall overshadow thee."

Whatever strikingly manifests divine love is attributed to the Holy Spirit, for he *is* God's love. These works we have

---

[1] Offertory, Roman Rite.   [2] Missal, *Prayer of St. Ambrose*, Friday.

mentioned are supremely great manifestations of divine love.

Therefore, St. Fulgence says: "When does Holy Church more fittingly ask for the coming of the Holy Spirit than when she asks him to come to consecrate the sacrifice of the body of Christ; for she, herself the body of Christ, knows that he, her Head, was conceived of the Holy Spirit." [3]

The miracle of forming the Eucharistic body of Christ, for the nourishment and growth of his Mystical Body, is most fittingly attributed to the same Holy Spirit who formed the natural body of Christ in Mary's womb and forms us in the likeness of the Son of God and Mary, so that we cry "Abba! Father!" These are all superb gifts of infinite love. That is why, after the Offertory, the Church prays: "Come, O Sanctifier, all-powerful and eternal God, bless this sacrifice," that is, come to sanctify this bread and wine by changing them into the body and blood of Christ, and thereby sanctify us who partake of them. The Church is thus asking the Holy Spirit to consecrate all of us, the Mystical Body of Christ, as a living sacrifice in union with our Head, the consecrated Victim on the altar.

St. Paul tells us that the whole purpose for preaching the Gospel is to make of all mankind a sacrifice to God, consecrated by the Holy Spirit. Preaching is a priestly action; it is the preparing of a sacrifice for the fire of the Holy Spirit which will consume it. For this reason, St. Paul calls himself "priest of God's Gospel, so that the Gentiles will become an acceptable sacrifice, sanctified by the Holy Spirit." [4]

This is precisely why Christ sent forth his apostles; he

---

[3] Gihr, *The Holy Sacrifice of the Mass* (St. Louis: Herder, 1943), p. 532, n. 4.

[4] Romans 15:16–Jerusalem Bible.

himself said so in his priestly prayer at the Last Supper: "Father, sanctify them in the truth. Thy word is truth. Even as thou hast sent me into the world, so I also have sent them into the world. And for them I sanctify myself, that they also may be sanctified in truth." [5]

Since they are works of divine love, the works of sanctification are always attributed to the Holy Spirit, the Sanctifier. So, too, even the sacrifice of Christ, in which he sanctifies or consecrates himself, is attributed to the Holy Spirit. Christ, says St. Paul, "through his eternal Spirit offered himself immaculate to God" to "purify our conscience from dead works, for the worship of the living God." [6]

Why is all sanctification, all consecration, all offering of sacrifice, even the offering of Christ's sacrifice on Calvary, attributed to the Holy Spirit? Because the purpose in offering sacrifice is sanctity, and sanctity is unity with God in love. But the Holy Spirit *is* Love. In fact, he himself is the bond of love making us one thing with God. "That all may be one, even as thou Father in me and I in thee, that they also may be one in us . . . that the love with which thou hast loved me may be in them, and I in them." [7] The love with which the Father loves the Son, and the Son the Father, is the Holy Spirit; they are one in the love which is the living Person of the Holy Spirit.

Our union with God in love which is the Holy Spirit is achieved only through the Incarnate Son of God. "There is only one God, the Father *from* whom are all things, and we *unto* him; and one Lord, Jesus Christ, *through* whom are all things and we *through* him." [8] Through Christ's sacrifice, in which he sanctified himself by the Holy Spirit, we are

[5] John 17:18–19.   [6] Hebrews 9:13–14.
[7] John 17:21–26.   [8] I Corinthians 8:6.

sanctified in that same Holy Spirit, whose work it is to form in us the perfect likeness of the Son of God. We are "predestined to become conformed to the image of his Son, that he should be the firstborn among many brethren." [9]

The Holy Spirit's work of sanctification, then, is accomplished by making us sons of God in the likeness of the eternal Word of God, not in any sort of similarity, but precisely in the likeness of his oneness with the Father in love. This is sanctity: unity with God in the Holy Spirit, in the way that the Son is eternally one with the Father in that Holy Spirit.

Wherefore, says St. Paul: "God has sent the Spirit of his Son into our hearts, crying, 'Abba, Father!' " [10] Impelled by the Holy Spirit, we rush in love to our heavenly Father.

In this we are like the eternal Son of God. In the same eternal instant, in the everlasting "now," in which the Son is begotten by the Father, he simultaneously goes back to the Father in that eternal embrace of love which is the Holy Spirit, crying out as it were, in love, "Abba, Father!"

And when the eternal Son proceeds from the Father into time by becoming Man, at the very instant of his entrance into time, he begins his return to the Father in love. "I came forth from the Father (by my eternal procession) and have come into the world (on my temporal mission). Again I leave the world and go to the Father." [11] The Son forever looks to the Father in love. He is forever giving himself to the Father in love, both in eternity and in time. The Holy Spirit is the eternal mutual gift of love between Father and Son. The Son gives himself to the Father eternally in this embrace of love and in the same Holy Spirit of Love he gives himself to the Father in time by doing his will.

"The Spirit of the Lord is upon me," he says.[12] "Full of the

[9] Romans 8:9.   [10] Galatians 4:6.   [11] John 16:28.   [12] Luke 4:18.

Holy Spirit," "led by the Holy Spirit," [13] "in the power of the Holy Spirit," he is always "about his Father's business." [14] "I do always the things that are pleasing to him; [15] my food is to do the will of him who sent me,[16] that the world may know that I love the Father, and that I do as the Father has commanded me." [17]

But the supreme gift of himself to the Father in the Holy Spirit of love is accomplished on Calvary, when "through his eternal Spirit he offers himself immaculate to God." [18] In eternity and in time, the Son forever goes to the Father in the embrace of love, the eternal Spirit of love.

It is the work of the Holy Spirit, the Sanctifier, to reproduce all of this in us, conforming us to the image of the Son of God, in his unity in love with the Father. This is sanctity. As the Son proceeds from the Father and goes back to him at once in love, so too, when the Father begets us as his adopted sons by sending the Spirit of his Son into our hearts, at once we start our return to the Father in love, crying "Abba, Father," running to him with the outstretched arms of desire, to receive the eternal embrace of love.

For this were we created: "He who made us for this very thing is God, who has given us the Spirit as its pledge." [19] We would never dare to aspire to this divine embrace if he himself did not inspire in us this desire and hope. "The Spirit himself gives testimony to our spirit that we are sons of God. But if we are sons, we are heirs also: heirs indeed of God and joint heirs with Christ." [20] We were "sealed in Christ with the Holy Spirit of promise, who is the pledge of our inheritance until its full possession is redeemed." [21]

[13] Matthew 4:1; Luke 4:1; 4:14.   [14] Luke 2:49.   [15] John 8:29.
[16] John 4:34.   [17] John 14:31.   [18] Hebrews 9:13.
[19] II Corinthians 6:5.   [20] Romans 8:16.
[21] Ephesians 1:14.

In the meantime, by inflaming us with the love of the Father, the Holy Spirit stirs up in us desire and yearning for the divine embrace. In eternity the Son of God's return to the Father is simultaneous with his eternal begetting; but when the Son entered into time by becoming Man, his return to the Father took time—the whole space of his life on earth, doing the will of the Father.

Our return, too, takes time; but it is always and only under the love-impulse of the Holy Spirit. From that first instant when he stirred up in us the desire for the divine embrace, making us cry, "Abba, Father," until in heaven, he himself becomes our embrace of God, the Holy Spirit is in us, yearning "with unutterable groanings." [22] That is, he stirs up in us burning desire, yearning hope, "hope which does not disappoint, because the love of God is poured forth in our hearts by the Holy Spirit who is given to us," even as the pledge of the ultimate, eternal embrace of love. The same Holy Spirit, who some day will be our peace and joy in the embrace of God, is now our longing, our unutterable groaning, our yearning, our desire. "And he who searches the hearts knows what the Spirit desires, that he pleads for the saints according to God." [23]

In other words, as St. Catherine of Siena and so many saints tell us, whatever holy desires are stirred up by the Holy Spirit will be fulfilled on condition that they are persevering and purified. The Spirit, who "pleads for the saints according to God," himself purifies our desires, teaching us how to desire "according to God," i.e., according to the will of God. Such a desire, if it perseveres, infallibly will be fulfilled.

True love desires only the will of the beloved; the desire of love is to give self totally to the beloved by doing his will.

[22] Romans 8:26.   [23] Romans 8:27.

Thus, the return of the Son of God to the embrace of the Father was accomplished by the total gift of himself in obedience unto death, even the death of the cross.

Nothing short of that is the giving which the Holy Spirit inspires in us, as the desires he inspires in us are more and more purified by fidelity to his inspirations. For he does his work of sanctification by conforming us to the likeness of the Son of God in his total gift of self in love to the Father, consecrating us as "an acceptable sacrifice, sanctified by the Holy Spirit." "For them do I sanctify myself," said Jesus of his sacrifice on the cross, offered in his Holy Spirit, "that they also may be sanctified in truth."

All of this was prefigured by the fires which came down from heaven to consume the holocausts offered by Moses and Solomon and Elias. The flames from heaven were the sign of God's acceptance of the sacrifice offered; he took the offering to himself, as it were changing it into himself, for fire was the symbol of the living God.

For the ancient Hebrews, fire symbolized God better than anything else they knew; God himself had manifested himself under this symbol when he appeared to Moses in the burning bush. The fire of God which consumed the holocaust, changing it into fire, symbolized that he who offers himself to God as a holocaust of charity is changed by charity into God himself, becoming one thing with God in love, in the Holy Spirit.

But the Holy Spirit first has to enkindle that fire of desire which makes us want to give self totally to God in love. He himself both enkindles the desire of love and accepts it, pouring out anew the flames of charity which complete the holocaust. One cannot embrace God and be embraced by him in such love, unless God converts our will to himself by pouring into it his own Holy Spirit of love.

St. Catherine of Siena relates in her *Dialogue* what the eternal Truth did one day at Mass to the desire that he had enkindled in her by his Holy Spirit: "Then the eternal Truth seized and drew more strongly to himself her desire, doing as he did in the Old Testament, for just as then, when the sacrifice was offered to God, a fire descended and drew to him the sacrifice that was acceptable to him, so did the sweet Truth to that soul, in sending down the fire of the clemency of the Holy Spirit, seizing the sacrifice of desire that she made of herself." [24]

St. Catherine is a living image of the Church. No wonder her prayer so clearly echoes the prayer in which the Church appeals to this same divine clemency for the fire of the Holy Spirit, to consecrate the sacrifice we offer. "Come, Sanctifier, all-powerful and eternal God, bless this sacrifice"; consecrate the host, the body of Christ, but consecrate also his Mystical Body as one living sacrifice with him, inflaming all of us with charity, the chief fruit of the Eucharist, the charity which makes all of us one thing with God, in Christ in the unity of the Holy Spirit.

[24] *Dialogue*, pp. 29–30.